Visions of Infancy

Visions of Infancy

A Critical Introduction to Child Psychology

BEN S. BRADLEY

Polity Press

First published 1989 by Polity Press
in association with Basil Blackwell.

Editorial Office:
Polity Press, Dales Brewery, Gwydir Street,
Cambridge CB1 2LJ, UK

Basil Blackwell Ltd
108 Cowley Road, Oxford OX4 1JF, UK

Basil Blackwell Inc.
3 Cambridge Center,
Cambridge, MA 02142, USA

British Library Cataloguing in Publication Data

Bradley, Ben S.
Visions of infancy: a critical introduction to child psychology
1. Children. Psychology
I. Title
155.4
ISBN 0-7456-0244-4
ISBN 0-7456-0245-2 pbk.

Library of Congress Cataloging-in-Publication Data

Bradley, Ben S.
Visions of infancy.
Bibliography: p.
Includes index.
1. Child psychology – History. I. Title.
BF721.B69 1989 155.4'22'09 88-34965
ISBN 0-7456-0244-4
ISBN 0-7456-0245-2 (pbk.)

Typeset in Plantin 10 on 12pt
by Hope Services, Abingdon
Printed in Great Britain by Billing & Sons Ltd (Worcester)

Contents

Acknowledgements

A book which has taken as long to write as this one inevitably incurs a large debt of gratitude. The research upon which it is based was begun under the supervision of Colwyn Trevarthen in 1974. Thanks to him and the late Margaret Manning for their supervision of my doctoral study of babies as social beings at Edinburgh University. I would like to thank various people linked with the Child Care and Development Group at Cambridge University, most obviously Denise Riley, Jane Selby, Cathy Urwin and Martin Richards. This book is to a large extent the product of my attempt to re-think my doctoral 'findings' about early interactions with babies as part of the critical tradition of thought about human development first represented for me in English by the work of Denise, Jane and Cathy. And Martin has been the main facilitator of this publishing exercise, efficiently making contacts and valiantly criticizing drafts. I would also like to thank various members of the department of the History and Philosophy of Science at Melbourne University for their help: Keith Hutchinson, Monica MacCallum, Janusz Sysak, to name but three. Thanks to John Thompson at Polity Press for his editorial skills and encouragement.

Others who have helped by word or deed include, amongst a cast of thousands, Klaus Neumann, Peter Gautry, George Pember Darwin, B. F. Skinner, Noam Chomsky, Patricia Cochrane, Gaby Lyon, Sylvia 'Agro' Stoikos, Jeno Felhosi, members of the Department of Psychology at the University of Melbourne. Thanks also to all the unnamed mothers, babies, friends, students and others who have helped towards completion.

The book is dedicated to Jane and Peter Selby.

The author and publishers are grateful to the following for permission to reprint previously published material in this book: International Universities Press, Inc., and International Thomson Publishing Services Ltd. for material from J. Piaget, *The Origins of Intelligence in the Child* (International Universities Press, Connecticut, 1966; Routledge & Kegan Paul, London, 1937/1953); International Thomson Publishing Services Ltd. and Humanities Press International, Inc., Atlantic Highlands, NJ, for material from J. Piaget, *Language and Thought of the Child* (Routledge & Kegan Paul, London, 1959; Humanities Press International, Atlantic Highlands, NJ, 1962); International Thomson Publishing Services Ltd. for material from J. Piaget, *The Child's Construction of Reality* (Routledge & Kegan Paul, London, 1937/1953) and J. Piaget, *Play, Dreams and Imitation* (Routledge & Kegan Paul, London, 1945/1951); Oxford University Press for 'The Blossom' by William Blake, from G. Keynes (ed.), *Blake: Complete Writings*, 2nd edn (OUP, Oxford, 1966).

1

Looking at Babies

This book probes the foundations of child psychology by looking into what scientists say about babies. It is concerned primarily with the kinds of arguments scientists have advanced about babies and the development of infants. Undoubtedly, an understanding of the institutional setting of such research would help us to piece together the motivations of the scientists who have studied babies and the changing social significance of their work. But it is the work itself that is at issue here: the key differences between the theories of major thinkers about infancy, the part played by observations of babies in their work and some of the tensions which make up contemporary debates about infant development in child psychology.

Observations of babies have been used by a variety of illustrious scientists as a canvas upon which to paint what seem to them to be the origins of human nature. The science of babies is like a microcosm of the science of psychological development. Findings about young children have figured in a variety of discussions, from the evolution of mind to the psychological foundations of learning, love, fantasy, language, reason, communication and social relationship. Today the scientific interest in infancy is matched by a booming popular interest in the first years of life. Car stickers, self-help groups, newspaper supplements, magazines devoted to parent and child, radio and television programmes and books on the birth, growth and care of babies – not to mention political debate – all attest to the importance currently attached to our understanding and care of young children. *Visions of Infancy* is written to provide a backcloth against which to set the modern fascination with childhood by discussing the main theories which have dominated scientific discussions about babies. Each chapter introduces readers to a different and distinctive scientific approach to the analysis of babyhood.

Well. How do you know that somebody has not ?

" But they would have put it into spirits, or into the *Illustrated News*, or perhaps cut it into two halves, poor dear little thing, and sent one to Professor Owen, and one to Professor Huxley, to see what they would each say about it."

Ah, my dear little man! that does not follow at all, as you will see before the end of the story.

" But a water-baby is contrary to nature."

Well, but, my dear little man, you must learn to talk about such things, when you grow older, in a very different way from that. You must not talk about "ain't" and "can't" when you speak of this great wonderful world round you, of which the wisest man knows only

Figure 1.1 'They would cut it into two halves, poor little thing, and send one to Professor Owen, and one to Professor Huxley, to see what they would each say about it' (Charles Kingsley, *The Water Babies*, 1863).

In *The Water Babies* the scientist-giant longs for one hour as a baby again but with full consciousness, because he would know everything then and be at rest.

Source: Victoria State Library.

As well as introducing leading scientific ideas about the beginning of human life, the following chapters explore an urgent debate about children in the study of mental growth. This debate is between those seeing child psychology as a branch of natural history, much like the study of shellfish or shore-birds, and those who see accounts of babyhood as serving primarily to anchor competing interpretations of adulthood in a convincing way. As natural history, the science of babies is simply concerned with what is true or false about infancy. But as an aid to the interpretation of our own lives, the science of babies serves more to draw out or make allegories of different thinkers' principal beliefs about the human condition.

The main issue in this debate is whether findings about babies primarily serve science as a means to construct a coherent picture of what goes on in the mental lives of babies themselves, or whether babies are mainly discussed in science to represent how scientists (not babies) see the world. In short, is the science of babies baby-centred or scientist-centred? And which should it be?

I argue that the science of babies is more scientist-centred than it admits. Scientific discussions of infancy make more sense as illustrations of what the world means to particular scientists than as products of a selfless attempt to describe what the world means to babies and their minders. Part of my evidence for this conclusion is the great diversity of opinions about babyhood, and part of it has to do with the way in which contemporary scientists often underestimate the important, obvious place of negative states in infancy as well as failing to explore the lives of the women who mind babies, lives which are so intimately entwined with babies' own lives.

But I am not simply proposing that child psychology should become more 'child-centred'.[1] Nor am I proposing that, if only scientists would throw away their prejudices and presuppositions, a new assumptionless science of babies would arise. The main use of criticizing research on babies is not to discover what babies are really like, something which I believe cannot be settled in theory but only approached in discussing the rights and wrongs of the practical care of particular babies. It is to illustrate what adult scientists think and feel about the mind. The value of stressing that infancy is not paradise or that babies are anxious or that baby-minders have complicated and ambivalent relationships with their charges is to remind us of facts (the problems of being looked after, negativity, the position of women) which bear on our own understandings and misunderstandings of ourselves. Such findings do not necessarily give us a glimpse of 'the truth' about childhood.

Central to my argument is the belief that human behaviour, including infant behaviour, is radically *ambiguous*. This belief defines what has been called an interpretative or 'hermeneutical' approach, more generally known as the 'new paradigm' in psychology.[2] According to this view, behaviour not only has meaning, but it makes many different sorts of sense, depending on how one views it. There is no single eternal and universal way to understand why a particular baby did a particular thing at a particular time, because each interpretation of infancy is partly shaped by the situation which provoked it. Infant behaviour cannot be used to settle once and for all what human beings are like.

An example

Suppose, for instance, that I wished to demonstrate that 'being able to describe one's own behavior' is the original root of what it is to be human.[3]

How might the study of babies contribute to such a demonstration? Would it be possible for me to find a kind of observation of infant behaviour which would prove that to be a 'mature adult' one must necessarily have learnt how to account out loud for one's acts?

More than one psychologist believes that it is possible to find this kind of observation. Thus, the English psychologists Gauld and Shotter argue that the central problem of psychology is to explain how

> within an extraordinarily brief period, a helpless and superficially inert neonate is transformed or transforms himself into a being who acts, has and implements intentions and desires, is capable up to a point of rational thought, and continually attempts to interact and communicate with other beings similarly endowed.[4]

Such an explanation is important because it would, in these authors' view, show that the way in which we become rational and intentional, the essential marks of maturity, is essentially bound up with interpreting the meanings of others' and our own behaviours.

To bear out this claim, Shotter and Gregory report an analysis of a mother and an eleven-month-old girl, Samantha, playing with a 'form-board'. The form-board is like a six-piece jig-saw puzzle that will only go together in one way. At one point in filling it in, Samatha accidently or not slips a piece of it into the correct slot. The mother says 'Clever girl!':

> But Samantha had not paused in her activity and signalled by eye contact and smiling that she had done something socially significant, she just went straight away onto manipulating something else. So her mother leant forward, caught her eye, and repeated her 'marker' i.e. 'AREN'T YOU CLEVER?'. Samantha then stopped and smiled.[5]

Shotter and Gregory remark that, in repeating herself, the mother marks one of her daughter's actions as having a significance (for the mother) above and beyond Samantha's other behaviour. It is by somehow 'taking note' of such emphases that babies are thought to gain an idea of themselves as persons, as agents who can act, and have social responsibility of their actions. This view of the origin of human relations had earlier been advanced by the American philosopher George Herbert Mead.[6] Similar ideas have been taken up and developed by a number of today's child psychologists (see especially chapter 8).

I argue that this kind of observation casts no direct light on the foundations of the human mind. As we shall see, infant behaviour can be described in ways which lead to quite different conclusions about the basis of mental life. The value of such observations is as reflections of the way in which scientists think about psychological change. Thus, the description of Samantha and her mother vividly illustrates Shotter and Gregory's belief that adults become what they are by coming to understand themselves in terms applied to them by others. But at the same time, what is missing or most unresolved in their account gives us insight into the main shortcomings of their theory and the questions which, as developmental psychologists, we must keep on asking.

For instance, what is the basis for a baby's coming to understand itself in others' terms? How is this effected? What are the underlying processes? Shotter and Gregory give us no clue. Is there simply an innate human faculty for understanding other people, present from birth? More particularly, in the case of Shotter and Gregory's work, what is the evidence that babies really do 'read' the emphases of their parents' behaviours in their parents' terms? Might it be that babies interpret others' social actions, but not in others' terms? Might Samantha *misinterpret* her mother's expression?

And what of the 'others' who interact with babies? How can we assess Shotter and Gregory's answer to what Gauld and Shotter call the central problem in psychology unless we have a prior (and therefore equally important) analysis of what the behaviour of these others means? Did Samantha's mother really think Samantha was clever? Or does she habitually make this kind of comment as a means of aiding in the management of her baby's fluctuating moods? Did she feel proud of Samantha? Or did she feel anxious in the experimenter's laboratory, and think this might be the kind of thing the experimenter wanted her to do? Did she think Samantha's behaviour was an accident? What does she imagine the experiment is about? And how come she is taking part in it?

Unless we have answers to these questions, we cannot be sure whether children ever come to understand themselves as their mothers do, let alone 'within an extraordinarily brief period' in infancy. And answers cannot be produced without doing a kind of research aimed to solve problems quite different from the one Gauld and Shotter claim to be so central to psychology. For instance, to determine whether and how well Samantha interpreted her mother's emphasized repetition, the mother would have to be interviewed to give the researchers a sense of what she meant by what she said and did. Such an interview would need an analysis which recognized the many, subtle, often distorted ways in which speech can be a medium of an adult's mental life.[7] Devising this analysis would lead us a long way from the topic of babies, not least because babies cannot speak.

The study of babies is not the royal road to understanding the basis of human knowledge. Rather, the analysis of how scientists have discussed infancy serves as a route to understanding the fundamentals and shortcomings of their theories about mental life. This is the route taken in the following chapters. The aim throughout is to discover the key themes and silences in scientific discussion of what children's minds are and how they change, as illustrated by theories of infancy.

Synopsis of the Following Chapters

Whilst the book is not primarily a history of child study and makes no detailed attempt to trace the influences of earlier scientists on later ones, or the changing political context of scientific work on infants, I have organized the chapters according to a rough chronology. Hence, Darwin (b. 1809) is discussed before Watson (b. 1878), Freud (b. 1856) before Piaget (b. 1896), Skinner (b. 1904) before Chomsky (b. 1928). Earlier work on babies is dealt with at the beginning of the book and current research towards the end.

More precisely, the book is organized around two nodal chapters, each presenting work which is generally taken to be a landmark in the history of child psychology: chapter 2 on Charles Darwin's discussion of early mental development and chapter 5 on Noam Chomsky's theory of language acquisition. Chapters 3 and 4 challenge and amend the idea that Darwin was the 'forefather' of child psychology, exploring the theory of association to which his own work appealed and its stepchildren, behaviourism and psycho-analysis. Chapters 6, 7 and 8 show how the research Chomsky inspired has led psychologists to go considerably beyond his initial formulations about child language in a variety of directions: cognitive, emotional and interactive.

Although the book does not itself discuss the social and intellectual changes which ground the history of child study, its chapters lay out some of the coordinates for that discussion. Hence readers will gain a sense of the links and contrasts between today's child psychology and work of an earlier era. It is this sense of contrast which I draw on in chapter 9 to argue that an idealizing theme is to be found in today's scientific picture of infancy. Such a theme was almost absent from the writings about babies of Charles Darwin.

Darwin was undoubtedly a pioneer of child study. He published two important analyses of infant expression during the 1870s.[8] By focusing on Darwin's work, chapter 2 investigates how evolutionary theory relates to psychological discussions about the genesis of human experiences. I argue that Darwin's interest in infancy was less promoted by an interest in the dynamics of mental development than by the need to demonstrate the truth of the idea that even the most peculiarly human of our mental faculties could have originated gradually and naturally, rather than being specially created by God. Nevertheless, Darwin's deliberations about babies draw on two theories of mental dynamics. The first is epitomized by the idea that infants are born with innate mental faculties or 'instincts'. The second assumes that mental characteristics are habits built upon association between events and reactions which have occurred together in the past. In the first case a child's pleasure in conversing with a friend would be explained as the natural consequence of an instinct to communicate and co-operate with other human beings, as both Darwin and some of today's scientists propose (see chapters 2 and 8). In the second theory, the child's pleasure might be the consequence of associating the friend or the conversation with pleasurable experience in the past, an exciting game, for example.

Chapter 3 explores the second of these two theories in more detail. Two different visions of mental development as the result of learning are discussed: associationism and behaviourism. 'Associationism' had its first flowering in England during the eighteenth century. It has informed many theories of mental growth, from Darwinian evolutionism to Freud's psycho-analysis. From the 1700s onwards, its exponents have illustrated their tenets by discussing the development of babies. But, unlike Charles Darwin's evolutionary theory, early associationism was part of a moral and political programme intended to provide a rational method of social change.

Similar aims, albeit differently framed, have shaped the twentieth-century approach to the explanation of development advanced by behaviourists. Like associationists, behaviourists base their account of adult actions on the particular history of learning which is supposed to have given all individuals their shape. But behaviourists deny the existence of the 'internal processes' which are the main topic of associationist explanation. Whilst this denial has led behaviourists to make discoveries of undoubted relevance to the psychology of development, such discoveries cannot contribute directly to a psychology which takes experience as its field of concern – where 'experience' is taken to mean, not simply 'the lessons of the past', but the perhaps idiosyncratic significances which structure the sense an individual or group currently makes of the world.

Chapter 4 examines another twentieth-century version of associationism: psycho-analysis. Freudian theories of childhood have had a great influence in shaping modern psychological visions of infancy. Even the American behaviourist J. B. Watson stated that he had accepted 'a large part' of Freudian theory.[9] But, unlike behaviourism, psycho-analysis is directly concerned with explaining the genesis and structure of mental states, particularly those of disturbed adults. By tracing the treatments of infancy to be found in the works of Freud, Melanie Klein and Jacques Lacan, I draw out a movement in European psycho-analytic thinking from seeing the patients's remembered childhood as literally *causing* adult illness, as in

Freud's early 'seduction theory', towards seeing accounts of infancy as analogies which derive their meaning from the present dynamics of the relationship between analyst and patient in which they are produced. This movement illustrates one of the book's central themes. For I wish to suggest that scientific findings about babies cannot be supposed simply to provide a factual basis for the explanation of adult characteristics. In what they ignore and what they accentuate, scientific visions of infancy reveal the preoccupations and desires of scientists themselves. This theme is further developed in chapter 9.

Chapter 5 focuses on the substance and style of Noam Chomsky's review of *Verbal Behavior* (1957) by B. F. Skinner.[10] Chomsky's critique of behaviourism as applied to the acquisition of language marks a well-acknowledged watershed in approaches to infant mind. But Chomsky's own explanation for language development is, in its dependence upon the idea that the brain is pre-programmed to process grammar, as much a barrier to the study of the experience of babies as is Skinner's overt opposition to the study of mental states. By proposing that the main course of language development was determined independently of the child's ability to learn, think or feel, Chomsky suggested that the deliberations of psychologists about experience were essentially irrelevant to explaining how humans acquire one of their most distinctive mental qualities. This challenge to psychologists has been met during the past three decades by an enormous outpouring of research into the mental and social lives of young children.

After a decade of research exploring Chomsky's speculations about the origin of language in young children, some psychologists began to say that the ability to speak must after all be a consequence of broad developments in the reasoning of young children. Chapter 6 reviews two different approaches to explaining this early growth of rationality. Perhaps the most influential formulations of early cognitive development were made by Jean Piaget who, in the 1930s, had conducted intensive studies of babies to investigate how intentional action, internal representations of the external world and the ability to represent the world symbolically grow in the first year and a half of life. After discussing Piaget's research, the chapter moves on to discuss more recent analyses of the growth of a rational understanding of the physical world, focusing in particular on the theory of infant cognition advanced by T. G. R. Bower. Bower's work is discussed as a contrast to Piaget's, both in method and explanation. But both Piagetian and post-Piagetian explanations of the formation of early ideas seem deficient in their failure to consider emotional life to play a part in the development of reasoning.

Chapter 7 discusses theories of emotional development. A wide variety of findings show the importance of affectionate care for the optimal growth of young children. These findings have in recent decades been most famously condensed into a theory of *attachment*. 'Attachment theory' states that babies will naturally grow up to be sociable, obedient and well-adjusted, provided that they have the consistent care of their mother or a mother-substitute. Since its proposal thirty years ago, attachment theory has been both challenged and changed by the observational studies it has inspired. In particular, increasing attention has been given to the unsuspected complexity and variety of the infant's early behavioural repertoire, including its negative aspects, and to the contribution of carers to the emotional growth of the child.

Chapter 8 discusses research on interactions between babies and adults. I discuss particularly a detailed analysis of a film of an early 'conversation'. Whilst not questioning the richness of expressive behaviour in early social interactions, the chapter is structured as a debate of the view that babies are born with a faculty for understanding other people. I argue that the evidence used to support the existence of such a faculty can equally well be interpreted as supporting the views that infants are born seeking, not an understanding of others, but conditions which either support and extend their own expressive displays and motivations or that lead to the transcendence of fear. My argument runs counter to the basic assumption of attachment theory: that babies are naturally oriented from birth to form a love-relationship with their carer(s).

Chapter 9 takes up the central theme of the book concerning the need to see modern theories of infancy as going beyond the facts which they try to explain. Scientists studying babies do not simply measure and calculate, they take part in a debate about the moral status of human life which stretches back through countless centuries of poetry and religious teaching. The chapter focuses in particular on the image of infancy as paradise.

It explores how some modern theories of babyhood might lead us to believe that the first year of life is the brightest and best of all those that are to follow. Such a vision excludes the dark side of the baby's early experience and of the experiences of those who look after babies. To make the negative secondary in formulations of infancy is to suggest from the beginning that sadness, frustration and violence are introduced into life from outside, often through those who are forced to take primary responsibility for child-care – namely mothers. An idealization of infancy would support a worrisome tendency amongst 'those who know' to blame mothers for the difficulties characteristic of childhood and later life.[11] It would allow development to be discussed without reference to the great obstacles to progress of poverty and disease which dominate the lives of millions of children and their minders.

The final chapter draws together the lines of my argument about infancy to illustrate the case against viewing developmental psychology as a science comparable to physiology or physics. I argue that scientific observations about babies are more like mirrors which reflect back the preoccupations and visions of those who study them than like windows opening directly on to the foundations of the mind. I suggest that it is the failure to recognize the study of infancy as a venture in self-reflection, rather than viewing it as a form of natural history akin to botany or bird-watching, that renders modern psychology susceptible to the short-comings I try to pinpoint in this book. These are:

1 the view that psychology can contribute to human understanding without making reference to how individuals understand their own experiences and mental life (see especially chapters 2, 3 and 5);
2 the emphasis on the form and instrumental functions of language as a tool of cognition rather than on its power to reveal to each of us differently the world and powers of our own being (see chapters 4 and 5);
3 the assumption that the significance of selected behaviours such as looking or crying can be judged independently from an analysis of the part they play in the wider subjective lives which give them sense (see chapters 6 and 7);
4 the belief that the understanding of others is naturally endowed by an inherited brain mechanism, rather than having to be repeatedly struggled for (see chapter 8); and,
5 the failure to account for the ways in which studies of infancy are shaped by the personal and historical conditions of those who conduct them (see chapter 9).

I conclude that, if these shortcomings are to be surmounted, developmental psychology must move beyond the model of itself as a science that merely looks at nature. It must become a self-conscious discipline advocating the grounds for change. Such a psychology would not content itself with supporting its theoretical statements by uttering general observations about the extraordinary capacities of babies. It would be a discipline intended to better the understanding, position and prospects of those most disadvantaged in human affairs – including, when babies are being discussed, the lot of those who look after them.

2

The Question of Genesis

From the publication of *Origin of Species* to the end of the 19th century, many thinkers were intrigued with drawing parallels between animal and child, between primitive human and child, between early human history and child development. The developing human being was seen as a natural museum of human natural history. Thus the child's development was believed to reveal the unfolding of the species. By careful observation of the infant and child, the descent of the human species could be traced. The search for biological and historical clues in the child's development marked the beginning of a science of child behaviour. Thus Darwin was truly the scientific forefather of child psychology.

A. Clarke-Stewart et al.,
Child Development: A Topical Approach

It was late on an August evening in 1831 that a young English naturalist and sportsman opened a letter which was to change his life. Recently graduated with an arts degree from Cambridge University, the twenty-two-year-old Charles Darwin's future was undecided. One possibility was that he would join the clergy. At Cambridge, he had pursued a wide range of interests, from reading theological treatises by William Paley to collecting rare beetles. Amongst the friends he had made were some of the leading naturalists of his day, including the Reverend J. S. Henslow, Professor of Botany at the University.[1]

It was Henslow's letter that he held in his hand on that fateful summer evening of 1831. Enclosed was an invitation to spend two years as ship's naturalist aboard the ten-gun brig HMS *Beagle*, shortly to set sail for South America and the Pacific Islands. Despite his father's misgivings about this 'wild and useless' scheme, the young man set sail with the *Beagle* two days after Christmas the same year.[2]

HMS *Beagle* took almost five years to circumnavigate the earth. During this time, her ship's naturalist industriously collected specimens of fossils, plants and animals which he later used as evidence to show that the world's living inhabitants had a history to which the book of Genesis gave no clue. His comparison of the animals on the west coast of South America with those on the nearby Galapagos islands was later used to show that both groups had members of the same species as distant ancestors but that the insular species had developed distinctive adaptations to exploit the peculiar advantages of their island environment. These advantages were different from those developed on mainland America, so that, in Darwin's day, mainland and island species sometimes looked similar but were physically different, and would not breed with each other.

The Royal Navy's HMS *Beagle* returned to Britain in 1836. Her ship's naturalist now had no doubts as to a future career. He began an arduous course of observations at the zoo, discussion with fellow naturalists and visits to the scientific museums in London. This course was to lead to the formulation of a theory which concluded that different species of plant and animal have evolved naturally and gradually from single filaments in a soupy sea. Forty years later he wrote that the two years and three months between his return in 1836 and his marriage in 1839 'were the most active ones I ever spent'.[3]

In 1837 Darwin began systematically to fill a series of notebooks which organized and developed his insights into natural history. Most of these were concentrated on the problem of the metamorphoses of species. But two, labelled 'M' and 'N', dealt almost exclusively with psychological, moral, aesthetic and metaphysical issues. Here we find that the focus of Darwin's interest could shift from biology to philosophy and materialism, dreams, conscience, reverie, association, the emotions, mental illness and the nature of beauty. Far from being marginal interests of a man concerned with the more important matters of biology, these are written by someone who calls the mysteries of the human heart 'the citadel itself'.[4] He describes the study of animals as merely a 'frontier instance', an oblique way of exploring the characteristic constitution and possibilities of the human species.[5] But he believed, as he told his friends and family, and later the public, with charming self-deprecation in *The Descent of Man*, that his gifts were not suited to the study of higher mental processes.[6]

Darwin's preferred method of research was observational.[7] Hence his interest in the *Beagle* assignment, his fossil-collection, his studies of orchids, climbing plants, barnacles and earthworms, his discussions with animal-breeders and his visits to the zoo. But notebooks 'M' and 'N' were preoccupied with problems to which observation was not an obvious solution. They focused primarily on the ways in which habits, patterns of feeling and behaviour, might be acquired and transmitted from generation to generation. His discussions of habit led Darwin not only to re-read the accounts of species-change given by his grandfather Erasmus Darwin (1731–1802) but to investigate a wide range of mental phenomena, including 'double consciousness' and mental disorders, as illustrated by the case-notes of his father, a medical practitioner.[8] He became particularly interested in how we often act in ways of which we are unaware or that we cannot control. He referred to dreams and introspective reports of his own and catalogues his sister's analysis of day-dreams and 'castles in the air'. He reflected upon drunkenness, memory and the difficulties of remembering what happened to us when children. He was even led to record his own memories of early childhood in a fragment of autobiography in 1838.[9]

As notebooks 'M' and 'N' progress, we find that the questions in which Darwin was interested led him to remark ever more frequently on the behaviours and attitudes of young children. By the end of 1838 Darwin was clearly regarding the 'natural history of babies' as a way to show that human habits or mental qualities are inherited in forms which from birth, 'before experience', show clear links with the habitual reactions of animals: 'Do babies . . . wink, when anything placed before their eyes, very young, before experience can have taught them to avoid danger. Do they know from when they first see it?'[10] The study of infants would also provide a testing-ground for associationist ideas about the growth of adult habits. Was grandfather Erasmus right to argue as follows?

> The origin of the smile has generally been ascribed to an inexplicable instinct, but may be deduced from our early association of actions and ideas. In the act of sucking, the lips of the infant are closed round the nipple of its mother, till it has filled its stomach, and the pleasure of digesting this grateful food succeeds; the the sphincter of the mouth, fatigued by the continued action of sucking, is relaxed; and the antagonist muscles of the face gently acting, produce the smile of pleasure which is thus during our lives associated with gentle pleasure.[11]

Direct observation might tell. So when in 1839, eight years to the day after HMS *Beagle* set sail, Darwin's wife Emma Wedgwood gave birth to their first child, William Erasmus, it was not surprising that the baby's father immediately began to fill a new notebook with detailed observations of his son's behaviours.[12] 'My first child was born on December 27th 1839, and I at once commenced to make notes on the first dawn of various expressions which he exhibited . . I could not at all agree that various muscles had been specially created for the sake of expression.'[13]

The notebook on William, who was nicknamed 'Doddy', shows that Darwin was exploring a variety of explanations for the form of early actions and expressions. He was certainly on the look-out for behaviours in the newborn which were instinctive or 'just like an old person's', but he also noted down behaviours which appeared to have been learnt or modified by experience:

> When nine weeks and three days old – whilst lying on his back cooing and kicking very happily – I happened to sneeze – which made it [*sic*] start, frown, look frightened and cry rather badly – for an hour afterwards every noise made him start – he was nervous. I think he certainly has undefined instinctive fears – as for instance when stripped naked – I think also when peeping under dark doorways.[14]

We find that Darwin's interest in his first-born son's 'vague fears' led him to make a 'wonderous number of strange noises and stranger grimaces' at Doddy, most of which were 'taken as good jokes'.

Darwin also explored baby William's ability to reason. The first sign of reason was recorded as follows:

> April 20th (aged 114 days) – Took my finger to his mouth and as usual could not get it in, on account of his own hand being in the way; then slipped his own back and so got my finger in – this was not chance and therefore a kind of reasoning.[15]

Ten days later, Darwin noted a new association: 'May 30th. He understands when his cloak is on, he is to go out and is cross, if not taken out immediately.'[16]

Darwin's further discussions of the capacity for deduction concerned his son's reactions to mirrors:

> When four and a half months old, he repeatedly smiled at my image and his own in a mirror, and no doubt mistook them for real objects, but he shows sense in being evidently surprised at my voice coming from behind him. Like all infants he much enjoyed thus looking at himself, and in less then two months perfectly understood that it was an image; for if I made quite silently an odd grimace, he would suddenly turn round and look at me. . . The higher apes which I tried with a small looking glass behaved differently; they placed their

Plate 2.1 Charles Darwin with his son 'Doddy' in 1841. Doddy was the main focus for the 'Biographical Sketch of a Baby' Darwin published a quarter of a century later in support of his evolutionary ideas.
Source: Cambridge University Library.

hand behind the glass, and in doing so showed their sense, but far from taking pleasure in looking at themselves they got angry and would look no more.[17]

Many of Darwin's observations of Doddy have been confirmed or extended by later investigators. They cover an impressive variety of behaviours: William's growing sense of humour and pleasure in games ('How can he find bo-peep amusing?'), his reflexes and first expressions, both of pleasure and annoyance, his first imitations, his memory, self-confidence, moral sense and jealousy, and his interests – particularly in music and in other people: 'He looks very much pleased after the performance of any of these accomplishments. He evidently studies expressions of those around him, especially if anything new is done before him.'[18]

Plate 2.2 Recent research shows that babies who are in a situation which is ambiguous inspect the faces of the adults around them in order to work out how to react. If the adults look worried, babies are more likely to cry or to break off what they are doing than if adults look happy or unconcerned. This kind of checking has been called 'social referencing'.[19]
Source: S. and R. Greenhill Photo Library.

The Publication of Darwin's Research on Babies

The basis of Darwin's theory of natural selection in plants and animals was worked out by the time of Doddy's birth in 1839. When this theory was published in *On the Origin of Species*, twenty years later, his notes on Doddy played no part in the evidence for evolution he reviewed. But when he sat down to marshal evidence for *human* evolution in the late 1860s, pride of place went to the argument that those who disbelieve in the natural and gradual evolution of human faculties would do well to study their development in young children.

It was Darwin's book *The Expression of Emotions in Man and Animals* (1872) that developed this point.[20] There he set out to prove in detail what *The Descent of Man* (1871) had argued more generally: that human minds, like human bodies, were products of an evolutionary history linking us to animals, not to to God. *The Expression of Emotions* concentrated on just one mental faculty. And Darwin did not focus upon the experience of emotion but on the anatomical structure of facial and other expressions. He aimed to demonstrate that expressions of emotion are not only shared by all kinds of human being, including different races and the insane, but show a systematic likeness to the expression of other mammals.

He described five methods to find out how far particular movements of the face and gestures are really expressive of certain states of mind. First amongst these was 'to observe infants; for they exhibit many emotions, as Sir C. Bell remarks "with extraordinary force", whereas, in after life, some of our expressions "cease to have the pure and simple source from which they spring in infancy".'[21] Chapter by chapter Darwin discussed the expressions of weeping, anxiety, high spirits, meditation, hatred and anger, disdain, horror and shame. He drew heavily on his notebook on Doddy, particularly in the chapter on 'suffering and weeping'.

Darwin's interest in infant suffering was primarily in showing that the characteristic muscle-movements which form cries have an intelligible natural history. He described these movements like this:

> Infants, when suffering even slight pain, moderate hunger, or discomfort, utter violent and prolonged screams. Whilst thus screaming their eyes are firmly closed, so that the skin round them is wrinkled, and the forehead contracted into a frown. The mouth is widely opened with the lips retracted in a peculiar manner, which causes it to assume a squarish form; the gums or teeth more or less exposed.[22]

Darwin spent much of his subsequent discussion of crying trying to explain why there was a contraction of the muscles around the eyes when

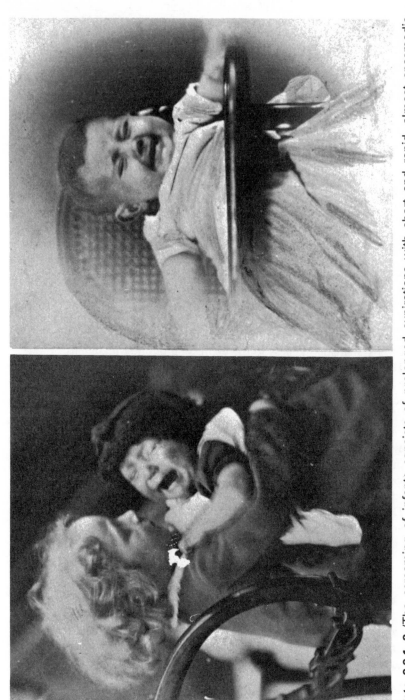

Plate 2.3.1-2 'The screaming of infants consists of prolonged expirations with short and rapid, almost spasmodic inspiration, followed at a somewhat more advanced age by sobbing'. Darwin, *The Expression of Emotions*, 1872, p. 158. *Source*: Cambridge University Library.

screaming. His favoured explanation was that the eyes close in order to protect the eyeball from injury by violent expiration. He went on to relate eye-closing to a topic that had exercised him thirty years earlier in his notebook on Doddy: the secretion of tears. Darwin's babies did not at first weep when they cried. But Darwin had noticed that at eleven weeks, one of Doddy's eyes formed tears after it had been accidentally brushed by the cuff of his father's coat. Meanwhile the other eye remained dry. This suggested that: 'As a slight blow on the eyelids causes a copious secretion of tears, it is at least possible that the spasmodic contraction of the eyelids, by pressing strongly on the eyeball, should in a similar manner cause some secretion.'[23]

Then, through 'numberless generations' of repeated association between eye closing whilst crying and tear-production, the link between weeping with distress would be born. (NB This involves the inheritance of acquired characters; see next chapter.) With age, we manage to 'repress' the muscular contractions associated with sorrow but we cannot stop our eyes forming tears. Yet, Darwin remarks,

> if, during an early period of life, when habits of all kinds are readily established, our infants, when pleased, had been accustomed to utter loud peals of laughter (during which the vessels of their eyes are distended) as often and as continuously as they have yielded when distressed to screaming fits, then it is probable that in after life tears would have been as copiously and regularly secreted under the one state of mind as under the other. Gentle laughter, or a smile, or even a pleasing thought, would have sufficed to cause a moderate secretion of tears.[24]

In concluding the book, Darwin went on to consider whether and how the *recognition* of facial expressions, like the expressions themselves, might have become instinctive. He reported that when Doddy was

> a few days over six months old, his nurse pretended to cry, and I saw that his face instantly assumed a melancholy expression, with the corners of the mouth strongly depressed; now this child could rarely have seen any other child crying, and never a grown-up crying, and I should doubt whether at so early an age he could have reasoned on the subject. Therefore it seems to me that an innate feeling must have told him that the pretended crying of his nurse expressed grief; and this through the instinct of sympathy excited grief in him.[25]

Communication in Infancy

Apart from essays about the power of movement in plants and the habits of worms, Darwin's last public statement relevant to human psychology was his *Biographical Sketch on an Infant* (1877).[17] This was a response to the translation of a brief article by the French philosopher Hippolyte Taine on the acquisition of language by his infant daughter.[26] Taine's essay stimulated Darwin to dust off his notes on Doddy and write an article which reads like a representation in miniature of all those grand metaphysical themes which had preoccupied him in the notebooks 'M' and 'N' begun forty years earlier. Aesthetics and morality, sympathy, sorrow and affection, play and jealousy all make their appearance in this sketch of Doddy's early months. But the overall argument has been clarified. By concentrating once again on the baby's expressions, Darwin points out that human language is built on a base which is not made up of words. Long before the one-year-old Doddy invented his first word ('mum' meaning 'food'), he had built up a rich and complex means of non-verbal communication – 'by the unconscious expression of the features, by gestures and in a marked manner by different intonations'.[27] Beginning from instinctive cries to express his wants, Doddy progressed towards speech through both the voluntary and the unconscious modification of his actions. And Darwin stressed once again that: 'An infant understands to a certain extent, and as I believe at a very early period, the meaning or feelings of those who tend him, by the expression of their features.'[28]

As evidence Darwin reported that, before sympathizing with the nurse's pretended grief at six months, his son also responded with pleasure to smiling from before two months of age and 'understood a compassionate expression at a little over five months old'.

> Before he was a year old, he understood intonations and gestures, as well as several words and short sentences. He understood one word, namely his nurse's name, exactly five months before he invented his first word *mum*; and this is what might have been expected, as we know that the lower animals easily learn to understand spoken words.[29]

By ending on this note, Darwin hoped not only to have described the first means of communication between adult and infant but also to have struck a conclusive blow to prove that one of the most human of faculties, the use of language, had evolved gradually and naturally from a basis which is already present in animals and which makes a reappearance at the start of human infancy.

Figure 2.1 An illustration from what is commonly regarded as the first alphabetic picture-book for children, devised by Comenius and published in 1623.[30] For Comenius, the defining characteristic of a baby was that it 'crieth' – 'Infans ejulat!'
Source: Melbourne University Library.

Questioning Darwin's Legacy

In the autobiography Darwin began to write in old age, he declared himself, like his grandfather Erasmus Darwin, a cautious optimist. He was well aware of the enormous suffering that humans undergo. Not without cause did he call mature existence a struggle, although, in his view, joy ultimately outbalanced suffering. But his view of infancy was bleaker. In his picture of infancy, suffering and weeping, or the custom of 'yielding when distressed to screaming fits', take the central place.[31]

Nevertheless, Darwin's work has been used to support interpretations of infancy that leave little room for suffering. These assume that natural selection normally ensures a harmonious fit between organism and environment, in which suffering is either unnatural or accidental. (Darwin himself explicitly denied that evolution makes all living things optimally adapted to the world they live in;[32] see chapter 9 for further discussion.) Or they leave no room for any mental state in their explanations of behaviour, whether suffering, joy or trepidation. Such interpreters include behaviourists like B. F. Skinner (see next chapter). They also include those who say that mental qualities, such as personality or intelligence, or depression are genetically determined 'before experience' (see chapter 5).

It is my argument that no mental quality can be fixed 'before experience'. On the contrary, personality and other such qualities are constituted in and by experience (past and present). To assume these traits can be biochemically fixed 'by evolution' is to forget that evolution is more than biochemistry. Worse, it is to nullify the entire venture of psychology as traditionally defined – which is the study of mental states, mental life or experience.[33]

The seeds in Darwin's work of the idea that human development can be scientifically explained without reference to mental life can be illustrated by his use of the word *instinct*. For example, he cites instincts of self-preservation, sexual love, the love of the mother for her newborn offspring, the desire possessed by the later to suck, and so forth.[34]

Instinct is a word whose scientific value has been questioned for centuries. Thus in *The Temple of Nature* (1803) Darwin's grandfather curtly dismissed the argument of those who tried to explain away parental care as the result of paternal and maternal 'instincts': 'These as well as many other animals facts, which are difficult to account for, have been referred to an inexplicable instinct; which is supposed to preclude further investigation.[35] In the elder Darwin's view, parental behaviour was most likely to have been acquired by learning in a state preceding the animal's present one and have been derived from the parents to the offspring 'by imitation, or other kind of tradition'.[36]

By modern students of animal behaviour too the claim that mental qualities are instinctive has been called 'merely a cloak for ignorance'.[37] To call behaviours 'instinctive' suggests that we can explain them in genetical terms, without reference to the psychological and social principles which give them their significance. As Robert Hinde observes, the term instinct is usually applied to behaviour that seems to be driven from within or develop independently of the types of experience that might be thought important for it. Thus, when we see a baby 'spontaneously' cry upon seeing its nurse feign tears, we might argue, as did Darwin, that this shows there is an instinct for sympathy. But this is to argue in a circle: 'We postulate the instinct because we observe the behaviour and then we explain the behaviour by the instinct we have postulated.'[38]

To claim sympathy is innate because it occurs without an obvious precedent, or in all members of a species, is to assume without evidence that early and widespread phenomena cannot be produced by psychological processes which are more basic than sympathy, such as sensori-motor learning or the struggle to transcend anxiety.[39]

The confusion which underpins Darwin's claim that mental qualities are inherited or 'instinctive' is linked to his failure to distinguish between what would now be called the 'genotypes' of organisms (their genes) and their 'phenotypes' (their observable appearance, including their body structure and other existential qualities as living, breathing individuals). Only genes are inherited. But it is as phenotypes that organisms take part in what Darwin called 'the struggle for life'. The links between the characteristics of genotypes and of phenotypes are all-important for evolutionary theory. But these links can only be studied once we have independently analysed both aspects of the organism.

In this connection it is important to note that the modern biochemical vocabulary which describes genes is quite inappropriate for the analysis of all the existential phenotypic qualities of living individuals. This is particularly true of behaviour. Only a vocabulary which adequately represents psychological events as such will put us in a position to decide whether or not a baby's behaviour is 'the same' as an old person's. For whatever the logical or the antomical similarities between expressions of 'emotion' or 'reason' in babies (or animals) and those of adults, to claim these expressions involve 'the same' mental operation is to ignore the possibility that the infant's subjective world is organized in ways which are profoundly different from those of adults, including scientists. In his discussion of instinct, Charles Darwin, and the 'socio-biologists' and 'psycho-biologists' who follow him today, commit what William James called the Psychologist's Fallacy *par excellence*: the confusion of his own point of view with that of the babies he describes.[40]

As part of a conscious policy to avoid arousing undue controversy, Darwin decided to side-line all discussion of the human mind in his first public formulation of evolutionary theory. This automatically suggested that evolutionary change could be explained without reference to mental life. Thus his main evidence for evolution was derived primarily from such non-psychological sources as geology, paleontology, the geographical distribution of zoological species and the study of domesticated animals. Nevertheless, when he published *The Origin of Species*, he could not completely avoid discussion of the mind. His concluding chapter contains this brief but tantalizing paragraph: 'In the distant future I see open fields for far more important researches. Psychology will be based on a new foundation, that of the necessary acquirement of each mental power and capacity of gradation. Light will be thrown on the origin of man and his history'.[41]

Darwin's idea that human intellectual faculties have been gradually perfected through natural selection has inspired and informed scientists up to the present day. But when Darwin and his successors have come to work out in more detail the implications of evolution for psychology, they have found that mental qualities are less marginal to the process of organic change than *The Origin of Species* suggested.

From a psychological point of view, the theory of natural selection is not all that is needed to explain the gradual and natural acquisition of intellectual faculties. Indeed, *The Descent of Man* draws heavily on pre-Darwinian psychological traditions which suggest that evolutionary developments may be directed by, not the cause of, mental processes. For example, organisms may at first adapt to their environmental conditions by learning new behaviours or imitating others, after which any heritable genetic variations or imitating others, after which any heritable genetic variations leading to structural changes which support the organism's new mode of life will be advantageous and have a better chance of being transmitted to future generations. This method of acquiring characters 'may closely simulate Lamarckism'.[41]

Thus, a ground-feeding bird that finds itself in a new environment rich in flowering trees may learn to sip their nectar, passing this on to its offspring by imitation. But as generation succeeds generation, any genetic change which renders the bird more agile or with a bill better adapted to eat its new food will be selected: 'Thus behaviour will always tend to be one jump ahead of structure, and so to play a decisive role in the evolutionary process.'[43] As Ernst Mayr wrote of the most advanced animal species: 'Much evidence indicates that most major evolutionary shifts began with a behavioural shift'.[44]

As noted above, Darwin's own historical reconstructions of how sexual differences in bodily form might have been selected show that mental qualities are intrinsic to the conceptualization of this kind of evolutionary change. Thus strength, size of body, deadly tusks and teeth, musical organs, bright colours and ornamental appendages have all been indirectly gained by one sex or the other through courage, pugnacity, perseverance, the exertion of choice, the influence of love and jealousy, and the appreciation of the beautiful in sound, colour or form.[45]

Of course, to accept that the mind has played a part in the origin of variations is not to deny that, once generated, adaptations will wax or wane in a given population subject to the laws of natural and sexual selection. But it is to suggest that there is an important degree of independence between the biological analysis of evolution and the analysis of its mental aspects. For the fact of evolution cannot figure in psychology as it does in biology. To say that a mental quality is coded in our genes, whether it be intelligence, altruism or manic-depression, tells the psychologist who is interested in how such qualities are generated nothing until the mental and social processes which produce these qualities have been clearly defined *in psychological terms*. Nor does it tell us how such qualities have come to be inherited.

Not surprisingly the evidence supposed to support the biochemical inheritance of mental qualities such as intelligence and personality is still so controversial as to be itself the focus of insistent critical enquiry.[46] This controversy partly arises from misconceptions about the explanatory relationship between the brain and the mind.[47] Thus, to argue that mental qualities are genetically coded is to argue that genes produce brain processes which, in turn, produce the mind. But the claim that the origin of mental states can be 'explained' by the evolution of the brain is once again to confuse different conceptual vocabularies between which the relationship is not causal.

Darwin's studies of babies give us an insight into the wonderful breadth of his interests. And they beautifully illustrate the idea that human beings are products of organic evolution. But they do not settle *how* human experience develops. Nor do they show that such faculties as language or reason can be acquired independently of or 'before' experience. Indeed, to say that mental abilities are 'innate' or determined 'in the genes' does not answer but closes off the most important psychological questions about human genesis in a way that does scant justice to Darwin's own open-minded standards of enquiry.

Darwin's work is often taken to be an unbeatable example of the way in which great minds deduce timeless scientific laws from painstaking enquiry into the phenomena of nature. Yet Darwin's project was more sophisticated than this image suggests. For the existence of evolutionary change had been talked about long before Darwin came to fame.[48] Darwin's great achievement depended on his use of evidence to convince the thinking public that evolution was a *scientifically reputable* idea. For Darwin, a bird or fossil was far from being an inert object waiting to have the law-like secret of its history deduced by the dispassionate eye of the scientist. In Darwin's hands a fossil was a way to change how humans understood their own status in the natural world. Likewise, when Darwin discussed babies, he did not do so simply as a dispassionate observer of nature. He used observations of babies as weapons in his war to wake humans up to the lowliness of their origins, to upset once and for all the idea that we are made in God's image, to challenge the proud illusions fostered by the religion of his day.

The Descent of Man was a book which made a point. Man has *descended* from the apes. Human life is not as marvellous ('advanced') as it might be. My point has been to argue that the problem of how human life might be made better, or of how 'new' life begins, is not solely a matter of chance or natural history. It is primarily a psychological problem, a problem which Darwin's theory does not directly address.

Summary

Was Charles Darwin the 'forefather' of child psychology? Such an assertion can be questioned on historical grounds. We might point, for example, to earlier writers who had published observations of infants as evidence for speculations about development of the mind, including Darwin's grandfather, the Scottish 'common sense' philosophers of the late 1700s and the German philosopher Tiedemann.[49] But the Darwinian paternity of developmental psychology is more directly disproved by the substance and direction of Darwin's own thinking about human beings.

Darwin's approach to humans was biological, not psychological. As he himself readily admitted, his own way of thinking about the mind was not particularly original because his gifts were not suited to psychology. From Darwin's point of view, the existence of mental faculties was an obstacle to widespread acceptance of his arguments about human evolution. Unless he could make it seem plausible that the unique intellectual abilities of human beings, such as speech, reason and morality, had been gradually and naturally acquired, few would believe that natural selection was a viable alternative to the idea that humans had originated in an act of special divine creation, as told in the book of Genesis.

Having postponed consideration of this problem by cutting psychological matters out of *The Origin of Species*, Darwin eventually opted to approach its solution from two directions. First, he up-graded animal behaviour, suggesting that birds, dogs, cats and monkeys showed many abilities which merited description as moral or intelligent. And secondly, he argued that human actions, particularly when emotional, clearly bore the marks of their animal origins. It was this second argument that led him to focus on infancy, because babies' behaviours are apparently relatively uncomplicated by culture or learning.

Darwin's discussions of infancy are aimed to show that much human behaviour is instinctive and derived from animals. More generally, by describing the first year of life in some detail, Darwin hoped to give his readers a plausible and vivid sketch of the way in which relatively simple behaviours could gradually and naturally develop into the faculties which seem most remarkable in adults. The implication was that, if the higher mental functions developed naturally during the individual life-span from a simple basis in babies, they could also have been acquired naturally by the species as a whole through evolution. Darwin did not explain how mental development came about in infancy, although he did refer to the theory of association to account for some new behaviours (the next chapter discusses this theory in more detail). The important thing was to show that there was no absolute gulf between the mental lives of humans and animals. In this respect, the mental development of babies provided a crucial bridge.

Exactly how the mind worked and grew or, indeed, the extent to which mental processes played a part in evolution, were matters beyond Darwin's range as a scientist. Hence his vision of infancy is much more concerned with the musculature of infant expressions than with their meanings in terms of the child's own mental life and environment or with the lives of those who look after babies. Nevertheless, his vision is a vivid one, demonstrating for all his successors the value of careful observation in natural surroundings and of clear description. At its heart is his analysis of the origin of the movements comprising infants' expressions of suffering. But many other observations are noteworthy, including his description of his son's behaviour in front of mirrors and the way that infants seek the reactions of others to their own feats. His work showed that observations like these raise the questions which any psychological science of babies must answer.

Further Reading

Darwin on Man: A Psychological Study of Scientific Creativity by H. E. Gruber and P. H. Barrett (Wildwood, London, 1974) is undoubtedly the best discussion of Darwin's psychological work. It includes transcriptions of and commentaries upon Darwin's three main notebooks on human psychology as well as his 'Biographical sketch of an infant'.

Evolution and Developmental Psychology edited by G. Butterworth (Harvester, Brighton, 1985) contains a series of papers assessing the place of evolutionary theory in modern child psychology. Of particular interest is A. Costall's chapter, 'Specious origins? Darwinism and developmental theory', which questions whether observations on children are ever appropriate evidence for analysing the course of human evolution.

Development and Evolution by J. M. Baldwin (Macmillan, New York, 1902) gives a fascinating early perspective on the connection between Darwin's ideas and the study of mental growth. Baldwin was one of the seminal thinkers in developmental psychology (read by both Freud and Piaget). He was the first fully to explore the idea that psychological processes make a direct contribution to evolution by natural selection.

The Biologising of Childhood: Developmental Psychology and the Darwinian Myth by J. R. Morss (Erlbaum, Hove, 1989) argues persuasively that the influence of biological thinking in child psychology is more massive than is generally acknowledged but that this influence is not truly Darwinian: the appeal to Darwin is not substantive but is used in a rhetorical way. Morss concludes that psychologists need to look for non-biological alternatives in thinking about mental change but stresses the difficulty of this task, given the pervasiveness of biological imagery in developmental psychology.

3

From Associationism
to Behaviourism

In anthropology, sociology, and psychology the preferred
formulations are those that do not dictate action. A thoroughgoing
developmentalism for example, almost denies the possibility of
effective action.

B. F. Skinner, 'Walden Two revisited' in
Walden Two (1976 edn)

How do we become the beings we are, with our current characteristic
physique, cares, life-style, desires, speech and idiosyncrasies? From one
venerable point of view, the answer is simple: *by association*. The way an
individual behaves today is a consequence of the way in which her or his
current circumstances correspond to or differ from previous events, events
which have gained significance by their associations with pleasure and
pain. If a child cries after seeing her father, that is because she associates
her father's appearance with sensations or ideas that have previously led to
cries: whether it be a coincidental pain in the gut, his angry expression, his
resemblance to a much-loved but recently deceased uncle or his function
as a comforter.

Associationism

According to the theory that the mind forms by means of the laws
governing the association of ideas, or 'associationism', one stimulus will

have as many different significances to different people as there are different learning-histories pertaining to that stimulus. We will very rarely be consciously aware of why we react as we do to a particular food, person or sound. But our reactions, even the most complex, are nevertheless the consequence of the consistent operations of simple laws under varied circumstances since the start of our lives.

For example, Charles Darwin's famous grandfather, the eighteenth-century associationist Erasmus Darwin (1731–1802), gives the following account of the adult aesthetic attraction to curved forms. Noting that the baby is given its mother's breast to suck 'soon after it is born into this cold world', the elder Darwin argues that it will then experience a lovely warmth, as well as tactile, olfactory and digestive pleasures:

> All these various kinds of pleasure at length become associated with the form of the mother's breast; which the infant embraces with its hands, presses with its lips, and watches with its eyes; and thus acquires more accurate ideas of the form of the mother's bosom, than of the odour or flavour or warmth which it perceives with its other senses. And hence at our maturer years, when any object of vision is presented to us, which by its waving or spiral lines bears any similitude to the form of the female bosom, whether it be found in a landscape with soft gradations of rising and descending surface, or in the forms of some antique vases, as in other works of the pencil or the chisel, we feel a general glow of delight, which seems to influence all our senses; and if the object be not too large, we experience an attraction to embrace it with our arms, and to salute with our lips, as we did in our early infancy the bosom of our mother.[1]

The first systematic presentation of an associationist psychology is said to have been published by David Hartley (1705–57) in his *Observations on Man, His Frame, His Duty, and His Expectations* (1749).[2] As the quotation from Hartley's follower Erasmus Darwin illustrates, the basic assumptions of associationism were two. First, even the most complex mental phenomena, including aesthetics, dreams and language, are formed from simple sensations (particularly pleasures and pains). Secondly, events which are similar or occur repeatedly together in time and space will become closely related in the mind.

These assumptions had been acknowledged by philosophers long before Hartley. But Hartley's *Observations* gave both new 'scientific' details and a suggestion of the possible profundity of the influence of association in human affairs. Like his predecessors, Hartley not infrequently chose to work out the implication of associationism through discussion of the effects on the mind of experiences in childhood. Thus Hartley explains the development of language as the result of a progressively more complex and refined association between mental pictures and repeated sounds:

> The name of the visible object, the nurse, for instance, is pronounced and repeated by the attendants to the child, more frequently when his eye is fixed upon the nurse, than when upon other objects. . . The association therefore of the sound *nurse* with the picture of the nurse upon the retina, will be far stronger than that with any other visible impression . . . and be so firmly cemented at last, that the picture will excite the audible idea of the word.[3]

Hartley goes on to argue that the child's idea of the nurse will be clarified and refined by successively ignoring variations in her more temporary characteristics, particular arrangement of hair, colour of clothes, and, more generally, physical background, to concentrate on her more consistent and directly available or 'essential' qualities: tones of voice, skin-feeling, smells, usual facial expressions, physical attitudes, characteristic actions (bathing, feeding, changing, punishing etc.) particularly those most closely associated with times of marked pleasure or pain.

The aim of early associationism was not simply to understand the mind but to understand the human mind *in such a way as would be morally progressive*. Hence Hartley's *Observations on Man* is divided into two parts: the first concerning a physicalistic 'doctrine of vibrations' and the association of ideas, the second about religious questions, using the first part to support its arguments. The second part, therefore, examines the 'Duty and Expectation of Man' mentioned in the title, whilst the first part discusses the human 'Frame'.

Hartley's 'frame' contains a theory of the development of ideas, sensations and muscular motions, based on Newton's reflections on physics. This scientific aspect of Hartley's thinking makes it original among the writings of the 'empiricist' philosophers who had previously discussed the association of ideas (including John Locke and David Hume), because he not only follows a scientific model, but also proposes a scientific theory to support his views. Hartley's psychology, like Locke's, is based on sensations, and, like Hume, he uses the theory of the association of ideas to explain the operations of the mind by demonstrating how a physical theory of vibrating particles accounts for the origin of ideas. But his aim in describing the mechanism of the white medullary substance of the brain is different from that of his scientific predecessors: his intention is to show how the association of ideas leads to the development of a 'moral sense' through the progressive association of pleasures and pains.[4]

Whilst Hartley wrote in a religious vein, his utilitarian and social-revolutionary followers viewed associationism in a legal or political light.

Thus Jeremy Bentham's thought was directed mainly towards legal reform, but his ideas on legislation involve a particular version of psychology which he put forward in *An Introduction to the Principles of Morals and Legislation* (1789).[5] In the preface to *Principles* Bentham writes that he is setting out to establish a 'new science'. This 'science of law' is to be as rigorous as that of anatomy or mathematics and will form part of a 'logic of the will' intended to replace the traditional 'logic of the understanding'. The aim of this 'logic' is to remove prejudice from language used in the application of human laws by describing all actions and their consequences in terms of pleasures or pains. These, for Bentham, are the only 'real' entities.

Bentham's view of psychology is akin to Hartley's in supposing that people's sensations, and hence ideas, are only determined by impressions originating from what is outside, external or peripheral to the ear, eye or other sense-receptor. The resulting organic vibrations are transmitted to and act on particles of the cerebral medulla which, depending on their relative familiarity, will evoke the two main different kinds of sensation; pleasure in repetition or pain and change:

> moderate and pleasant impressions may agitate the medullary particular in so moderate a degree, as that they shall again return to their former situations and corrections, when the agitation is over; whereas violent and painful ones may force the particles from thence, and give rise to new ones, i.e. to the solution of continuity.[6]

The implication of associationism is critical of contemporary behaviour-patterns. The mental associations of ideas which dominate society are both relics and causes of social behaviours and prejudices which are less then morally acceptable. These included, for the utilitarians, those patterns of behaviour and thought reproducing the subjection of coloured people by whites and of women by men. Then as now, the past yields an unwelcome legacy, including racial prejudice, sexual jealousy, war, many kinds of ignorance and too little sympathy with our fellow beings. The evidence for the existence of this negative inheritance was presented in considerable detail by Erasmus Darwin in the course of working out his associationist formulation of evolution in the prose work *Zoonomia* (1796) and his annotated poem on the evolutionary and psychological origin of society *The Temple of Nature* (1803).[7]

The critical intentions of early associationists should be remembered when considering the claims they make about babies. As we have noted regarding Charles Darwin, early writers about babies were not simply scientists making dispassionate statements about physical reality. They were trying to persuade women and men of the possibility of and need for a social and psychological metamorphosis of modern civilization – what

The Temple of Nature called a 'new age'. They wrote to: 'Rouse the dull ear, the hoodwink'd eye unbind, and give to energy the public mind'.[8]

The scientific examples they chose were not simply facts but parables. In Darwin's *Temple*, the 'cradles of nature' were explicitly opposed to her 'coffins'.[9] The discussion of babies was used to counter-weigh the poet's despair over the perpetual destruction of organic life. Observations on infancy were used as self-conscious allegories for the enormous potential in nature for improvement and delight. (One of Darwin's footnotes defines the state of infancy as 'a state of progressive improvement'.) Babies were interesting because of what they, and changes in their behaviours, could be used *to illustrate* about the dynamics and potentials of human nature: 'since natural objects are allied to each other by many affinities, every kind of theoretic distribution of them adds to our knowledge *by developing some of their analogies*'.[10] From the associationist point of view babies are interesting, not because they reveal a divinely or diabolically fixed pattern of human nature, but because they can be used to convince adults that nature is changeable.

Behaviourism

In modern times, the application of the principles of learning to child behaviour has been most extensively pursued by scientists calling themselves 'behaviourists'. Behaviourism subtracts from associationism the belief that scientists can study and learn how to control human actions by reference to hypotheses concerning invisible 'mental states', 'internal processes', or 'faculties' such as perception, cognition and fantasy. Whereas associationists are interested in explaining why particular ideas are linked together, what 'mental events' make a tune remind us of a person for example, behaviourists aim to deal only with the connections between observable stimuli (the tune) and observable behaviours (of people). No reference is made to mental events. This difference has important repercussions for scientific method and, as we shall see, for psychological vocabulary. Associationists largely depend for data on individuals' own reports or 'introspections' about their mental states. Behaviourists draw their information wholly from the observation and experimental control of measurable behaviours. Nevertheless, both associationists and behaviourists lay their main emphasis on learning from the past in their explanation of psychological growth.

Pavlov

Behaviourism is usually thought of as a North American phenomenon. But it was built on the work of Russian physiologists such as Ivan

Michailovich Sechenov (1829–1905) and Nobel-prizewinner Ivan Petrovich Pavlov (1849–1936). A famous experiment of Pavlov's can be used to illustrate the behaviouristic approach.

Amongst Pavlov's main concerns at the start of this century was a wish to know why dogs salivate. To this end he kept a small colony of captive dogs. One day he noticed something new. He observed that a dog who was used to being fed at a certain time of day began to drool, not at the sight, smell or taste of food, but at the sounds of its keeper's feet. Pavlov noted that this was a reaction which had no necessary link with the event that seemed to trigger it, footfalls. He therefore suggested that: 'When the body of an animal or human being has been exposed sufficiently often to two stimuli which occur at roughly the same time, the earlier of them alone tends to call out the response previously called out by the other.'[11] Pavlov went on to get his underlings to show that captive dogs could easily be trained to salivate upon all sorts of odd occasions, such as when a bell rang or when a light flashed. All one had to do was regularly pair in time a sound or a sight with food, and wait. Eventually the dogs would drool at the flash or ring alone. This kind of behaviour came to be called a 'conditioned response'. The method of training that produced such responses is called 'classical conditioning'.

But Pavlov went further than showing that mammalian reflexes could be experimentally controlled. He argued that this kind of change could be described and explained without any reference to states of mind. The idea that dogs had feelings, plans, intelligence, moral understanding or 'inner states' was to him both needless and unscientific:

> To understand these things, are we obliged to enter into the inner state of the animal, and to fancy its feelings and wishes as based on our own?
>
> For the investigator, I believe there is only one possible answer to the last question – an absolute 'No'. Where does there exist so incontestable a criterion that one may judge by it, and may use it in understanding the internal state of an animal by comparison with our own, even though the animal be so highly developed as the dog? And further: does not the eternal sorrow of life consist in the fact that human beings cannot understand one another, that one person cannot enter into the internal state of another?[12]

Watson

At the same time as Pavlov was working with dogs in Moscow, a young American hailing from South Carolina was just starting his career in the behavioural sciences. Like Pavlov, J. B. Watson (1878–1958) wanted to study animals. He wrote to a university in New Jersey but was put off by the requirement that he study Greek. Instead he went to Chicago and began to study rats. Like Pavlov, Watson tried to avoid mentalistic vocabulary in explaining the behaviour of his charges. Their behaviour could and should be explained in biological terms, without reference to states of consciousness.

For more than a decade, Watson's crusade was to banish introspection and the appeal to mental states from the study of animals. But in 1913, he raised a new cry. In his classic lecture 'Psychology as the Behaviourist Views It', he proposed that human psychology too would only become an objective science if it was based on the direct observation of behaviour which was perceptible to more than one person.[13] All behaviour could and should be defined in physiologically-based terms, without reference to personal states in mind. Most importantly, Watson believed that all but the most primitive adult characteristics could be explained as the products of complex histories of environmental conditioning and patterns of stimulation.

To make his approach convincing, Watson had to show that human beings were like animals and could form new habits by classical conditioning from the start of life. With Ruth Morgan he began energetically to observe small infants, soon concluding that human nature had very simple beginnings:

> After observing a large number of infants, especially during the first months of life, we suggest the following groups of emotional reactions as belonging to the original and fundamental nature of man: *fear, rage,* and *love* (using love in approximately the same sense that Freud uses 'sex'). We use these terms which are current in psychology with a good deal of hesitation. The reader is asked to find nothing in them which is not fully statable in terms of situation and response. Indeed we would be willing to call them original reaction states, X, Y, and Z.[14]

Whilst Watson and Morgan were able to describe and classify the babies' emotional reactions to different situations into these three categories (noting for example that rage was the natural response to physical restraint), Watson had yet to show that these reactions could be changed by conditioning. For this purpose, Watson and his colleague Rosalie Rayner selected a baby called Albert who, because his mother was a wet nurse in a Home for Invalid Children, had been reared almost from birth in hospital. At eight months of age, Albert was normal and well-developed, 'stolid and unemotional'.[15] In the first part of Watson's experiment, Albert was confronted one by one with a series of things: a white rat, a rabbit, a dog, a monkey, masks having hair and without hair, cotton wool and burning newspaper. Albert showed no fear in any of these situations, most usually trying to handle the 'frightening' stimuli. Only when the experimenters unexpectedly struck a large metal bar with a hammer behind Albert's back did he cry or show any signs of fear. Watson then decided to pair the frightening clang of metal with a stimulus which was not frightening – a white rat – to see whether Albert could be made to fear the rat.

At weekly intervals Albert was presented with the rat and, just as he looked at or reached towards the animal, the metal bar would be struck. The rat would then be presented soundlessly and Albert's reaction recorded. On the second week, after five 'joint presentations' of the rat with the sound, the rat was presented alone with the following results: 'The instant the rat was shown the baby began to cry. Almost instantly he turned sharply to the left, fell over on his left side, raised himself on all fours and began to crawl away so rapidly that he was caught with difficulty before reaching the edge of the table.'[16] As Watson and Rayner exultantly conclude: 'This was as convincing a case of a completely conditioned fear response as could have been theoretically pictured.'[17]

But Watson and Rayner were not satisfied with this demonstration. They wanted to see whether and how this new negative reaction transferred to other stimuli. They soon found that whilst Albert would still play fearlessly with wooden blocks, he showed signs of terror when confronted by a rabbit, a dog, a seal-skin coat, cotton wool or human hair. The experimenters concluded that there was selective transfer of the new 'conditioned reflex' to all fur-like objects. They went on to show that even after a month's lapse without seeing the rat or hearing the dreaded metal bar struck, Albert was still frightened of furry objects, although his fear seemed weaker. These results put Watson in a strong position to claim that 'the early home life of the child furnishes a laboratory situation' for turning the simple emotional reflexes of the newborn baby into the complex 'emotional compounds' which structure the behaviour of adults.[18] On the other hand, if the home-life of the baby could be changed, the end-product of behavioural development should change correspondingly. As Watson later put it:

> Give me a dozen healthy infants, well-formed, and my own specified world to bring them up in and I'll guarantee to take any one at random and train him to become any type of specialist I might select – doctor, lawyer, artist, merchant, chief and, yes, even beggar-man and thief, regardless of his talents, penchants, tendencies, abilities, vocations and race of his ancestors.[19]

Whilst this flamboyant challenge had no chance of being met in the American society of his day, Watson's advice to mothers had a more serious note. In his best-selling book, *Psychological Care of the Infant and*

Child, Watson told parents that, if they wanted their babies to become adults, they must:

> Treat them as though they were young adults. Dress them, bathe them with care and circumspection. Let your behaviour always be objective and kindly firm. Never hug and kiss them, never let them sit in your lap. If you must, kiss them once on the forehead when they say good night. Shake hands with them in the morning. Give them a pat on the head if they have made an extraordinarily good job of a difficult task. Try it out. In a week's time you will find how easy it is to be perfectly objective with your child and at the same time kindly. Your will be utterly ashamed of the mawkish sentimental way you have been handling it.[20]

Such a regime would not only reduce the child's dependence on the mother but, Watson argued, liberate the mother from the child.

Watson himself was dismissed from his job as a professional psychologist in 1920 (for having an affair with his student Rosalie Rayner) and became an advertising executive. But work on the classical conditioning of babies has continued to the present day. For example, following the example of Pavlov, babies have been taught to suck at the sound of a buzzer in the first ten days of life by pairing the buzzer with, or slightly before, the offer of milk from the nipple of a bottle.[21]

Skinner

Watson's influence on scientific thinking about babies has been much magnified through the work of Burrhus Frederic Skinner (b. 1904). Spurred on by praise for an early story from the eminent writer Robert Frost, Skinner began his career with literary ambitions. But, having failed to become a successful writer in a year, he venomously rejected art and turned to psychology.

For Skinner, Watson's behaviourism did not go far enough. Watson was still trying to *replace* the introspective description of mental faculties and consciousness favoured by William James and associationists with a physiological description. Skinner was simply interested in studying definable behaviours.

Equipped with considerable literary skills, great technical ingenuity, a combative spirit and undoubted intellectual brilliance, he soon conjured a host of experimental results from studies of the rat which had his scientific colleagues gasping with both indignation and admiration. His greatest discovery was a new kind of behavioural conditioning or 'reinforcement' which occurred at lightning speed and therefore gave a far more convincing explanation of what Watson called the 'formation of habit-

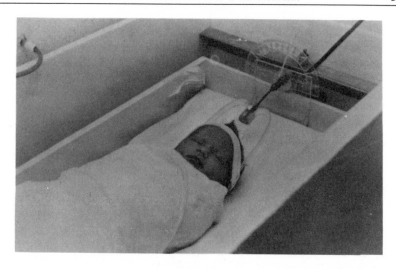

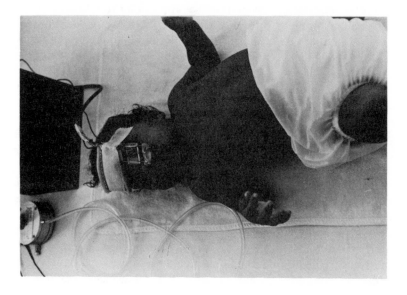

Plate 3.1.1–2 Babies rigged out for two kinds of modern experiment on early learning. The apparatus attached to their heads allows the experimenter either to measure their head-turning as a response to an experimental stimulus or to puff air lightly at the face so as to associate their blinking response with experimental stimuli.
Source: L. Lipsitt.

systems' than the much slower and more painstaking 'classical' conditioning discovered by Pavlov. Classical conditioning paired a known reflex (salivation, sucking) with a new stimulus (a sound from bell or buzzer). So-called Skinnerian or 'operant' conditioning could be used to shape previously unformed responses.

Skinner's discovery grew from his construction of a rat-cage which was bare except for a bar and a food dispenser. Whenever the bar was pressed, a pellet of food dropped into the cage. Skinner found that, provided his rats were calm and familiar with the cage, they would often recognize immediately that there was a link between bar-pressing and getting fed. Skinner had taken an apparently random piece of behaviour and shown that it could swiftly be shaped by an appropriate schedule of rewards and punishment. As Chapter 5 shows, Skinner was later to suggest that even language could be learnt in this way provided that the necessary range of speech-sounds were to be found in the spontaneous vocalizations of the baby. In a similar vein to Hartley, he wrote: 'A child acquires verbal behavior when relatively unpatterned vocalizations, selectively reinforced, gradually assume forms which produce appropriate consequences in a given verbal community.'[22]

Much of Skinner's success depended on his ability to produce machines which allowed him precisely to control the stimulation which his experimental animals received. By gradual changes in patterns of reward, he was able to produce relatively complex 'new' behaviours in rats and pigeons. These successes led him to assert that behaviourism could supply humankind with a new 'technology of behaviour'. According to Skinner's blueprint, behavioural experts could organize a schedule of social rewards and punishments in modern society which would ensure an end to social ills such as violence, sloth and misery.

In 1943, Skinner's fame was assured. He was married and had one child Julie. Skinner debated with his wife whether they should have a second child. Yvonne Skinner said that she did not mind the idea but dreaded the drudgery of the first year or two. So Skinner swiftly set about modifying the task of child-rearing. Arguing that the human species evolved in a warm, tropical climate and that the clothing necessitated by keeping warm in colder temperatures not only created a lot of needless laundry and clothes-changing but seriously immobilized babies' movements, Skinner sat down to design a new kind of crib. It was completely enclosed, had sound-absorbing walls and a large picture window. A strip of sheeting ten yards long passed over the canvas floor, so that a clean section could be cranked into place in a few seconds. Air which had been filtered, moistened and warmed under careful thermostatic control flowed up through the baby's living compartment.

Advantages were immediate. The risk of people 'sneezing all over'

Plate 3.2 Skinner's second daughter Debbie in the 'heir conditioner' where she spent much of her infancy.
Source: B. F. Skinner.

Skinner's younger daughter was eliminated, and air-control also lessened the risk of other air-borne infections. Debbie Skinner remained free of colds as a baby and was able to establish her own daily routine, sleeping and playing as she liked – her parents merely closing or opening the curtain on her picture window as they saw fit. Another discovery was that she was able to move around, roll over and kick much more than if she had been hampered by clothes. Most significant was the importance of temperature in controlling Debbie's crying. She was very sensitive to temperature, a variation of a little as 2°C making the difference between her being too hot or too cold. On the very few occasions when she did complain 'crying and fussing could always be stopped by slightly lowering the tempereature.'[23]

Whilst Skinner did see possibilities of his 'baby tender' for experimental studies, these never took serious form. His notes mention the possibility of conditioning emotional reactions such as 'crying for attention', 'tolerance for frustration', 'eating and sleeping' and 'achievements with body, turning over etc.'. But only one feature of the tender was specifically designed to be reinforcing:

> One toy is a ring suspended from a modified music box. A note can be played by pulling the ring downward, and a series of rapid jerks will produce Three Blind Mice. At seven months our baby would grasp the ring in her toes, stretch out her leg and play the tune with a rhythmic movement of her foot.[24]

The practical advantages of the 'baby tender' outweighed the scientific ones. Skinner believed that his new device would have many benefits – 'not only in easing the lot of the young mother but in building happy and healthy babies even in otherwise unsatisfactory circumstances'.[25] He explored its commercial possibilities, the tender becoming known as the 'baby box' and the 'Heir Conditioner' before successfully being marketed as the 'Air Crib'. Yet, behind all these practicalities, lay an ulterior motive:

> If, as many people have claimed, the first year is extraordinarily important in the determination of character and personality, then by all means let us control the conditions of that year as far as possible in order to discover the important variables.[26]

The 'baby tender' was a first small but significant step towards what Skinner saw as a perfectly practicable new kind of human community (described in his novel *Walden Two*).[27] The community would be small and largely self-governing. Numbering around one thousand persons, its philosophical basis would be the belief that undesirable human behaviours will change if the rules that dictate how human societies run are changed.

Amongst the social rules that Skinner was keenest to challenge were the rules dictating the modern laissez-faire system of child-care. In *Walden Two*, babies are housed in centrally heated, glass-fronted cubicles watched over by specially trained attendants, not by parents. On their first birthday they graduate to small 'toddler' play-rooms equipped with miniature furniture and a new set of trained overseers.

Skinner pointed out that there are good reasons why 'home is not the place to raise children'. Group care is better than parental care for children because they have more adults to depend on. The child-minders are better off, both because they earn a fair wage and respect for performing a difficult job and because they are trained and have the support of trained colleagues. Child-care is an 'intricate science' into which any adult cannot be initiated without systematic education. In Skinner's ideal community, children are unspoilt by unfair favours or handicaps resulting from their particular family setting. And no stigma attaches to childless adults, who can express their affection toward children like anyone else.

Assessing Behaviourism

Watson's dictums on child-care and Skinner's utopian schemes mark the kinship of their ideas with those of the early associationists. But, unlike their predecessors, neither Skinner nor Watson suggested that psychologists should engage in political struggle for a new kind of government. The need they see is for further scientific knowledge about human behaviour and new ways of applying it to the design of cultural practices. Skinner explicitly rejects the ideas of communism (though not those of Thoreau[28]) and thereby distances himself from those who believe that the socialization of housework – including meal preparation and child-care – could already be incorporated in industry, were it not for the profit-motive's reign over advanced capitalist economy.[29]

Whilst many other criticisms have been levelled at behaviourist accounts of human development, from the libertarian to the logical, there can be little doubt that learning plays a crucial role in forming the mind.[30] Thus experimental studies have shown that even the youngest infants can be swiftly taught to change their behaviour by Skinnerian methods. On this basis, one expert has gone so far as to argue that 'the newborn human creature is about as competent a learning organism as he can become.'[31] Like Skinner's rats, babies often learn new sequences of behaviour at the first try.

Nevertheless, the best studies of infant learning reveal features of infant behaviour which are difficult for a behaviourist to explain. In 1969 the Czech psychologist Hanus Papousek reported two observations of this kind. Papousek took the 'random' head-movements of young babies as his focus for study. He set up a situation in which a buzzer told babies that they would be rewarded with milk if they turned their head to the right side, and a bell signalled a milk-reward on the left. Papousek found that many babies quickly learnt the meaning of bell and buzzer. He also noticed that babies would continue to perform very well in the task long after they were too full to drink any more milk. Every time they turned to the correct side, they 'smiled and bubbled' with obvious signs of pleasure yet they would refuse to take a drop more milk. Papousek remarked that 'it looked as if some motivation other than hunger was involved, some demand to respond correctly or solve a problem'.[32]

Papousek's conclusion was expanded by a further observation. Bell and buzzer sounded in a random order so as to avoid any simple regularity in the baby's sequence of responses. Yet the infants seemed to pick up an occasional accidental sequence of the conditioning signals, suggesting a problem-solving strategy which led them to look for regularities, and to carry out the next responses in accord with this strategy, regardless of the real values of buzzer and bell. For instance, some infants turned regularly once to the left and once to the right. An accidental reward for their strategy elicited signs of pleasure whereas its failure produced signs of displeasure. This observation led Papousek to explore the question whether infants were able to detect rules in environmental stimulation and adapt their behaviour to them. He set up a situation in which four-month-olds were expected to turn their heads three times in succession to the left or once to the left and once to the right in order to switch on a panel of flashing lights overhead. Results confirmed that babies recognized that they were being asked to solve a problem and solved it with obvious signs of pleasure.

Papousek's was only one of many studies which suggested that children contribute more complex activity to their own development than behaviourism suggests. The very young child's behaviour is much too subtle, variable and finely structured to be described as random, reactive or reflexive. Skinner himself reports a suggestive observation of this kind:

> One day I had opened the window of the baby-tender and was talking to Debbie, I wrinkled my nose. To my amazement she immediately wrinkled hers. At the time I was not convinced that there was any innate tendency to imitate, but it seems impossible that she could have *learned* that the muscles she moved produced an expression on her face like the one she had seen on mine.[33]

Considering behaviourism in general, it is certainly true that Watson's initial description of infant behaviour underestimated the sophistication of the young child's repertoire. But this does not undermine the behaviourist project as a whole. It is still perfectly possible to explain an adult or older child's current behavioural responses in terms of their history or experience, however highly strutured the individuals's movements were at birth.

If behaviourists are to be criticized for misrepresenting the complexity and activity of human faculties, their deficiency has less to do with the associationism of behaviourism than with its denial of mental states. In the last chapter we saw how Darwin's theory of evolution can be taken to explain organic change (which includes behavioural change) without reference to the study of experience. In behaviourism, this tendency has been taken to be the founding principle of scientific enquiry. Hence the structured complexity of infant action is important, not because it disproves learning-theory accounts of development, but because it suggests that babies have fluid and complex mental lives to which the work of behaviourists gives no clue.

The behaviouristic denial of mental life cuts two ways in development psychology. Not only does it lead to a science which has nothing to say about states of mind; it also exempts scientists from seeing their work as reflecting their own states of mind and values. Somehow, by refusing to discuss their own feelings and experience or those of their experimental subjects, behaviourists are supposedly elevated into a domain where all observations are objective, unaffected by personal motives or ambitions. Yet the work of Skinner and Watson is only too obviously a vehicle for their values, including the thoroughly commendable values of achieving a more effective science of psychology and of lessening the maternal burden of child-care.

On the other hand, to admit that mental states are relevant to the explanation of behaviour is not only to change the behaviouristic perception of children. It is to call into question the very status of developmental theory. For if the mental states of adults, like infants, are determined by processes akin to imitation and association, then there is no easy way to tell whether a particular scientific statement (e.g. infancy is bliss) or perception (e.g. a baby that smiles is happy) is the product of some reaction to the scientist's own social and personal conditioning or a genuine discovery.

In the next chapter we see that there is a kind of associationism which differs from its North American cousin both in its use of complex formulations about inner states and in its development of a self-critical method of inquiry: psycho-analysis.

Summary

Speculations about mental growth have for centuries been illustrated and supported by observations of infants. The first thinkers to work records of infant behaviour into a systematic theory of mental process were the associationists. A century before the publication of *The Origin of Species*, associationists argued that our current mental life, our ideas, memories, fantasies and expectations, can best be explained by the analysis of their co-occurrence with or similarity to events we have previously experienced, particularly events giving rise to pleasure or pain. It was this theory to which Charles Darwin turned when he wanted to explain why babies shed tears when they cry or why Doddy grew impatient when his coat was put on.

Whilst associationists accepted that human behaviour was not random at birth, they believed that the main laws of mental growth were laws of association or learning and that the main substance of psychological development was shaped by training. This was a vision shared by behaviourists such as Pavlov, Watson and Skinner. Behaviourists, however, did not phrase their descriptions of human life in mental terms.

Human actions were first and foremost *behaviours*, physical movements, and could be explained without reference to the various meanings of the world to human individuals. But, as with associationists, these explanations were analyses of the previous history of rewards and punishments associated with the pattern of behaviour to be explained.

For Watson and Skinner, as for the early associationists, observations of and experiments upon babies were primarily analogies for the shaping power of learning in human development. Both early associationists and the founders of behaviourism were driven by a zeal to reform the societies in which they lived. The demonstration that infant behaviour could easily and radically be shaped by experience provided a vivid parable for the radical changes they believed scientifically designed educational changes could make it society, whether this was the elimination of slavery (as for Erasmus Darwin) or an end to nucler war (as for Skinner).

As we shall see later, the ideas that human development is mainly the result of learning and that human behaviour can be described without reference to mental states have come in for a great deal of criticism. But research on infants has left little doubt that babies are extremely able learners and that learning makes a considerable contribution to psychological development, however sophisticated the psychological qualities of the baby may be at birth.

Further Reading

The *Dictionary of the History of Ideas* edited by P. P. Wiener (Scribner's, New York, 1973) contains an excellent chapter on the 'Association of ideas' by R. M. Young. Young summarizes the ideas of Hartley, his precursors and successors, and traces the development of associationism in later intellectual climates.

The Shaping of a Behaviourist, the second volume of Skinner's eminently readable autobiography (Knopf, New York, 1979), gives a good insight into the balance between his humanitarian concerns and his vision of behaviourism. The book contains a full account of his invention of the 'baby box', how it was used, the controversy it aroused and its potential for making observations of early development.

Images of Man in Psychological Research by J. Shotter (Methuen, London, 1975) develops a vision of a psychology which is simultaneously scientific and humanitarian, very different from that of Skinner. Shotter, who opposes behaviourism, argues that psychology should become 'hermeneutical' or a 'moral science of action', being based upon the interpretation of others' mental states, with a view to expanding the domain of human responsibility.

The Pseudo-Science of B. F. Skinner by T. R. Machan (Arlington House, New Rochelle, NY, 1974) is, as its title suggests, an attack on the basic philosophy of the behaviouristic approach to the study of human action.

4

The Dynamics of Desire

If there is no interpreter, the speaker had better not address the meeting at all.

1 Corinthians 14:28

The word 'infant' has its roots in the Latin *infans*, meaning 'unable to speak'. From this fact of etymology scientists often take infancy to be the period which lasts from birth until the child's first use of recognizable words. Such a definition predisposes us to see infancy as a time of gathering the abilities necessary for speech. Thus our understandings of what language is and what speech requires of us become crucial to formulation of the psychological tasks confronting the newborn baby.

In the next chapter we will discuss a theory of infant development based on the view that the essential mark of linguistic expression is grammar. This chapter explores theories of infancy which are based upon a view of language as determined by intentions and patterns of desire that may be profoundly unconscious. These are theories of psycho-analysis.

Psycho-analysis is doubly indebted to language. Not only does the whole venture of psycho-analytic therapy, including the possibility of cure, focus upon and have its roots in the resources of language, but psycho-analysis owes much of its fame to its status as great literature. For, whilst Sigmund Freud (1856–1939), the 'father' of psycho-analysis, had good claims to be a scientist (both as a research neurologist and as an experimental psychotherapist), he was undoubtedly a writer of extraordinary originality. (In 1927 he won the prestigious Goethe Prize on these grounds.) As one commentator has remarked:

> If it is the highest art to conceal art then Freud succeeded more completely than most, more completely, probably, than any writers save Milton and those earlier law givers who wrote the Old Testament, and who are, as the late *Moses and Montheism* attests, the only conceivable rivals so far as Freud himself is concerned.[1]

When we read Freud, we meet part of our own cultural heritage, a heritage that is both more ancient and more contemporary than Freud himself. Just as the Bible provided our ancestors with a means of analysing and judging their own actions, so Freud's writing is furnished with a kit of concepts which seem peculiarly applicable to our own self-examination. For Freud, like his biblical precursors, and like Goethe, was first and last a great moralist, a diviner of human ignorance.[2] His intellectual kinship is thus as much with the renowned moralists of the past as with the medical and scientific contemporaries to whom he is commonly compared.

Witness for instance a posthumous publication of the eighteenth-century preacher and satirist Jonathan Swift (1667–1745). Entitled 'The Difficulty of Knowing One's Self', this never-delivered sermon illustrates the way in which we humans typically deceive ourselves.[3] Swift begins by commenting on the Old Testament story of Hazael, servant to the King of Syria. In the story, the King, who was ill, sent Hazael to ask the prophet Elisha whether he would get better. At their meeting, Elisha foretold that Hazael would do great evil to the people of Israel. Hazael, not understanding himself as well as Elisha did, was amazed and could not believe that he, 'a dog, a mere nobody', would ever perform the monstrous cruelty Elisha prophesied. The next day, Hazael suffocated the King and began a reign of unparalleled bloodshed and terror.

The moral of the story, Swift pointed out, applies to the majority of humankind. Despite years of turning over new leaves, despite the sturdiest belief in our own virtue, despite conscious repentance, despite the sincerest intentions to learn to be happier, less violent, love more, exercise harder, eat, drink or smoke less, the average person trips over the same pitfalls and temptations again and again:

> Every man's life is an imperfect sort of a circle, which he repeats and runs over every day; he has a set of thoughts, desires, and inclinations, which return upon him in their proper time and order, and will very hardly be laid aside, to make room for anything new and uncommon.[4]

This kind of repetition is as central to the theory and practice of psychoanalysis as it is to the analysis of sin.

For example, in 1910 Freud described a kind of romantic passion which he found more than once amongst neurotic men. These patients repeatedly fell in love with women seemingly chosen to fulfil a set of unconsciously selected criteria:

1 the woman was always one whom another man could claim as his own, either as husband, fiancé or friend;
2 the woman was never one 'whose reputation is irreproachable' – she may simply have enjoyed flirtations or she may have been 'openly promiscuous';
3 these women were not blamed by the man for their lack of sexual integrity but considered to be 'love-objects of the highest value';
4 like the legendary knight on a white charger, these men felt an urge to 'rescue' their loved-ones: 'The man is convinced that she is in need of him, that without him she would lose all moral control and rapidly sink to a lamentable level. He rescues her, therefore, by not giving her up.'[5]

Freud suggests that these four conditions of loving seem unintelligible and indeed bewildering until we trace them back to their source in childhood. They are derived, he tells us, from 'the infantile fixation of tender feelings on the mother, and represent one of the consequences of that fixation'.[6] The conditions he has described are all characteristics of the small boy's first love for his mother, a love which creates what Freud calls the Oedipus complex.

The Greek myth of Oedipus to which Freud referred told of an abandoned son growing up to kill his father and marry his mother without recognizing either of them.[7] In a similar way, Freud suggested that adult men are unaware that, as small boys, they wished to be sole lovers and possessors of their mothers and saw their fathers as hated rivals. Upon acquaintance with the facts of sexual reproduction, the boy is supposed to have felt that his mother had proven unfaithful to him, or been 'promiscuous', by granting sexual favours to his father rather than himself. Freud concluded that it is as a result of repeated attempts to resolve the buried and conflicting feelings of an Oedipal boyhood that the type of male love he described as neurotic had arisen.

The purpose of Freud's therapy was to change each patient's unconscious agenda of self-sabotage, to lessen their guilt, to make them happier with themselves. This was to be achieved by developing a strong emotional relationship between the patient and the analyst in which the fixed symbolic dynamics dominating the unconscious life of the patient could be repeated or played out one more time. In therapy, these dynamics should be recognized, interpreted and re-understood by both analyst and patient in such a way as to produce happier dynamics in the future. It was this practice of therapy which underpinned all Freud's psycho-analytic writings.

Freud's Early Career

Freud had begun his working life as a doctor, and the psycho-analytic method is in part an extension of traditional methods of medical interview. Freud had finished his medical training in 1885 (aged 29) by winning a scholarship to study with the great French physician Jean-Martin Charcot, in Paris. It was Charcot who had introduced Freud to the idea that there were close connections between the symptoms of psychosomatic or 'hysterical' illnesses and the effects of hypnosis. When Freud returned to Vienna in 1886 and began to take in private patients for the first time, he was faced with a variety of different kinds of mental illness, including people with incapacitating obsessions, phobias, anxieties and 'hysterical' or psychosomatic paralyses. Before long he was experimenting with all manner of techniques of treatment, including electricity, baths and hypnotism, which he used to help patients recall the exact circumstances surrounding the onset of their symptoms.

With the help of his colleague Josef Breuer and some insightful female patients, he eventually developed a technique he called 'free association'. His clients would simply be asked to relax and say whatever came into their heads with respect to their symptoms, however irrelevant, embarrassing, stupid or disconnected their remarks might seem.

Freud adopted a receptive attitude to his patients' speech. And, as his experience grew, he began to see patterns and links in the preoccupations of his patients, whatever the topic of their remarks. Very often what they said would suggest in a round about way that days, months or years ago something had happened which was intimately connected with one of their symptoms but which the patient had completely forgotten. The event in question may to the outsider have seemed perfectly innocent but will have occasioned feelings in the patient which were upsetting or 'traumatic'. These feelings proved traumatic because they were completely at variance with the patient's moral beliefs and style of life.

In one example, Freud traced the acute psychosomatic pains in the legs of a dutiful and cultivated Viennese spinster to a long walk two years previously, during which she fleetingly realized that she was in love with her brother-in-law. Freud concluded that she had fended off the painful recognition that she desired her sister's husband by inducing physical pains in herself instead, pains which replaced but were symbolically related to the forbidden or 'repressed' ideas surrounding her erotic feelings.[8] Freud's method as a therapist was to encourage his patients to speak out the previously unspeakable 'repressed' ideas and feelings which were linked to their neurotic symptoms. This was a form of catharsis which often led to the disappearance of the unwanted paralyses, pains and anxieties which Freud was hired to cure.

Freud's early enthusiasm for his cathartic method did not last long. Whilst the so-called 'talking-cure' could remove particular symptoms in a matter of weeks or months, his patients did not lose their tendency to form new symptoms. Freud was certain that he had to excavate deeper and deeper into his clients' unconscious desires in order to cure them permanently. As he did so, the traumas he uncovered seemed to have occurred earlier and earlier in their lives. These traumas were frequently sexual. Thus, in 1896, Freud was led to conclude that the problems of his patients were caused by sexual experiences in early childhood, experiences which involved sexual advances by adults or older children.

Freud's 'seduction theory' of mental illness was only the first and simplest of three theories he advanced about the links between childhood and the emotional associations of his patients. Why he abandoned it in 1897 has recently become a topic of considerable debate.[9] According to one argument, Freud abandoned it because it implied that the sexual abuse of children was astonishingly widespread amongst the parents of the Viennese upper-middle class. Even Freud's own father fell under suspicion by virtue of the hysterical symptoms to be seen in Freud's brothers and sisters, not to mention Freud's own neurotic forebodings that he would die at the age of 51, his anxieties over travel, his phobia of large open spaces, his impotence and occasional fainting fits.

Freud also suspected that the memories of childhood recounted by his patients or recalled by himself were 'emotionally-charged fictions', motivated by desires which had little to do with historical accuracy, fictions which seemed like screens to hide the secrets of early infantile experience.[10] (See pp. 59–60 below.) Furthermore, Freud was having little therapeutic success with the interpretations inspired by his seduction theory. He therefore supposed that his clients' common claims to have had sexual experiences when very young were not evidence for perversity in parents but of the perversity of his patients: patients only told tales of sexual adventures with their parents in infancy because they *wanted* to have had such sexual adventures *when they were very young*.[11] Partly on this basis, Freud hypothesized that babies were born with sexual feelings. This was a revolutionary idea.

Sexual Life in Infancy

Freud was led to the study of babies as sexual beings from more than one direction. During his practice as a therapist, he had been impressed by the frequency with which his clients told him their dreams in connection with their symptoms. He noticed that the analysis of dreams often provided an invaluable means for overcoming resistance to his method of therapy. He therefore launched himself on a large-scale study of dreaming – both his own dreams and those of his patients. His project was completed in 1899 with the publication of his masterpiece, *The Interpretation of Dreams*.[12] This long book concludes with an argument that dreams are distorted images of situations which are unconsciously wished-for.

Freud saw a parallel between the forbidden wishes underlying mental illnesses and the distorted wishes which give a meaning to dreams. He went on to propose that the human mind was governed by two processes – a primitive, pleasure-controlled 'primary process' and a civilized, scientific 'secondary' process.[13] The primary process is regulated by an effort to avoid excitation. Any internal need or external demand, any 'unpleasure', will by met by an attempt to re-establish a mental state of equilibrium by the quickest possible means. For example, you are asleep and your alarm-clock rings. Because you are unwilling to go to work, you dream that the clock is a telephone and that you are already at work. The primary process has protected your sleep from an unwelcome interruption by constructing a hallucination which explains away the external demand.

Freud believed that the primary process was not only to be seen at work in dreams but also dominated the mental lives of babies. For example, a tiny baby suddenly feels hungry. She screams and kicks helplessly, powerless to find a source of food. But if she remembers or acts out what it is like to be fed, she can re-experience the taste and warmth of food by means of a hallucination. The primary process thus protects the baby against the fear of recognizing her vulnerability to bodily needs.

Slowly the 'bitter experience of life' will convince babies that hallucination is not a satisfactory method of seeking food and comfort.[14] We are forced to develop a more efficient 'secondary' process. As their physical powers grow, children will try to work out more effective methods to influence the external world so that they get what they want. They will develop sounds and gestures which tell their parents what they want, they will learn to crawl towards and grasp desired objects. They will begin to take a scientific interest in getting their way in the world. But even in adulthood, when rational thinking and knowledge of the world are at their most advanced, the infantile process of wishful hallucination still recurs – in sexual life, in irrationality, in reveries, in jokes and, most vividly of all, in dreams:

> What once dominated waking life, while the mind was still young and incompetent, seems now to have been banished into the night – just as the primitive weapons, the bows and arrows, that have been

abandoned by adult men, turn up once more in the nursery. Dreaming is a piece of infantile mental life that has been superseded.[15]

From two directions then, Freud's thinking had been led to focus on the mental and sexual life of young children. But as yet he had not considered this topic in its own right. So when, in 1905, Freud published his *Three Essays on the Theory of Sexuality*, the central essay was entitled 'Infantile Sexuality'.[16]

Freud introduced his ideas about the mental lives of children by discussing sexual perversions in adults. He argued that normal sexual development involved a narrowing down of sexual interest from the 'polymorphous perversity' of infancy to the genitals of the opposite sex, but that very often adults gained 'perverse' pleasures from stimulation of the lips, being beaten, looking at pictures, licking the anus and so on.

Freud used observations of young children to support his claim that infants gain erotic pleasure from many zones of the body including the genitals, the mouth and anus, which adults would consider perverse (e.g. the erections of boys only days old). To begin with, Freud argued, these pleasures are mainly produced by 'masturbation' or self-stimulation of pleasure-zones. But by three or four years of age, children start to desire *others* sexually, particularly their mothers. But these desires are mixed with a conflicting fear of castration by figures of authority, symbolically, the father. Now begins the Oedipal conflict which ends with the repression of loving feelings for the mother in favour of a relationship with the father, either erotic, wanting to possess the father sexually (in girls), or of identification, wanting to become like the father (in boys). This repression also leads to the forgetting of most early childhood experiences.

Freud and evolutionary theory

Freud's description of infantile sexuality was profoundly influenced by evolutionary theory. Freud had read and admired Darwin's main published works on psychology as well as many post-Darwinian works on the behaviour of young children. The historian Frank Sulloway has presented persuasive evidence that many of Freud's central ideas are part of this evolutionary tradition.[17] Perhaps most central are the three ideas; that we possess a bestial unconscious; that the two basic roots of mental life are sexuality and self-preservation; and that there are oral, anal and genital stages of childhood development.

The words 'unconscious' and 'repress' had occurred frequently in Charles Darwin's writings on psychology. The theory that humans have descended from animals has as natural consequences both the idea that humans function much as we presume animals to do, in ignorance of their own motives, and the corollary that human wisdom has for millenia been blind to this obvious insight. Darwin's work also stressed the centrality of struggle and conflict to the formation of the human mind. Thus it was not an enormous departure from evolutionary thinking for Freud to suggest that the human unconscious is constituted by the repression of a conflict between a sexual instinct (which led to desire for the mother) and a self-preservative instinct (which led to fear of the father). Sexual instincts could be seen as the evolutionary product of sexual selection. In contrast, self-preservation or 'ego' instincts would parallel the results of natural selection.

Freud's theory of the development of these instincts in childhood also shows strong marks of the idea that the individual's development repeats in brief the evolution of the species. Freud commented that both sexual and ego instincts 'are at bottom heritages, abbreviated recapitulations, of the development which all mankind has passed through from its earliest days over long periods of time'.[18]

Following biological ideas current in Europe when he wrote, Freud believed that the evolution of animal sexuality went through three stages. At the simplest level, sexual reproduction occurred by the fusion of two organisms – 'a sort of higher eating'. In more complex animals, sex through unification was impossible. Instead an organ developed which combined the functions of excretion and copulation. The sex act was a pressing of cloaca to cloaca. Finally, the sexual organ proper evolved, as in mammals. Freud again: 'Consider how in one class of animals the genital apparatus is brought into closest relation to the mouth, while in another it cannot be distinguished from the excretory apparatus, and in yet others it is linked to the motor organs.'[19]

The 'Stage' Theory of Infantile Sexuality

Equipped with the idea of repression and a tripartite picture of sexual evolution, Freud felt in a strong position to argue that, before passing through the Oedipus complex, the human child must pass through two earlier sexual stages: an oral stage and an anal stage.

The oral stage occupied the early months of life up to and including weaning. The baby gained its strongest sensual pleasures from feeding. According to this view, sex and the satisfaction of hunger were to begin with synonymous. Just as Darwin had reported in 1877 that the 'swimming eyes' of young babies when sucking shows that they feel pleasure in the earliest weeks of life, so Freud wrote: 'No one who has seen a baby sinking back satiated from the breast and falling asleep with flushed cheeks and a blissful smile can escape the reflection that this picture persists as a prototype of sexual satisfaction in later life.'[20]

Before long, however, the pleasures of the mouth are interrupted by the frustrations of weaning. Food begins to appear in solid form and the baby is expected to eat with a spoon. She/he can no longer rely on breast or bottle. Nevertheless Freud noted that children continue to obtain oral pleasure from sucking thumbs, blankets and other inedible objects from birth right up to school age.

The next site of sexual pleasure to exert its influence on mental development is the anus. Unlike feeding, excretion is more under the baby's control than that of the surrounding adults. Two pleasures therefore attach to functions of the anus. Firstly there is the simple pleasure of emptying the bowels of accumulated waste, including the possibly blissful sensation of moist warmth as its contents pass over the responsive membranes in the anal passage. Secondly there is the meaning of the faeces as a part of the baby which is presented to those who are *in loco parentis*. The contents of the bowels 'are clearly treated as a part of the infant's own body and represent his first "gift": by producing them he can express his active compliance with the environment and, by withholding them, his disobedience.'[21]

The great crisis of this stage is the time of potty-training. This may often take on the character of a battle of wills between baby and parents. Toddlers may refuse to excrete for days or, alternatively, may hourly dirty their clothes. Long after individuals have stopped wearing nappies, heightened emotion may lead them to become constipated or to regress to the uncontrolled defecation of babyhood.

Finally, young children enter the genital stage, marked observationally by the increase of early genital masturbation and the passions of the Oedipus complex. Masturbation draws upon the child fears of retribution, not only for masturbation itself but for the child's lust for the mother. These fears are fuelled by any adult admonishments concerning the genitals. Such admonishments later help form the voice of the child's conscience (the 'super-ego').

The repression of sexual feeling which ends the Oedipus complex also closes the period of infantile sexuality (around the age of six). According to Freud, sexual feelings will not re-emerge until puberty. But when they do, the particular experiences and anxieties of infancy will stamp their influence on the proclivities of adults. Thus Freud describes sexual fetishes and character-types corresponding to disturbances in all three stages of childhood.

Children who have experienced either too much or too little anxiety in early infancy may grow up to be unduly dependent on others or on the stimulation of cigarettes, drink or drugs. Alternatively they may suffer disturbances in eating behaviour, becoming anorexic or obese as the case may be. An anal character, on the other hand, is likely to develop peculiar relationships to hygiene and money, becoming fastidious and miserly, for example, or spendthrift and untidy. As for the genital stage, we have already read Freud's analysis of a disturbance in adult male amours, behaviour rooted in the failure satisfactorily to resolve the Oedipal situation.

Revisions of Freud's Theory

The idea that children progress towards maturity through three stages of infantile sexuality is undoubtedly Freud's most famous vision of infancy. But before long, Freud and others began to recognize it had serious shortcomings. Their revisions focused on three main issues: Freud's self-confessed difficulties in accounting for the desires and mental development of *women*; deficiencies in the observational evidence and logic supporting Freud's theory of *instincts*; and doubts about the *causal relationship* between patients' accounts of childhood and their neuroses.

Concerning women

Freud aligned masculinity and femininity with activity and passivity in a way that even he realized was arbitrary, for both men and women were, according to Freud, bisexual.[22] Nevertheless, this alignment reflected a general tendency in Freud's thinking to see women as more passive and less intellectually and morally able than men. Typically, Freud's account of infantile sexuality is based on the boy's development: the father's control of the son gathers force from the son's realization that the father really is capable of castrating or killing him. The boy believes that such violence is possible, not from experience but, according to Freud, by the false deduction that girls lack a penis, having 'already been castrated'.

Early on the little girl is also supposed to rival her father for sexual possession of her mother, but in her case, exposure to anatomical differences between men and women forces her into a realization that she has already been castrated. As a result, she is furious with her mother for not having given her a penis, and turns to her father, proud owner of such an object, to give her one. In this account of gender, the girl's repressions of her desire to have sex with her father is less strong than the boy's repression of his incestuous longings, as she, the girl, has nothing to lose. She has *never* had sense of having a penis. Having less incentive to identify with the father, she lacks a strong super-ego and conscience. One outcome

Plate 4.1 Freud with his grand-daughter Eve (*c.*1924). Freud confessed late on in his life that he found the psychological development of girls particularly difficult to understand.
Source: Mary Evans Picture Library.

of this is that she has less of a sense of morality and justice, and is less able to think objectively.

Despite his overvaluation of penises, Freud can be thought to have drawn his shortcomings, as well as his insights, from a doctor's practice in turn-of-the-century Vienna. This has opened up the possibility for sympathetic female critics to see his work as partly a product of that place and epoch. Indeed, his emphasis on the strength of unconscious processes in constructing the meaning of what was expressed in the analytic situation has been taken up by some feminists to explain the hold of patriarchal values and practices on contemporary women, or the 'collusion' of women in their oppression. The aim of these writers is to find ways of surmounting the lack of social change achieved by campaigns aimed only at the more obvious material and social injustices representing women's oppression: to achieve equal financial resources, access to power and properly organized child-care facilities.

Central to the feminist re-evaluation of psycho-analytic theory is the distinction Freud made in 1925 between the penis (a bit of flesh) and the phallus (a symbol of the point at which repression of fantasies of domination allows individual entry into the vicissitudes of social life in a man's world).[23] This distinction has been used to shift the emphasis of political discussions about sexual inequality from the straight-forward facts of inequality to the way in which men and women represent themselves and each other in psychic life. In this way, the Oedipus complex may become a myth, not to be taken literally, but holding a subtle truth about gender through which individuals may read and understand the roots of their continuing masochistic compliance and collusion in situations which are not to their advantage.[24]

Concerning instincts

Freud's own revision of his theory of instinctual development was first broached in a series of papers on 'metapsychology', introduced in 1914 with a paper 'On Narcissism'.[25] This was concerned both with the beginning of babyhood and with adult states of mind associated with: homosexual love, schizophrenia, a preoccupation with appearances (particularly in women) and the egocentrism of parents.

Schizophrenia posed particularly difficult problems for Freud. Psycho-analysis is a therapy which depends upon exchanges of conversation to effect improvement. Thus it is the mental illnesses which most profoundly disturb conversation that prove hardest to cure (e.g. those that are shared with no one or are unrecognized by everyone). Freud's difficulty with schizophrenics was that these patients seemed to feel wholly alone. They showed no desire to form an emotional relationship with him. His other patients sometimes had difficulty in speaking and sometimes said nothing at all but their hesitations and silences could always be interpreted, provided that these gestures were at least partly aimed at Freud. In contrast, schizophrenics seemed to talk only for their own benefit, as if they had withdrawn their hearts from the world. In 1914 Freud proposed that, in their self-absorption, schizophrenics were recreating the baby's first psychological state. Freud compared this state to that of the mythical Greek actor of tragedies, Narcissus.

The myth of Narcissus tells us that, before Narcissus was born, his mother heard that her son would only thrive provided that he did not know himself. He was from birth someone so beautiful that many fell in love with him. Amongst these, the most famous was the nymph Echo (who, owing to the curse of a goddess, could only echo what others said).

Narcissus rejected all his suitors until he caught sight of a face reflected in a pool of water. He loved the elusive reflection passionately. But when he saw that he had fallen in love with himself and that his passion was futile, he drew a sword and killed himself.[26]

Freud's notion that babies are 'narcissistic' has proved very important: *in psycho-analysis*, informing the thinking of such maestros as Melanie Klein and Jacques Lacan; *in academic psychology*, as adapted by Jean Piaget, for example (see chapter 6); and *in cultural criticism*, where it has been used to typify contemporary life as one of 'inner emptiness, fear of dependence, fascination with celebrity, decline of the play spirit and deteriorating relations between men and women', not to mention famine and nuclear war.[27] But it undermined Freud's earlier explanation of the Oedipal repression as being the consequence of conflict between 'ego' and 'sexual' instincts. By suggesting that at the start of life, the object of sexual and self-preservative desires are the same, namely, the baby's own self, his idea that the sexual and ego instincts *conflict* in infancy became a superfluous contradiction. Yet instinctual conflict remained indispensable as the core of psycho-analytic explanations for the repressions which occur in the Oedipal situation and constitute the adult unconscious.

In 1920, after the terrible violence of the First World War in which three of Freud's sons risked their lives and many others were psychologically damaged, Freud proposed a new division of the instincts.[28] On the one side were the Life instincts, including the formerly opposed aims of sex and self-preservation. On the other were the Death instincts, including aggression, hate and destructiveness. The Oedipus complex could now be explained in the old way again, as the product of conflict between vital love for the mother and mortal hatred of the father. But his new theory of instincts posed a host of questions about early infancy. In particular, how does the Death instinct manifest itself before the Oedipus complex? The fullest answer to this question was formulated in the writings of Melanie Klein (1882–1960), who was born in Vienna but spent the second half of her life working in London. (Klein later supervised some important figures in British psychology, including Donald Winnicott and John Bowlby; see chapters 6, 7 and 9.)

Klein's work is particularly important to the science of babies because, unlike Freud, she devoted her talents to the detailed observation and interpretation of the actions of very young children. Her success depended on the invention of a new technique of psycho-analysis specifically adapted to the treatment of little children. This was the 'play technique'.[29] Instead of interpreting the verbal associations of adults, as had Freud, Klein interpreted the imaginative play of young children with simple toys which could be used to represent family-members, pets, monsters or other people and events. Very soon she had concluded that the Oedipus complex occurred much earlier than Freud had thought, even during the first year or two of life.[30]

Klein was particularly impressed by hints of deep anxiety in the early months, by the intensity of frustrations caused at weaning and by signs that children desire their fathers from very early in life. She first proposed that, as a response to weaning, babies turn away from their mothers as love-objects to their fathers.[30] Later she distinguished between two types of anxiety felt by everybody, from birth onwards: 'persecutory' anxiety and 'depressive' anxiety. This distinction led her to argue that the first year of life is dominated by two successive 'positions', characterized respectively by persecutory and depressive feelings.[31]

Klein believed that we begin life with an orientation to the source of food which is extremely fragile. Stirred up by the pains of birth, we are led by the overwhelming nature of our demands and frustrations to imagine the world to be very different from the 'reality' traditionally accepted by adults. Klein described a number of psychological ploys or 'defences' against the anxiety of recognizing our almost total lack of control over the people and the world upon which we first depend. The baby's main defence is to split the world into two halves. Under favourable circumstances, when the baby is well-fed and comfortable, the world or, more accurately, the 'mother-figure' will be idealized and imagined as loving and always available to comply with the baby's every desire. The baby feels omnipotent, that the mother-figure is under his or her exclusive control. Food is like nectar and the possibility of frustration is wholly denied. Under unfavourable conditions, the baby's world is more sinister. When the baby does not receive the food or comfort she or he wants, the mother-figure is imagined to be a persecutor who is feared and attacked in fantasy with any means at the baby's disposal, including 'explosive urine and faeces'.[32] In this state of mind, any food will be rejected as poison. The baby will refuse to suck, struggling and biting at the breast. The 'bad' mother completely replaces the 'good' mother so that any connection between the 'two' mothers is not recognized.

Klein found evidence for these views in such commonplace sights as the baby who, on seeing an unfamiliar face or a familiar person, such as a grandmother, under unusual circumstances (e.g. poor lighting), screams with fear – of the 'persecutory' mother. Or of a hungry child who, having worked herself or himself up into a range of frustration, only *attacks* the breast or bottle when it is finally offered. Klein thus describes in detail the various mechanisms which make up what Freud called the 'primary process'.

During the second six months of life, the 'secondary process' develops and the child's grip on reality grows firmer. The baby starts to realize that he or she has only one mother and lives in one world. Now begin 'depressive' anxieties. The baby feels guilty for hating and wishing to kill the loved mother and fears that he or she will be abandoned. Whereas in the early 'persecutory' months the baby's parents are combined in fantasy, mother and father are now distinguished as separate individuals for the first time. Babies' fears that their mothers will desert them make them turn to the father as a substitute, a situation which foreshadows the Oedipus complex. But babies simultaneously begin to experience feelings of gratitude to their mothers for standing by them and tolerating their destructiveness. As later observational studies confirm, it is at around nine months of age, when the 'depressive position' is first at its height, that babies begin to give food, toys and other valuables to their caretakers. In Klein's theory, such gifts serve as 'reparations' for the baby's early acts of real and imagined violence.[33]

Klein describes the persecutory and depressive anxieties of babies as typical of the relatively transitory occupation of mental 'positions' which may be taken up throughout life. She thereby distinguishes them from an ineluctable progression of oral, anal and genital 'stages' as described by Freud, which are supposedly outgrown for ever by adults (though note that these stages gain much significance from their supposed effects on the 'characters' of adults). Klein argues that adults under stress may quite easily slip into the split patterns of feeling and fantasy which she found in babies – as in superstition or racial prejudice for example. Alternatively, adults may never rise above depressive or persecutory anxieties, in which case they will be more or less seriously ill.

Concerning causality

Klein's idea of 'position' brings to a head a third kind of hypothesizing about infancy that runs through Freud's writings on psycho-analysis. This concerns causal relations between present and past in discussing patients' accounts of childhood produced in the psycho-analytic setting.

As early as 1897 Freud had suspected that adults' accounts of their infantile feelings might well have more to do with their own current desires and preoccupations than with what really happened in the past:

> Our childhood memories show us our earliest years not as they were but as they appeared at the later periods of revival, the childhood memories did not, as people are accustomed to say, *emerge*; they were *formed* at that time. And a number of motives, which had no concern with historical accuracy, had their part in forming them as well as in the selection of the memories themselves.[34]

It was partly this suspicion that had led him to drop his 'seduction theory'.

In 1918 he published a lengthy case-history of a man whose symptoms

seemed to have been shaped by a series of events occurring in early
infancy, including a dream featuring wolves and the sight of his father
entering his mother from behind.[35] The case of the 'Wolf Man' was
remarkable for both the patient's and Freud's own inability to provide a
convincing chronological record of these early events. In Freud's
discussion of the case, he concludes that such a chronology is not crucial
for a successful outcome in treatment. Certainly the analyst must
provisionally accept recollections of infancy as truthful, but their real
value is as illustrative stories made necessary by and gaining meaning from
the state of the patient's current relationship to the analyst.

This is known technically as the 'transference' relationship. In it the
patient transfers her or his usual thoughts and feelings about other people
on to the person of the analyst. All relationships involve 'transference' but,
by refusing to do anything other than interpret and analyse, the analyst
allows patients much more space than usual to develop their transferences,
both loving and hostile. The analytic setting is therefore designed to
facilitate the kinds of repetition we discussed at the start of this chapter:
'The patient cannot remember the whole of what is repressed in him, and
what he cannot remember may be precisely the essential part of it. . . He is
obliged to *repeat* the repressed material as a contemporary experience'.[36]

Patients live out their illnesses in the vagaries of a new relationship with
the analyst, thus making immediate their hidden and forgotten impulses.
The cure depends wholly on the timing and type of the analyst's
interventions in the field of their immediate relationship. It is on this field
that the therapeutic battle is won or lost.

Lacan on Infancy and Science

But what does this notion of the past mean about babies and babyhood?
And what does it mean about the genesis of human knowledge? An answer
to these questions was proposed late in the 1940s by the Frenchman
Jacques Lacan. Lacan's own interest in mental development grew from his
consideration of rage and aggression, experiences that are subjective
through and through, coming over people in an instant, for reasons which
they may never understand.

Lacan understood aggression as the correlative tendency of narcissism.
Narcissus falls in love with his reflection. But then, upon recognizing that
it is a reflection, he becomes violently suicidal. One's attachment to one's
reflected image is very fragile. One gets tired of one's self. The mirror is
dirty, the record of the song which holds for us the deepest sense of our
being is scratched, our favourite toy smells wrong or is lost, the wife goes
too far . . . and violence erupts.

Lacan illustrated his understanding of aggression with careful observations of babies, observations by himself, Henri Wallon, Charlotte Buhler and, particularly, Melanie Klein. But, from the beginning of his work, Lacan was clearly aware that his references to infancy were *only* illustrations:

> The subjectivity of the child who registers as defeats and victories the heroic chronicle of the training of his sphincters, taking pleasure throughout it in the imaginary sexualization of his cloacal orifices, turning his excremental expulsions into aggressions, his retentions into seductions, and his movements of release into symbols – this subjectivity *is not fundamentally different* from the subjectivity of the psycho-analyst.[37]

Indeed, Lacan's most famous paper on infancy, 'The Mirror Stage as Formative of the Function of I as Revealed in Psycho-Analytic Experience' (1949), is well read as a commentary, not on babies, but on the state of mind of Freud and other scientists who, in order to understand their patients' expressions, tried to reconstitute 'the forms of love' of little children.[38]

Lacan owed a large debt to Klein. This was for her demonstration, both theoretically and observationally, that the child, before the appearance of language, manifests a complex subjective life having a structure comparable to adult mentality. With respect to aggression, subjectivity was evident to Lacan in the simple facts that: a child who does not yet speak reacts differently to punishment as opposed to brutality; in the imagery of early play with toys, and in the incidence of infantile depression – all of which were discussed by Klein.

Lacan's interests in 'narcissism' and in the common structure of adults' and the babies' subjective lives made it important to him that babies, like adults, can become absorbed in their reflections. In his paper on the Mirror Stage, Lacan, like Darwin, drew observational comparisons between the reactions to mirrors of human infants and young apes:

> This act, far from exhausting itself, as in the case of the monkey, once the image has been mastered and found empty, immediately rebounds in the case of the child in a series of gestures in which he experiences in play the relation between the movements assumed in the image and the reflected environment. . . Unable as yet to walk, or even to stand up, and held tightly as he is by some support, human or artificial, he nevertheless overcomes, in a flutter of jubilant activity, the obstructions of his support and, fixing his attitude in a slightly leaning-forward position, in order to hold it in his gaze, brings back an instananeous aspect of the image.[39]

Plate 4.2 After the early months, babies often become fascinated to look at themselves in a mirror. This observation helped Lacan to flesh out his belief that human knowledge has its roots in what Freud called 'narcissism' – the search for an image of one's self.
Source: Author.

For Lacan, this phenomenon is linked to the child's very early attention to the human form, a form which, in the case of the human face and voice, holds the child's interest from the earliest days after birth. But it is the signs of triumphant jubilation and playful discovery in babies' encounters with their images in mirrors that demonstrates for Lacan the kind of recognition and absorption representing the basis of human knowledge and science in general. Such knowledge is based upon a fundamental misunderstanding of the kind basic to the myth of Narcissus, a taking-as-true of what is immediately seen or given without exploration of how or why it might have been created as it seems. Hence the infant takes as its 'self' a visual image that bears hardly at all on who or what the infant deeply 'is' (viz. a nexus of existential problems).

According to Lacan, the individual's (or infant's) route out of these misunderstandings is through involvement in language and other forms of social communication. But this is far from being a direct route. In entering the domain of language and symbols, individuals must submit themselves to a regime of rules and conventions which pre-date and operate without reference to the individual's own concerns and needs. Yet language and social life does offer the possibility of self-correction, deepened understanding and genuine communication, difficult though these may be to achieve. For Lacan the potential transforming-power of discourse is as essential to the infant's acquisition of language as it is to the struggle to develop communication in psycho-analysis. In both cases this struggle demands a movement from the falsity of imaginary mirror-knowledge towards the fullness of a discourse in which the individual's speech draws its meaning from, and allows individuals to realize, their fates.

The power of Lacan's writing about children's reactions to mirrors comes partly from his self-conscious recognition that children, even more than animals, have for so long been taken as the mirror of human nature. His illustration that the drama of human knowledge, as revealed in psycho-analytic experience, is set upon a narcissistic stage, used observations of infants in its support, suggesting that babies were like adults in this crucial respect. But simultaneously, Lacan put in question any easy scientific conclusion about the origins of human nature from reporting and discussing observations of infancy, as is traditional in the discipline of child study hailing Charles Darwin as its forefather.

If Freud saw himself as an Old Testament prophet, Lacan can be seen as a New Testament teacher, as is well captured in his Rome discourse 'The Function of Language in Psycho-analysis' (1953). For, whilst following Freud, Lacan saw the dynamics of desire as best understood to be dynamics of what St John and later Christian theologians have called The Word or *logos*. Both the practice of psycho-analysis and the illnesses it is used to treat are phenomena manifested in speech and language.

Lacan's work focused attention on the centrality and creative power of language in adult mental functioning. In his view, the terms of biology such as 'instinct', should not be used to explain how therapeutic language works, being themselves products of that language. Likewise Lacan was critical of the idea that love, the all-important quality in Christian theology, could be automatically and inevitably produced as a phenomenon of natural history. Love was an unnatural gift which reconciled an otherwise confused and fragmented nature: 'Perfect love is not a fruit of nature but of grace – that is to say, the fruit of an intersubjective accord imposing its harmony on the torn and riven nature which supports it.'[40]

Chapter 7 illustrates how developmental psychologists have come to assume love *is* a natural product of instinct, not the supreme aim of moral striving. It argues that such a reading of love into babies has been supported by a selective, not to say distorted sampling of the lives of babies and the adults who care for them. Chapter 8 reviews recent empirical evidence from film and TV records casting light on the kinds of 'intersubjective accord' which may obtain between babies and adults. Particular attention is paid to recent arguments about the kind of understanding of other people that babies achieve in the first year of life. In chapter 9 I ask whether studies of infancy that side-line the central concerns of mothers and the poor can give anything approaching a true picture of the origin of social being.

As with the work of Lacan on infancy, my argument questions both the view that human faculties are produced 'naturally', without struggle, and asks how it is that psychologists can feel satisfied with this anodyne view of human development. For Lacan's conception of the Mirror Stage challenges not only our vision of the child's mind but our expectations of science too.

In Lacan's view the discipline of psycho-analysis foreshadows a new kind of 'positive' science, a science that does not simply add data to the fund of human knowledge but which changes the experience of those who participate in it, the changes being transmitted through dialogue between individuals and potentially 'verifiable by everyone'. In such a science, the scientist is no longer the observer of psychological development but its subject and agent. Of the Freudian method, Lacan asks:

> Can his results form the basis of a positive science? Yes, if the experience is verifiable by everyone. But his experience, constituted between two subjects one of whom plays in the dialogue the role of ideal impersonality, may, once it is completed, and providing that it fulfils the conditions of efficacy that may be required of any special research, be resumed by the other subject with a third subject. This apparently initiatory way is simply a transmission by recurrence.[41]

Lacan's optimism for psycho-analysis as the technique of a practical science of individual transformation, through the alchemy of language, at once echoes the exalted aims of earlier moral reformers and defines a new horizon for the science of human development. Whilst we are still a long way from devising a society in which therapy is available to everyone, the ideal of a psychology which does not merely observe and prescribe but aims actively to participate in and facilitate the improvement of human experience is one with which it is not hard to concur.[42]

Summary

This chapter discussed the development of Freud's ideas about early childhood and those of his disciples Klein and Lacan. It showed that there is more than one psycho-analytic vision of infancy and traced a movement in Freud's own thinking from hearing his patients' accounts of childhood as referring to real occurrences in the past to hearing them as more or less unverifiable constructions which serve mainly to cast light on the patients' current fantasies and preoccupations.

Whilst psycho-analysis clearly owes a debt to associationism, it has developed in a very different direction from that taken by Pavlov, Watson and Skinner. In psycho-analysis, the emphasis is primarily on mental states and mental dynamics, of which a patient's 'free associations' are the product. Combined with this stress on internal processes, psycho-analysts have increasingly stressed the emotional complexity and ambiguity of spoken communication and the difficulty of acquiring any direct knowledge of one's self. Hence, in psycho-analysis, the analyst's interpretation of what others say is as much a moral exercise, leading to the acquisition of self-knowledge and emotional balance, as a scientific one. Indeed, Lacan has argued that Freud's work provides the basis for a new kind of science, a science which sets out not so much to explain human experience as to transform it for the better.

The place of infants in such a science would, as Lacan points out, be fundamentally the same as that of any other human being. The behaviour of infants can hence be used to illustrate or mirror adult states of mind but not to explain them. Klein's observations are particularly important in this respect, illustrating from observations of young children that the most basic modes of human experience are profoundly ambivalent.

My aim in this chapter has been to show that Freud and his followers have not simply developed a new description of infancy, highlighting for example oral, anal and genital behaviours; they have questioned the very status of infancy as the 'foundation' of human development. It is this line of questioning in psycho-analytic work which should make it possible to question the kind of misunderstanding pinpointed by Mircea Eliade and Richard Shweder:

> One of Freud's discoveries above all has had portentous consequences [in psycho-analysis and development psychology], namely, that for man there is a 'primordial' epoch in which all is decided – very early childhood – and that the course of this infancy is exemplary for the rest of life. Restating this in terms of archaic thinking, one might say that there was once a 'paradise' (which for psycho-analysts is the pre-natal period, or the time before weaning), ending in a 'break' or 'catastrophe' (the infantile trauma), and that whatever the adult's attitude may be towards these primordial circumstances, they are nonetheless constitutive of his being.[43]

We return to the possibility of mis-reading infancy as paradise in chapter 9.

Further Reading

Freud's work is best read at first hand. Two contrasting visions of infancy are to be found in his case-studies. 'Analysis of a Phobia in a Five-Year-Old Boy' (in *Case Histories I: 'Dora' and 'Little Hans'*, Penguin Freud Library, 8; Penguin, Harmondsworth, 1977), also known as the case of 'Little Hans', was first published in 1909 and illustrates how Hans's fear of horses related to Freud's most widely known stage-theory of infantile sexuality. In contrast, 'From the History of an Infantile Neurosis' (in *Case Histories II: 'Rat Man', Schreber, 'Wolf Man', Female Homosexuality*, Penguin Freud Library, 9; Penguin, Harmondsworth, 1979), also known as the case of 'the Wolf Man', was first published in 1918 and shows Freud trying and failing to find a verifiable history underlying his patient's 'memories' of early childhood. Alternatively, readers new to Freud can begin with his *Introductory Lectures on Psychoanalysis* (Penguin Freud Library, 1; Penguin, Harmondsworth, 1973).

The Selected Melanie Klein edited by J. Mitchell (Penguin, Harmondsworth, 1986) contains Klein's most important papers on infancy, showing how observations of babies can illuminate adult mental processes, together with brief historical introductions and an excellent introductory essay by the editor.

Changing the Subject: Psychology, Social Regulation and Subjectivity by J. Henriques, W. Hollway, C. Urwin, C. Venn and V. Walkerdine (Methuen, London, 1984) contains a number of attempts to sum up Lacan's position. The best is to be found in Urwin's chapter, 'Power relations and the emergence of language'.

Freud on Femininity and Faith by J. van Herik (University of California Press, Berkeley, 1982) presents an elegant analysis of Freud as a moralist in the Mosaic tradition.

Freud and Man's Soul, a short book by B. Bettelheim (Chatto & Windus, London, 1983), argues that Freud's translators have led English-speakers to ignore his aspirations as a moralist in order to represent psycho-analysis as a science.

5

Before Grammar

The previous three chapters explore arguments about infancy by thinkers whose work preceded the modern boom in scientific research on babies. The analysis presented in each chapter showed a different tension between fact-gathering about babies and the representation of adulthood: Darwin published his notes on Doddy in trying to convince his contemporaries that the human mind had originated like the human body through millenia of natural selection and other evolutionary processes. The early associationists discussed infancy to illustrate their belief that links in consciousness grew up as a result of the co-occurrence of events in time and space, a belief that they used to support campaigns for social reform based on re-education. Likewise, behaviourists used observations of infancy to support their claims that learning was all-powerful in shaping adult character. Alternatively, the last chapter showed how psycho-analysts have turned from representing the events of early childhood as causing later developments of the personality to treating discussions about infancy as part of the symbolic language which their patients use to represent their current preoccupations and concerns.

This and the following three chapters discuss contemporary approaches to the scientific study of infancy, approaches each having a different debt to the visions of infancy entertained by their intellectual predecessors. Such modern research can be seen as being inaugurated by a debate about the development of language which had as its starting point a reaction against Skinner's account of verbal behaviour. The present chapter describes this debate, which is in marked contrast to the debate about language among psycho-analysts.

The Form of Language

For centuries scientists and thinkers interested in the structure of language have, usually on the birth of their own children, noted down the development of word-like sounds, first words, and early combinations of words to fuel their speculations. As we have seen, it was publication of notes of this sort by the French philosopher Hippolyte Taine that prompted Charles Darwin to publish his 'Biographical Sketch of an Infant' in 1877.[1] The fullest 'diary study' of a child's language was published between 1939 and 1949 in four volumes by the German-American linguist Leopold, describing the development from birth of his daughter Hildegard as she learnt both German and English.[2] Like Leopold's work, most diary studies focused almost exclusively on the changing distribution of sounds and words as babies developed, taking particular interest in the changing distributions of nouns, verbs, adjectives and other linguistic units in the increasingly sophisticated speeches of growing children. When larger samples of young speakers were examined, they focused on the normal 'milestones' of language development; average ages for the first word, the first question, for first incorrect and correct uses of 'I' and so on.

Interesting though these studies are, they were not inspired by any special theory of language development. Children were believed to learn language much as they learnt everything else. Leonard Bloomfield added that children must be capable of classifying grammatical units together and be able to form new utterances by anaology with sentences they had already heard.[3] But his account of the special difficulties with which language faced the developing child was not distinct enough to prompt any new theoretical work by scientists studying children. That there was a need for such work was made clear by Noam Chomsky in his review of Skinner's book on language, *Verbal Behavior*.[4]

Skinner's view

In *Verbal Behavior* Skinner had argued for a radical revision of the terms traditionally used to describe language by scientists. Language learning was not to be seen as depending on the child's own sense of meaning or the recognition of meanings intended by others. Speech was just one outcome of the subjection of a malleable and quick-learning organism to a lengthy and intricate history of conditioning by adults who themselves used speech. From a scientific point of view, Skinner said, language was just one amongst many products of the subtle ways in which behaviour can be shaped by punishment and incentive. All that is unique about verbal behaviour is its relationship to the reinforcement it receives in the human community that supports it. Verbal behaviour is behaviour that has been changed 'through the mediation of other persons' needs'.[5]

Skinner illustrated the change of view he was advocating by translating a traditional description of language development into behaviourist terms. Here is the traditional version:

In many countries it has been observed that very early a child uses a long *m* (without a vowel) as a sign that it wants something, but we can hardly be right in supposing that the sound is originally meant by children in this sense. They do not use it consciously until they see that grown-up people, on hearing the sound, come up and find out what the child wants.[6]

And here is Skinner's version:

It has been observed that very early a child emits the sound *m* in certain states of deprivation or aversive stimulation, but we can hardly be right in calling the response verbal at this stage. It is conditioned as a verbal operant only when people, upon hearing the sound, come up and supply appropriate reinforcement.[7]

Underlying this new description was a behaviourist theory of language learning very simple in conception but enormously complicated in implication.

Skinner illustrated this theory with the example of crying. Vocal behaviour of this sort, is, in his terms, an 'unconditioned response' in the newborn baby. Then for some time it is a function of varying amounts of deprivation and aversive stimulation. But when crying is characteristically followed by parental attentions which are reinforcing, it becomes *verbal* according to Skinner's definition:

It has become a different behavioural unit because it is now under the control of different variables. It has also probably acquired different properties, for parents are likely to react differently to different intonations of intensities of crying.[8]

Verbal Behavior was written to advance a conception of psychology which subsumed language under the general principles of animal adaptation. Skinner's aim was to use his discussion of speech to illustrate the unifying psychological principles he had characterized in his earlier work on rats and pigeons. Central to this aim was the wish to devise an *effective* science of human action, a science which crusaded for planned changes in human behaviour. He argued that, faced with world war and mass starvation, psychology should build the foundations of its theory upon the need to rationalize human behaviour. Hence scientists could not say that they understood behaviour, whether verbal or otherwise, until they knew how to change it predictably:

> The extent to which we understand verbal behavior in a 'causal' analysis is to be assessed from the extent to which we can predict the occurrence of specific instances and, eventually, from the extent to which we can produce or control such behavior by altering the conditions under which it occurs.[9]

Chomsky's review

Chomsky's famous review of Skinner's book concentrated on Skinner's critique of traditional grammar and his attempt to give an account of language learning without reference to such 'internal' mental processes as intention or understanding. Chomsky conceded that learning played a part in structuring speech. But he argued that the terminology devised to describe experiments on learning in rats and pigeons only confused the issue when used to describe the structure and maintenance of language:

> If we take his [Skinner's] terms in their literal meaning, the description covers almost no aspect of verbal behavior, and if we take them metaphorically, the description offers no improvement over various traditional formulations. . . What has been hoped for from the psychologist is some indication how the casual and informal description of everyday behavior in the popular vocabulary can be explained or clarified in terms of the notions developed in careful experiment and observation, or perhaps replaced in terms of a better scheme. A mere terminological revision, in which a term borrowed from the laboratory is used with the full vagueness of the ordinary vocabulary, is of no conceivable interest.[10]

But Chomsky's review was more than a criticism of Skinner. It proposed an alternative model for the acquisition of language, a model which seemed to many psychologists to be an excellent basis for research on little children:

> As long as we are speculating, we may consider the possibility that the brain has evolved to the point where, given an input of observed Chinese sentences, it produces (by an 'induction' of apparently fantastic complexity and suddenness) the 'rules' of Chinese grammar, and given an input of observed English sentences, it produces (by, perhaps, exactly the same process of induction) the rules of English grammar; or that given an observed application of a term to certain instances it automatically predicts the extension to a class of complexly related instances.[11]

Plate 5.1 Noam Chomsky holding . . . a Language Acquisition Device? (According to Chomsky, the LAD is not the baby itself but a hypothetical 'black box' in the brain of the newborn child.)
Source: Noam Chomsky.

To many the idea that babies were born with a so-called Language Acquisition Device in the brain seemed a far more plausible idea than that of language acquisition by means of learning from the 'careful arrangement of contingencies' or 'meticulous training'.[12] To Skinner's critics there was nothing careful or meticulous about the way in which babies were brought up to speak:

> It is a common observation that a young child of immigrant parents may learn a second language in the streets, from other children, with amazing rapidity, and that his speech may be completely fluent and correct to the last allophone, while the subtleties that become second nature to the child may elude his parents despite high motivation and continued practice. A child may pick up a large part of his vocabulary and 'feel' for sentence structure from television, from reading, from listening to adults, etc. Even a very young child who

has not yet acquired a minimal repertoire from which to form new utterances may imitate a word quite well on an early try, with no attempt on the part of his parents to teach him. It is also perfectly obvious that, at a later stage, a child will be able to construct and understand utterances which are quite new, and are, at the same time, acceptable sentences in his language.[13]

Chomsky's view of language learning was based on a parallel he drew, like Bloomfield before him, between the task facing a linguist who sets out to describe a new language and a baby trying to learn a first language. Both baby and linguist cannot know immediately when they have heard the utterances which are closest to the true or most enlightening grammar of the language they don't know. Both will get very little direct evidence as to the 'deep structure' of the language being spoken all around them. Under these circumstances, both baby and linguist must make some strong assumptions about the relative values of the sounds they hear. As an academic who had spent much of the 1950s working out in detail the kinds of assumption a linguist needed to make in order to describe a language, and by virtue of his equation between baby and linguist, Chomsky felt in a strong position to make fairly detailed claims about what a baby must be born knowing if he or she is to be able to learn any human language with equal ease.

Chomsky's message to psychologists was that when a baby learns to talk, she or he learns more than the distribution of nouns, verbs and other parts of speech in a sentence. Babies must also develop a sense of the various rules by which the 'deep' grammatical structure of an utterance (such as 'Jane sees movies') can be transformed into different surface structures (e.g. 'Movies are seen by Jane'). Once the rules of transformation between deep and surface structure have been learnt a child is able to sense the difference between superficially similar sentences such as 'John is eager to please' and 'John is easy to please' and to detect ambiguities in sentences such as 'We fed her dog bones' or 'Flying planes can be dangerous'.

Psychologists' response to Chomsky

The impact of Chomsky's work was not immediately felt in the science of pre-verbal babies. The first response by psychologists to Chomsky's review of *Verbal Behavior* and his own book *Syntactic Structures* was that they began to look for evidence of rule-use in the early utterances of children who had just begun to speak.[14] By the mid-1960s they were claiming that even small children's two-word utterances do show a simple grammatical structure. So-called 'pivot-grammar' distinguished between two sorts of words: a small class of frequently used 'pivot' words such as *more* and *Mummy* and a larger class of 'open' words such as *juice*, *birdie* and *ball*. Pivot words were divided into two sub-classes: those which always appeared first in a sentence and those which always appeared second (e.g. *gone* in *juice gone*, *birdie gone*, *ball gone*).[15]

For a while it seemed that pivot grammar fulfilled all Chomsky's predictions. Toddlers were producing grammatical sentences and, moreover, forming a unique grammar of their own which could not have been learnt directly from adults, as adults use a very different grammar. This was surely proof that babies were born with a rule-generating capacity of which their linguistic feats were the product. But scientific enthusiasm for pivot grammar has waned because it is, like the diary studies which preceded Chomsky, merely a description of the surface distribution of different kinds of word in the utterances young children make. Pivot grammar has nothing to say about the child's knowledge of the 'deep structure' of language, the relationship between subject, verb and object, for example.

By the end of the 1960s, research had begun to suggest that the 'deep' rules that underlie what children say and understand might not be grammatical rules at all. For example, scientists interested in the grammar of toddlers' utterances found that the 'native speakers' of child language, children themselves, seldom gave useful answers to questions about grammar:

Interviewer: Adam, which is right, 'two shoes' or 'two shoe'?
Adam: Pop goes the weasel.[16]

Such examples illustrate a lack of match between the focus of the scientist's interest in the words of children – in this case, the grammar of plurals – and the child's own foci of interest.

Even for adults, answers to questions about what is grammatical often are blurred or hard to give unless one can clearly visualize different conditions under which the constructions might be used. Words are conglomerates of sound and meaning. Chomsky's concentration on adult grammar gave no clue to the way in which babies develop their senses of what expressions can mean, something which could not happen 'to a large extent independently of intelligence', as Chomsky proposed for grammar.

Early in the 1970s, research was published which further challenged the assumption that how infants begin to organize words could be discussed quite separately from what young children mean by what they say. In particular, Lois Bloom's diary study of the little girl Kathryn showed that for children, as for adults, the same words and phrases often have very different meanings. For example, the four utterances *no fit*, *no dirty soap no pocket* and *no Mommy* would all be classed as the same in pivot grammar (pivot + open word). Yet Bloom's descriptions of the circumstances in which these utterances occurred made plain that Kathryn was using the same word *no* to code very different meanings. She said *no fit* when unable to put a toy lamb into another toy, using *no* descriptively. *No dirty soap* took its meaning from Kathryn pushing away a piece of worn soap in the bath, wanting to be washed with new pink soap. Here *no* coded disinclination. *No pocket* referred to Kathryn's inability to find a pocket in her mother's skirt, *no* coding an apparent absence. And *no Mommy* was a comment made when Kathryn refused to have her hair combed by someone other than her mother, *no* coding preference for Mommy. Similarly, Kathryn made the identical remark *Mommy sock* on two very different occasions. First when she picked up her mother's dirty sock and second when her mother was putting Kathryn's sock on Kathryn.[17]

Whilst Bloom's research did not answer all the questions it posed, these questions set a new standard for research on infancy and early childhood. Scientists clearly had to consider the context as well as the content of children's utterances if they were to gain any insight into the way in which babies learnt how to mean with words. Moreover, it seemed that, early in life, childrens' understanding of their environment and the demands they expressed were far more complex and remarkable than their grammatical capacities. In seeking the origins of the young child's prococious sense of what is appropriate and meaningful in different circumstances, scientists were forced once again to reconsider how language is learnt.

Flaws in Chomsky's argument

The next three chapters review different bases for revising the Chomskyan picture of language. But before proceeding we should ask what it was that made Chomsky's work such a landmark in psychological studies of children. And why was it that his own formulations about the Language Acquisition Device (or LAD) failed to explain the development of communication in infancy?

We can approach an answer to both these questions by attending to the letter of Chomsky's utterances about language. These utterances are clearly made chiefly to define a point of view which contrasts with the explanation of language acquisition as a process of animal learning. They are made with considerable vehemence, a vehemence that impresses us as much by the energy of its expression as by argument or evidence. Upon reflection, Chomsky's evidence for the LAD often seems less convincing than it does at first sight. For example, we are told that small children may imitate new words at an early try, with no help from others (see above). But babies imitate gestures and facial expressions long before they imitate language.[18] So is the imitation of words evidence for an early ability specifically to handle grammar? Or is verbal imitation one product of a capacity with a far broader psychological purchase?

Chomsky's review of *Verbal Behavior* has been called 'perhaps the single most influential psychological paper published since Watson's behaviorist manifesto of 1913'.[19] One reason for this judgement is that since 1960 the vision of the brain as an information-processing device, intrinsic to Chomsky's conception of the LAD, has increasingly come to dominate scientific thinking about cognition (see next chapter). But whilst Chomsky's analogy of the brain as computer may seem peculiarly prescient to historians of the modern 'cognitive revolution' in psychology, it is also the root of his failure to explain the baby's approach to language. For models of the brain as a computer simultaneously assume that the language and logic of computer-programming naturally matches the running of the mind and that a model of the brain is the same as a model of the mind. Chomsky's approach to language undoubtedly leans more towards engineering and physiology than it does towards the interpretation of experience.[20] Like most cognitive psychologists, Chomsky is keen to vault over an analysis of the idiosyncratic significances which structure the mental lives of individual speakers and the role these significances play in generating action. Hence, he implies that this kind of analysis is irrelevant to working out how well-formed sentences might mechanically be produced.

An example of Chomsky's inappropriate reliance on parallels between the brain and the computer is to be found in his incomplete interpretation of the following quotation from his philosophical hero René Descartes.[21] Chomsky is arguing against the criticism that the concept of 'innate grammar' is incomprehensible:

There is nothing incomprehensible in the view that stimulation provides the occasion for the mind to apply certain innate interpretive principles, certain concepts that proceed from 'the power of understanding' itself, from the faculty of thinking, rather than from external objects directly. To take an example from Descartes:

When first in infancy we see a triangular figure depicted on paper, this figure cannot show us how a real triangle ought to be conceived, in the way in which geometricians consider it, because the true triangle is contained in this figure, just as the statue of Mercury is contained in a rough block of wood. But because we already possess within us the idea of a true triangle, and it can be more easily conceived by our mind than the more complex figure of the triangle drawn on paper, we, therefore, when we see the composite figure, apprehend not it itself, but rather the authentic triangle. [emphasis added (BSB)]

In this sense the idea of a triangle is innate. Surely the notion is comprehensible; there would be no difficulty, for example, in programming a computer to react to stimuli along these lines.[22]

Here we find Chomsky arguing that, because he can imagine how to build a computer to do something, then Nature or Evolution must be able to build the same ability into the newborn baby. But this is to suppose nature at large is equipped with an intelligence like Chomsky's, a most anthropocentric supposition. On the other hand, the use of computers as a model of a human process like the perception of speech dehumanizes it, asking us to imagine that speakers have no qualities which cannot be modelled by the machines we ourselves have invented. The production of such machines would, in any case, only be possible after their designers had attained perfect self-knowledge, a task for which neither humans nor computers seem particularly well-designed.

An additional irony in Chomsky's selection of this quotation from Descartes to support his views is that Descartes himself seems here to be making a crucial distinction between infant and adult perception which runs directly counter to Chomsky's argument. Descartes's argument can be read as follows: When infants see a drawing of a triangular figure, the figure cannot show them how a real triangle ought to be conceived; the triangle is as invisible to infants as is the image of a statue of Mercury to all but the sculptor who envisages it whilst looking at a raw block of wood. But we adults are like the sculptor. By virtue of our education, we already possess the idea of a true triangle. Therefore, when we see a drawing of a triangle, we see an authentic triangle, not merely pencil strokes on paper. Read in this way, Descartes is illustrating the view that babies do *not* have innate knowledge of a kind which parallels the knowledge of adults, whether they be geometricians or grammarians.

But perhaps the most important plank of Chomsky's argument that grammar is innate is his insistence that the experience of children is 'meagre and degenerate':

> I think if we contemplate the classical problem of psychology, that of accounting for human knowledge, we cannot avoid being struck by the enormous disparity between knowledge and experience – in the case of language, between the generative grammar that expresses the linguistic competence of the native speaker and the meager and degenerate data on the basis of which he has constructed this grammar for himself.[23]

By running down the importance and richness of our experience of environmental structure in this way, Chomsky implicitly excuses himself from having to account for its role in shaping language. Nevertheless, his is a most incomprehensible belief. Surely we are all inundated with incomparably copious, varied and minutely structured data from the moment we are born. To argue as Chomsky does is to count as nothing the exquisite abundance of nature as well as all the human sophistications of strategy and ritual which surround us on every side. It is only by denying this abundance that Chomsky is able to shift our attention to the 'amazing complexity' of the abilities he imputes to the newborn child.

Babies are the most ungrammatical of human creatures. Whilst grammar must clearly be the measure of all things linguistic *for grammarians*, it is surely a mistake to make this the scientific measure of infant or pre-verbal expression. Chomsky writes; 'Anyone concerned with the study of human nature and human capacities must somehow come to grips with the fact that all normal humans acquire language, whereas acquisition of even its barest rudiments is quite beyond the capacities of an otherwise intelligent ape.'[24] But he is only able to maintain this view by clinging to a purely grammatical definition of language.

The Origins of Meaning in Early Language

If language is seen as something that mediates the subject-matter of pain, desire, intelligence, affection and the many other subtle senses that can be conveyed by non-verbal means, there can be no doubt that apes and many other animals have a great deal more than its barest rudiments. Likewise when we consider the cries, coos, gurgles, babbles and even the first words of human infants, grammar seems peculiarly inappropriate to their analysis. When a baby begins to say 'Mum' or 'juice' or 'Pss', surely we most want to know what he/she was doing or wanting or thinking or feeling when he/she made the sound, not whether he/she was using it as a sentence or a phrase.

Thoughts

If the precursors of language in infancy are not primarily grammatical, what are they?

Linguists studying early speech have for decades remarked that toddlers extend their first vocabulary by using the same word in a variety of ways. Various theories have been advanced to explain the thinking behind the 'over-extension' of these early words. In some cases it seems that all the word's referents share a common feature which the word denotes.

For example, a small girl studied by Melissa Bowerman used the word 'ball' to refer to a variety of rounded objects suitable for handling and throwing: a rounded cork pincushion, a round red balloon, an Easter egg, a small round stone, a plastic egg-shaped toy and a round canister lid.[25] In

Figure 5.1 Some of the things most commonly named when babies begin to speak.[26]
Source: Author.

other cases, there seems to be no common feature underlying word-use, merely a changing chain of associations. Thus another child used the sound 'bébé' to refer to a sequence of objects; first, a photograph of himself, then all photos, then all pictures, then all books with pictures and finally all books.[27]

Such examples illustrate how important the way in which babies reason may be in explaining how babies acquire language. They also show that babies may think in ways that are unfamiliar to adults. Thus toddlers quite often use words in ways which suggest they use categories which seem to us odd. One baby is reported to have invented a word to refer to railway steam-engines, boiling coffee pots and anything else that hissed or made a noise. And babies not uncommonly develop uses of language to refer to prohibitions, interference or physical restraint by adults. For instance one little girl cried 'too tight' when her mother tried to wash her ears.[28]

Feelings

Another kind of research on early speech suggests that emotion and emotional attachments may be an important feature in structuring the mental life of the speaking child. In 1966 Leslie Ames published an analysis of over two hundred stories told by children aged between two and five.[29] He found that the predominant themes in these early stories were violence and aggression. For example, a two-year-old girl says:

> About a girl. I think she frightened a rabbit. In the woods. He was eating the carrots. The rabbit ate all the little girl up. Then a fox came out. The fox bited the rabbit. Cause the little rabbit aten the little girl. The fox wanted to go back in his wood cause he wanted to west. Then he waked up. The bunny wanted a west. He got into his woods and he wested. Then he woke up again. A witch was coming. She stole the little bunny. He was all eaten by the witch. The witch was killed by a fox. They had to put that witch in jail. They had to.[30]

And when Ruth Weir came to analyse the soliloquies of her two-year-old son Anthony alone in his crib before sleeping, she found that they were a complex commentary on his feelings about and attitudes to salient characters and events in his life: his parents, their relationship, his dog, his toys, his food, and so on:

> That's for he . . . Mamamama with Daddy . . . Milk for Daddy . . . OK . . . Daddy dance . . . Daddy dance . . . Hi Daddy . . . Only Anthony . . . Daddy dance . . . Daddy dance . . . Daddy give it . . . Daddy not for Anthony . . . No . . . Daddy . . . Daddy got . . . Look at Daddy [*falsetto*] . . . Look at Daddy here . . . Look at Daddy . . . Milk in the bottle . . . I spilled it . . . etc.[31]

Chapter 7 discusses the contribution of science to our understanding of the emotional lives of babies.

Social life

A third approach to the explanation of development towards language as more than grammar has seen the growth of communication between adult and child as a joint achievement, not as something occurring solely in the head of the child. Jerome Bruner has wittily represented the bones of this approach by suggesting that, to understand what Chomsky explained with the LAD, we must consider the child's 'language acquisition support system' (LASS), the contribution of those who look after the child.[32] In chapter 8 we consider some of the views of scientists who believe that the most significant pre-verbal regularities relevant to the attainment of speech are to be found in the routines of interaction between infants and their familiars, as seen in games of peek-a-boo or the rituals surrounding nappy-changing, bathing, feeding, and giving and taking.

Perhaps the most important reason for revising Chomsky's low estimate of the mother's (and/or other adults') contribution to the development of the child has been provided by research on what some Americans dub 'motherese': adult speech to infants. In direct contrast to Chomsky's belief that the linguistic 'input' to the LAD is degenerate, researchers like Catherine Snow have collected substantial evidence that adults and even older children talk to babies from birth onwards in a specially modified way: talking predominantly about the baby, using short simple utterances, often repeating themselves, speaking slowly and stressing what they say with characteristic patterns of intonation, gesture and facial expression.[33] Clearly babies do get considerable help in learning language from their minders. Hence the contribution of minders must have an important place in any theory of language acquisition (see chapter 9).

For all the shortcomings of Chomsky's view of child language, his review of *Verbal Behavior* undoubtedly awoke psychologists to the complexity of the child's achievement in learning to speak and the importance of understanding the status of language as a mental process. The heat and clarity of his opposition to learning-theory has proven a major factor in forging the interests of many of the main exponents of the modern science of infancy.

Summary

Chomsky's review of Skinner's *Verbal Behavior* marks the start of a great surge of interest in the psychological prerequisites for the infant's acquisition of language. Chomsky argued that language was too complex and too quickly learnt to be acquired 'like everything else', through the administration of rewards and punishments. In direct contrast to behaviourism, he argued that the learning of language could only be explained if it was granted that babies are born with a brain already adapted to the formulation of grammatical rules. His review made further points against behaviourism. He accused Skinner of inventing a bogus, pseudo-scientific vocabulary for the description of language which was if anything an obstacle to understanding. And he argued that no comprehensible explanation of human mental faculties could be made without reference to 'internal operations' of the kind he thought responsible for the child's construction of syntax. He suggested that these operations could be thought of as analogous to those going on in computers.

The debate which Chomsky's critique stirred up soon produced a host of studies on young children. By the end of the 1960s, psychologists were starting to question whether the child's early speech was indeed the consequence of the operation of a computer-like mechanism in the brain, programmed to abstract grammatical rules from the talk of adults. Rather than reverting to behaviourism, they began to suggest that the child's speech might be the product of mental operations not specifically adapted to the production of speech. The child's language did not primarily reflect a grammatical intelligence. Early speech combined what children knew (their cognitions) and what they wanted to say in a way that owed as much to their general understanding of their own and others' actions as to their grasp of grammar.

Evidence for this argument was collected in a variety of ways. First, it was shown by Bloom that what toddlers meant by what they said could often only be deduced from the context in which they spoke. The same set of words could be used to code a number of different linguistic functions for the child. Secondly, studies of relatively long sequences of early speech, as in the stories collected by Ames and the 'cradle talk' collected by Weir, showed that young children's speech contains emotional themes to which grammar can give no clue. And, thirdly, analysis of how mothers spoke to children showed that the first words emerge in a highly structured social relationship where some form of communication has been going on for many months.

The line of argument supporting the critique of Chomsky's speculations about a 'language acquisition device' led scientists to focus more and more on what was going on in the pre-verbal period of childhood. When they did so, the questions they had in mind were of three kinds: concerning cognition (What must children know before they can understand and use speech? And how do they gain this knowledge?); concerning emotion (What is the emotional basis of language learning? What do children want to speak about?); and, concerning social interaction (How do pre-verbal interactions between infants and adults assist the child to speak? And what are the psychological prerequisites for these interactions?). The next three chapters deal with these three kinds of question in turn.

Further Reading

Chomsky: Selected Readings edited by J. P. B. Allen and P. van Buren (Oxford University Press, London, 1971) contains extracts from Chomsky's seminal writings on linguistics, including his vigorous review of Skinner's *Verbal Behavior*.

Chomsky by J. Lyons (Fontana, London, 1977, revised edn) is an expert but readable introduction to Chomsky's linguistic project as a whole.

Child Language by A. J. Elliot (Cambridge University Press, Cambridge, 1981) is a useful and comprehensive student's introduction to the study of early language.

Language Development: Form and Function in Emerging Grammars by L. Bloom (MIT Press, Cambridge, Mass., 1970) is an example of research on early language showing the clash between seeing children's first utterances as formal grammatical structures and seeing them as motivated to mean different things.

6

Babies as Thinkers

In his review of *Verbal Behavior*, Chomsky suggested that human babies are born with a species-specific brain mechanism purpose-built for detecting in speech the rules of grammar. The idea of the mind as an information-processing unit is a popular one amongst academic psychologists. The beginnings of this popularity have been traced to the participation of behavioural scientists in the Second World War.[1]

Between 1939 and 1945 many academic psychologists turned their minds to helping their nations win the war. Some of their enterprises succeeded whilst others failed. After the armistice, these war efforts were to have effects which carried over into the science of psychology. In the United States, Skinner spent years training pigeons to sit in the noses of missiles which they could guide to destroy enemy targets. His pigeons were never used by the American armed forces but, after the war, pigeons replaced rats as the most popular animal for behavioural research on learning.

In Britain, psychologists were employed to solve a different set of military problems. Their task was to design a machine which might replace the people who spent hour after hour watching radar screens to distinguish from clouds and flocks of birds the patterns of dots which signalled marauding formations of enemy bombers and fighter planes. Human pattern-detectors easily lapse into sleep or inattention. A machine which 'knew' what enemy aircraft looked like would clearly be more efficient. Psychologists were also asked to design a machine which could predict the movements of fast-flying planes so that anti-aircraft shells could be fired an appropriate distance in advance of targets to hit them.

Success in these two tasks started a new train of research in the science of mind. Before the war, the argument that scientists could not helpfully study mental processes, because they were unobservable, seemed conclusive. The influence on psychology of Watson's and Skinner's decision to base their work only on observable behaviours bears witness to this fact. But the discovery that machines could be constructed which themselves had 'internal representations' (of aircraft) changed all this, a change further advanced by the invention of problem-solving computers in the 1940s. There is nothing more objective than a machine fashioned from metal, wire, glass and plastic. And if machines can be built to visualize and plan ahead, it makes little sense to deny that humans reason and intend. This insight set the stage for the so-called 'cognitive' revolution in psychology which has inspired research based on the idea that our mental operations may be viewed in the same light as and modelled upon the workings of complex machines.

It is only a short step from recognizing that scientists can study 'internal representations' to asking whence comes the human capacity to represent the world internally? Are children born with mental representations? If not, how do these develop after birth?

Chomsky's answer to these questions was, yes, babies are born with an innate mental representation of the grammatical structure of phrases. But, as we saw in the last chapter, intensive research on young talkers, stirred up by Chomsky's work, suggested that how children acquire grammar (syntax) could not be explained without understanding how babies develop their sense of meaning. This chapter examines the idea that the child's understandings and uses of words are consequences of the infant's advance towards complex pre-verbal thought-processes not directly related to grammar.

The Cognitive Basis for Learning Language

One of the strongest cases that there is a broad 'cognitive basis' for language learning rather than the specifically grammatical basis proposed by Chomsky was made by the American John Macnamara in 1972.[2] Macnamara argued that infants learn language by first working out, independently of language, the meaning which a speaker intends to convey to them, and later working out the relationship between meaning and words. He was particularly interested in the difficulties young children face in understanding rather than speaking language. His evidence focused on three types of ambiguity which children must unravel if they are to learn how to speak.

The first ambiguities affected vocabulary. For example, adults often point to an object – a rabbit, for example – in teaching a child its name.

Yet, how is the child to know whether the sound 'rabbit' means rabbit rather than fur, head, animal or rabbit-shape? Grammar or even a pointing-finger is not itself enough to distinguish between these possibilities. And how do children learn that adults name independently movable objects, such as a lamp, rather than conglomerates such as a lamp-surrounded-by-light?

Macnamara's second source of evidence concerned grammatical complexities. How is a child to learn that the same words in the same grammatical construction can have very different meanings (as in *The girl struck the boy* versus *The boy struck the girl*), while different grammatical constructions using different words can have the same meaning (for example, *The cat climbed the tree* means much the same as *The tree was climbed by the cat*)? Alternatively the same words may have a variety of meanings in different company: for example, *In a box, In a temper, In a minute* (time when) and *In a minute* (time how long). Macnamara argued that a sense of grammar alone could not provide the child with a way to solve these unpredictable puzzles.

Macnamara's final set of ambiguities concerns the sounds that words have. For example, the word *watch* has different meanings as a verb and as a noun, yet sounds identical in both cases. Alternatively, some variations in speech-sound in different dialects or different languages carry no meaning whereas others do. When the English say *sheep*, they do not mean *ship*. Yet, in Spanish, the sound-difference between *ship* and *sheep* never carries meaning. So children must in some countries learn to distinguish sounds which in other countries must be ignored, without assistance from the language itself.

By painting a vivid picture of the problems faced by infants learning language for the first time, Macnamara made a persuasive case for shifting the scientific focus from grammar to meaning in linguistic studies of babies. He pointed to the work of Jean Piaget (1896–1980) on early cognitive development as the best aid for understanding how babies build up knowledge of the world before they can speak. During the 1920s and 1930s Piaget had published a series of brilliant experimental studies of babies' thinking. These studies gave a definitive answer to the questions about the origins of thinking which began to preoccupy the critics of pivot grammar in the late 1960s and early 1970s.

Piaget on the growth of rationality

Piaget's first extensive scientific work concerned the biology of freshwater shellfish living in the lakes around his home in Switzerland. He began publishing articles about these molluscs at the age of fifteen.[3] By the age of twenty-one he had completed a prose-poem and a philosophical novel entitled *Recherche*.[4] But his first experimental work on children was conducted in Alfred Binet's old laboratory in Paris. His initial aim was to find out how Parisian children performed on the reasoning tests devised in London by Cyril Burt to test intelligence. But he soon realized that

> though Burt's tests certainly had their diagnostic merits, based on the number of successes and failures, it was much more interesting to try to find the reasons for the failures. Thus I engaged my subjects in conversations patterned after psychiatric questioning, with the aim of discovering something about the reasoning process underlying their right, but especially their wrong answers.[5]

Piaget was amazed to find that even simple reasoning tasks, such as finding the part common to two wholes, presented normal children with unsuspected difficulties up to the ages of eleven or twelve. He concluded that logic was not inborn, but develops little by little according to biological laws, the discovery of which would provide the basis for 'a sort of embryology of intelligence'.[6]

Piaget's first psychological book, published in 1924, was entitled *The Language and Thought of the Child*.[7] It revealed that Piaget's thinking about children was strongly influenced by Freud's ideas. Yet is was not a psycho-analytic book. As a youth, Piaget was intensely interested in notions of the unconscious. In his autobiography he relates this interest to having had a mother with a 'rather neurotic temperament'. But, he writes, 'I have never since felt any desire to involve myself deeper in that particular direction, always much preferring the study of normalcy and of the workings of the intellect to that of the tricks of the unconscious.'[8]

Piaget's aim was to plot, step by step, how normal human beings progress towards rationality. One of his greatest debts to Freud was the notion that young children are narcissistic or, as Piaget termed it, 'profoundly egocentric'.[9] This was the main claim in Piaget's first book. Early speech is egocentric 'partly because the child speaks only about himself, but chiefly because he does not attempt to place himself at the point of view of his hearer'.[10] Piaget noted that children often do not seem concerned when their remarks are unanswered or bear no relation to those around them. For example, a teacher tells a group of six-year-olds that owls cannot see by day. One of her pupils who is drawing then remarks:

> Well, I know quite well that it can't. I've already done 'moon' so I'll have to change it (referring to his work. Then picking up some crumbs of barley-sugar). I say, I've got a lovely pile of eye-glasses. I say, I've got a gun to kill him with. I say, I am the captain on horseback. I say, I've got a horse and a gun as well.[11]

This kind of language is dominant from three to seven years and, to a lesser extent, from seven to twelve years.

In contrast, socialized speech is when the child 'really exchanges his thoughts with others, either by telling his hearer something that will interest him and influence his actions, or by an actual interchange of ideas'. According to Piaget, socialized speech only begins to appear in the child's repertoire at ages of seven or eight and the change from egocentrism to a truly social orientation is not complete until eleven or twelve. Critics of Piaget have pointed out that egocentric speech is much reduced when small children are expected to co-operate rather than work alone, as were Piaget's subjects.[12]

Shortly after Piaget's first book on children was published, his first daughter was born (1925). A second daughter followed in 1927 and a son in 1931. With the help of his wife, Piaget observed his children closely from birth onwards and subjected them to many experiments. Whilst Piaget was hardly the first scientist to note the behaviours of his own children, it says much for his originality as a thinker and his powers of observation and deduction that his descriptions of these three babies still provide the classic basis for modern research on mental development in infancy.

Piaget's main interest was in the origin of the human capacity to represent the world in the mind. Like Watson, Piaget believed that at birth, human beings are endowed only with simple reflexes and an ability to learn. Yet if they are to learn how to speak in eighteen months they must swiftly build up the basis for understanding symbols and signs. Piaget's three books on infancy each concentrated on a different aspect of this process.

The first was called *The Origins of Intelligence in the Child* (1937).[13] It focused on the growth of babies' ability to represent the goals of their actions independently from the means to reach those goals. Piaget described six stages of progress towards what he called genuinely intentional action.

His first observations were of the sucking reflex, concentrating on the slow adaptation of the reflex to external reality. He took particular interest in the way in which babies locate what they want to suck, whether it be a nipple or their thumb. If thumb or nipple is removed from their mouths, are their searches completely random? And how do they recognize the suckable object once their face brushes against it? How soon do they realize that, rather than their mother's nipple, they are sucking their father's finger? Piaget observed that his children showed a marked improvement in identifying nipples and thumbs during the first month of life.

By the second month of life, Piaget's interest had turned from the sucking reflex to the baby's first acquired skills. He described his children's newly learnt abilities to locate their father's voice, to grasp what they touched, to make characteristic vocalizations, to follow the movements of a hand-held flame. The hallmark of this second stage in the development of infantile intelligence is the *repetition* of learnt behaviours. Just as Freud described the 'primary process' as being the hallucinated repetition of a previously satisfactory experience, so Piaget noted that babies seek to repeat new patterns of behaviour. For example, at two months and eighteen days, Piaget's son Laurent repeatedly plays with his saliva, letting it accumulate within his half-open lips and then abruptly swallowing it. A month earlier Piaget had recorded a parallel phenomenon: 'Laurent's arm is stretched out and almost immobile while his hand opens, half closes and then opens again, etc. When the palm of his hand strikes the covers, he grasps them, lets them go in unceasing oscillating notion.'[14]

Piaget describes this behaviour as 'grasping for the sake of grasping'. The baby shows no interest in using grasping to achieve an independent goal. Yet these movements are very similar to intentional actions. One might say that the baby repeats its motions in order to achieve a desired result. And this would sound as if the result were the 'reason' for the action. Piaget's careful observations suggested that this would be an over-interpretation. The baby's repeated or 'circular' reactions were entirely caused by the impact of a familiar impression on his or her nervous system, whether it was the accumulation of saliva in the lower lip or the feeling of cloth on the palm of a hand.

The first signs of genuinely intentional actions are seen in babies of three or four months of age. This is the third stage in Piaget's framework for the development of intelligence in infancy. Now, for the first time, babies begin to coordinate more than one behaviour to repeat interesting experiences. For example at five months of age Piaget's daughter Lucienne tries to grasp a rattle which is attached to the hood of her crib and hangs in front of her face:

> During an unlucky attempt she strikes it violently: fright, then a vague smile. She brings her hand back with a doubtless intentional suddenness: a new blow. The phenomenon then becomes systematic: Lucienne hits the rattle with regularity a very great number of times.[15]

In Piaget's view, incidents such as this show that a baby has begun to recognize the difference between means and ends. These repetitions depend on the baby recognizing that a chance effect of an accidental action is caused by that action.

The fourth stage of the development of intention begins around eight or nine months of age. The baby's sense of a goal becomes more obvious in her or his actions. Babies will begin to apply a variety of known means to attain a new end. For example, at nine months of age, Jacqueline Piaget

> tries directly to grasp her celluloid duck when I put its head between the strings [which attach some dolls to the hood of her pram]. Not succeeding, she grasps both strings, one in each hand, and pulls. She looks at the duck who shakes when she shakes. Then she grasps both strings in one hand and pulls, then grasps them in the other hand a little higher up and pulls harder until the duck falls.[16]

The penultimate stage of mental development in infancy involves the discovery of new means to attain a desired goal through active experimentation, a stage occupying the first half of the second year. An example is seen when Jacqueline, aged fifteen months

> discovers the possibility of making objects slide on the floor by means of a stick and so drawing them to her; in order to catch a doll lying on the ground out of reach, she begins by striking it with a stick, then, noticing its slight displacement, she pushes it until she is able to attain it with her right hand.[17]

Finally the invention of new means by thought alone is observed around eighteen months of age. An example is seen when Lucienne Piaget, aged eighteen months,

> tries to kneel before a stool but, by leaning against it, pushes it further away. She then raises herself up, takes it and places it against a sofa. When it is firmly set there she leans against it and kneels without difficulty.[18]

It is when young children begin mentally to envision means of reaching their goals, as does Lucienne in this example, that Piaget deems them to have acquired the ability to represent actions internally.

Piaget's most famous demonstration that infants acquire the ability to think by interacting with the world in ever more complex ways over the first year of life was published in 1937 as *The Child's Construction of Reality*.[19] This book covers the same period of childhood as Piaget's study of intentional action but first focuses on a single problem: how babies think about inanimate things such as apples, toys and bottles. Adults believe that such objects have substance, are permanent and of unchanging shape. But for the young baby, a rattle or a ball does not have a permanent existence but is seen as part of the structure of the baby's own acts or like a picture which disappears and reappears without obvious reason. For example, the five-month-old Lucienne Piaget is feeding at her mother's breast. She

> turns when I [Piaget] call her and smiles at me. Then she resumes nursing, but several times in succession, despite my silence, she turns directly to the position from which she can see me. She does it again after a pause of a few minutes. Then I withdraw; when she turns without finding me her expression is one of mingled disappointment and expectation.[20]

On the basis of observations like these, Piaget suggests that young babies try to find a missing object simply by repeating the act which was previously successful in 'producing' it. The baby is like an unskilled magician who imagines that vanished things can be recaptured merely by waving a conjuror's wand.

Between six and nine months of age babies begin to develop a more sophisticated attitude to invisible things. For example, babies begin to predict that a fallen object will be found on the floor and to show that they have an idea that moving objects follow a predictable trajectory. But they show a surprising lack of intelligence when an object of interest is screened from them by a hand or a cloth. For example, seven-month-old Jacqueline

> tries to grasp a celluloid duck on top of her quilt. She almost catches it, shakes herself, and the duck slides down beside her. It falls very close to her hand but behind a fold in the sheet. Jacqueline's eyes have followed the movement, she has even followed it with her outstretched hand. But as soon as the duck has disappeared – nothing more! It does not occur to her to search behind the fold of the sheet, which would be very easy to do.[21]

To Piaget, such observations prove that for children less than eight months old, out of sight is out of mind. They have no internal representation of hidden objects.

When babies do begin to look for objects that are hidden behind screens, they still make mistakes which show that their ideas about things are very different from those of adults. For example, at nine months of age

> Laurent is placed on a sofa between a coverlet A on the right and a wool garment B on the left. I place my watch under A; he gently raises the coverlet, perceives part of the object, uncovers it, and grasps it. The same thing happens a second and third time but with increasing application. I then place the watch under B; Laurent watches the manoeuvre attentively, but at the moment the watch has disappeared under garment B, he turns back towards coverlet A and searches for the object under that screen.[22]

This kind of error is made continually by children of Laurent's age. Such children seem to believe that the reappearance of a hidden object depends more on the repetition of a previously successful action than on tracing the movements of the object itself. At this stage of intellectual development babies still superstitiously believe that the reappearance of hidden objects is an effect created by their own actions.

The next step towards understanding that objects exist independently from the baby are taken when the baby looks for objects where they were last hidden. Finally babies are able to work out that objects may be found in a variety of possible hiding-places. At nineteen months, for example, Piaget tested his daughter Jacqueline's ability to find a coin as follows:

> I place the coin in my hand, then my hand under a cushion. I bring it forth closed and immediately hide it under the coverlet. Finally I withdraw it and hold it out, closed, to Jacqueline. Jacqueline then pushes my hand aside without opening it (she guesses that there is nothing in it, which is new), she looks under the cushion, then directly under the coverlet, where she finds the object.[23]

Piaget argues that, when children pass a test like this, they have developed a true mental representation of physical objects. Objects are no longer seen as events created by the baby's own actions. The baby's universe becomes a place filled with things that have lives of their own.

Piaget's third source of evidence that the ability to represent the world mentally first develops in the middle of the second year of life was the study of imitation and play.[24] Piaget argued that whilst young babies might imitate others' actions they could already make themselves, only around eighteen months could they base their imitations on true mental representations. For example, Piaget found that his attempts to get his children to retaliate when he stuck his tongue out at them were first successful when they were around eight months old. Eight months later, Piaget observed a new kind of imitation which he called 'deferred': for example, at sixteen months of age, Jacqueline Piaget

> had a visit from a little boy of eighteen months whom she used to see from time to time, and who, in the course of the afternoon got into a terrible temper. He screamed as he tried to get out of a play-pen and pushed it backwards, stamping his feet. Jacqueline stood watching him in amazement, never having witnessed such a scene before. The next day, she herself screamed in her play-pen and tried to move it, stamping her foot lightly several times in succession. The imitation of the whole scene was most striking. Had it been immediate, it would naturally not have involved representation, but coming as it

did after an interval of more than twelve hours, it must have involved some representative or pre-representative element.[25]

Piaget noted that 'make-believe' games – the use of one thing to represent another – also begin in the first half of the second year of life. This observation reinforced his conclusion that the slow elaboration of increasingly complex forms of action in infancy eventually produces a capacity to picture the world in the mind at about the time babies first begin to speak. The convergence of these different kinds of evidence gave weight to this conclusion, which, as we saw in the last chapter, supports the view of linguists that early speech depends on the development of pre-verbal intellectual abilities.

Piaget himself never wrote a study of language acquisition as such. But a study using Piaget's theory of infant development to explain language development was published in 1975 by Elizabeth Bates and her colleagues in Italy.[26] These researchers suggested that speech acts are built up from three components: a capacity to cause effects in other people, the capacity to use others as means to achieve one's own ends and the ability to use conventional sounds to refer to external objects. Bates then illustrated that the development of these communicative abilities runs parallel to key stages in Piaget's embryology of infant intelligence. Thus even the smallest baby can cause effects in adults by crying or smiling. But only when she or he begins to realize that means are independent from ends (Piaget's Stage IV) do we find that the baby begins to use looks, sounds and gestures such as pointing to direct the actions of adults. For example, at one year old,

> Carlotta is seated in the corridor in front of the kitchen door. She looks toward her mother and calls with an acute sound 'ha'. Mother comes over to her, and Carlotta looks toward the kitchen, twisting her body and upper shoulders to do so. Mother carries her into the kitchen and Carlotta points towards the sink. Mother gives her a glass of water, and Carlotta drinks it eagerly.[27]

We get a strong impression that this sequence of gestures is organized by well-formulated intentions in Carlotta's mind – as well as a desire to control her mother! Having tested Carlotta on Piaget's tests for the ability to intend, Bates feels able to argue that communication grows with and depends on the growth of the intellect.

Finally, Bates's babies begin to use recognizable words at around the time when they begin to play symbolically. For example, at thirteen months, the baby takes a spoon, holds it against her ear like a telephone and begins to 'talk'. At around the same age, she develops words with different meanings. For example, in the bathtub she is handed a rubber duck by her father. As she reaches to take it, she says 'qua qua'.

Beyond Piaget

When Piaget died in 1980, he left a sequence of publications about the mental development of children which, in detail and extent, are without parallel in the library of science. Yet there are many grounds upon which to question Piaget's work. Some of these are simply matters of observation. For example, Piaget argues that babies do not stick out their tongues in imitation of adults until eight months of age. Contemporary observers argue that babies perform this feat in the first month of life (see chapter 8).

Perhaps the largest volume of research has been generated by Piaget's contention that babies are profoundly egocentric, having no idea of the independent existence of other things or people until the last quarter of the first year. This research has featured a relative neglect of Piaget's ideas about biology, an increase in the artificiality of the apparatus and procedures used in experiments, and a willingness to draw general conclusions about infant reasoning from changes in frequency of a far narrower range of behaviours than used as a basis for generalization by Piaget.

Piaget's theory of mental growth was put forward within a biological framework. For Piaget, intelligence was the product of a process of biological adaptation. The structure of intelligence at any age consisted of schemes or 'schemas' representing in knowledge the basis of a baby's response to, let us say, the movements of a mobile. These schemas change through interaction and conflict with other representations of the world, becoming increasingly elaborate as the children find ways of extending their rudimentary understanding to gain more mastery over the objects and events which affect them. Such extension occurs in two main ways: *Assimilation* occurs where an already existing scheme of action like patting a dog incorporates a new object such as patting piano keys. *Accommodation* occurs where a scheme of action changes to match an external object, as in imitation. All developments in intelligence involve both assimilation and accommodation in varying degrees. Thus a child may pat a dog with a flat hand but later a piano with an angled hand (accommodation). Alternatively, imitation inevitably draws to a certain extent on familiar patterns of action (assimilation), however much these are changed in the act of copying.

Those who have criticized Piaget's treatment of the 'object concept' have generally done so without reference to his biological formulations. They do not observe the careful distinctions he made between the non-conceptual sensori-motor intelligence of young infants (0–18 months) and the stages of concrete (2–11 years) and formal operations (12 years onwards) which are supposed to grow from it. Their vocabulary is more

akin to that of Chomsky and information-processing, the aim being to
establish what forms of knowledge must be 'built in' to the brain of babies
to explain their reactions to variously contrived displays of objects.

One of the neatest experiments of this kind has suggested that babies
considerably younger than nine months have an idea that the world exists
independently from their own actions. Working in Australia, Bernadette
Keating, Beryl McKenzie and Ross Day placed four-month-olds and six-
month-olds in their mothers' laps on a swivel-chair in the middle of a small
round room with a plain white wall and ceiling.[28] In their set-up the only
obvious features were eight identical red balls hung at equal distances and
equal heights around the wall. Each mother was asked to sit so that her
baby was facing one of the balls, which was then jiggled up and down.
When the jiggling stopped someone popped up over the wall at Position
X, smiling and teasing the baby. The baby turned to look at her. After two
seconds she vanished and another ball started jiggling. Mother and baby
swivelled on their chair to face the moving ball. When it stopped the
experimenter popped up again at Position X and renewed her routine. The
baby turned to look once again. After two seconds, the experimenter
disappeared and a third ball started moving up and down. The sequence of
jiggles and teases was repeated enough times to teach any child capable
of learning the lesson that whenever and wherever a ball moved,
entertainment would shortly reappear at Position X.

The crucial moment came when a previously unjiggled ball is jiggled in
a new place and the experimenter did *not* pop up at Position X. Where
would the baby look? Most six-month-olds and even some four-month-
olds looked expectantly towards Position X. This showed that young
babies are aware that they must take changes in their own orientation into
account when looking for a remembered location.

In other words, contrary to the claims of Piaget, young babies are aware
that their physical environment has a structure which is independent of
their own actions. How they work this out in a round room without any
distinctive landmarks is a question to which no one has an answer! Even
adults have difficulty in matching the performance of six-month-olds on
this task.

Another challenge to Piaget's belief that babies view the physical world
'egocentrically' has come from Elizabeth Spelke in the United States.
Spelke was interested in Piaget's claim that, before eight months of age,
babies have no idea that an object which is out of sight continues to exist.[29]
Piaget believed that young babies behave as if their own acts of looking
magically create the things they see and that to blink is to abolish the
visible world. In her study Spelke repeatedly showed four-month-olds a
stick moving back and forwards behind a stationary block which hid the
middle of the stick. When the babies were familiar with this display,

Spelke showed them two new displays. The first was what the babies had previously seen but without the block: that is, two short aligned sticks, separated by a gap, moving back and forth in mid-air. The second display was of a whole stick moving back and forth, including the bit that had previously been hidden by the block.

Spelke argued that babies should be more interested in looking at the display which they felt was more unlike what they had seen before. If they had no idea that objects may exist whilst hidden from the eye, then they should be more interested in the second display of a whole stick. But if they thought that what they were first shown was a block hiding a whole stick, then the two sticks-ends should attract more attention than the whole stick.

Spelke's results showed that most four-month-olds look more at the two short stick ends than at the one long unbroken stick. She concluded that babies view the first display as a stick moving behind a block, not as a block with two moving parts. Therefore babies must have some idea that objects, or parts of objects, may exist whilst unseen.

Bower's theory

While the studies of Keating, McKenzie and Day and of Spelke serve to question the findings which are the basis for Piaget's theory of infancy, they do not constitute an alternative to that theory. One of the most interesting theoretical alternatives to Piaget has been developed by Tom Bower and his colleagues in Scotland.

Bower argues that we do not begin life able only to respond reflexively to a few specific stimuli, as Piaget argues. Influenced by the information-processing model of intelligence, he marshals evidence to show that babies are born with a very high-level abstract picture of the world. Rather than development going from specific reflexes to abstract concepts, as in Piaget, Bower argues the opposite. Babies develop their thinking by learning to make their abstract ideas more specific as they become familiar with the particular contexts in which they must act.[30]

The first step in Bower's research was to collect evidence which challenged Piaget's belief that babies are born only with independent reflexes, which must be slowly combined to create more complex forms of behaviour. For example, Piaget claimed that the five-month-old's ability to reach and grasp what he or she wants depends not only on the growth of intention in babies but on their coordination of hand and arm movements by sight. Bower pointed out that even ten-day-old babies may reach towards suspended objects, long before they have had time to achieve such coordination by eye. He drew two conclusions from this observation. First, even very young babies have rudimentary intentions, many months

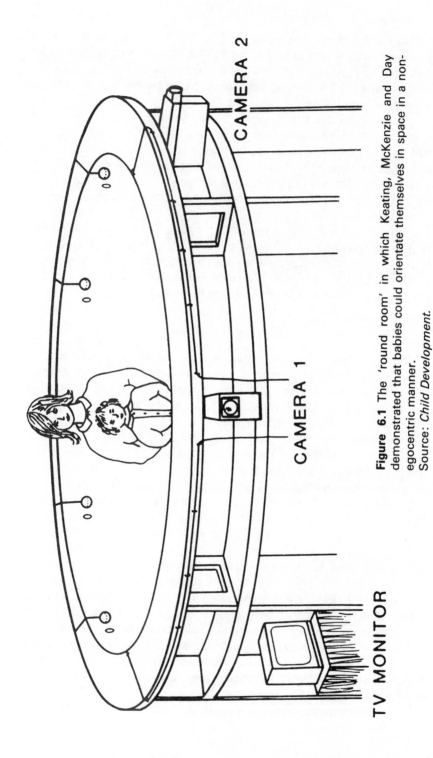

Figure 6.1 The 'round room' in which Keating, McKenzie and Day demonstrated that babies could orientate themselves in space in a non-egocentric manner.
Source: *Child Development.*

CAMERA 2

CAMERA 1

TV MONITOR

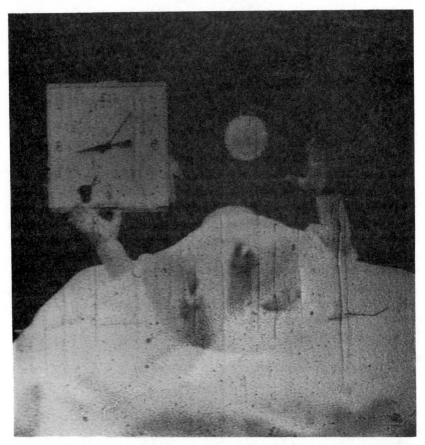

Plate 6.1 Radical ambiguity? Or a two-week-old baby reaching towards a slowly moving ball? This kind of behaviour has been used to support the idea that even tiny babies do not simply react to stimuli but act intentionally to affect the world in which they live.
Source: Author.

earlier than Piaget claimed. Secondly, babies must be born with the idea that what is visible must be tangible.

Having established that babies have intentions long before they are supposed to by Piaget, Bower was faced with the problem of re-interpreting Piaget's developmental account of the object concept. Suppose we consider the five-month-old who, according to Piaget, will only successfully grasp a desired object so long as it is at least partly visible. When it is completely covered behind a screen or under a cloth, she or he will not search for it. According to Piaget, this kind of 'error' results from the young baby thinking that because a thing can't be seen, it no longer exists and so believes all searches will be fruitless. But Bower wonders whether babies are simply unable to make the delicate movements necessary to lift up covers: the baby knows where the hidden object is but doesn't know how to get it. What is needed to distinguish between these two explanations is some kind of behaviour other than hand-searches to show that the baby knows the object exists. Bower proposes two candidates – expressions of surprise and eye-movements.

First of all he slowly covered an object with a screen in front of the baby and then compared the baby's reaction, when the screen is lifted, to seeing either that the object is there or that it has vanished. If babies imagine that covered things disappear – as Piaget suggests – then the reappearance of a hidden object should surprise them more than evidence that it really has vanished. Alternatively, if they really do believe that it is still there behind the cover, then they should be more surprised when the curtain lifts to reveal an empty stage. Bower's measure of surprise was change in heart-rate. His results showed that babies were less surprised to see the hidden object again than to find it had gone. Further research seemed to have supported this disproof of Piaget by interpretation of five-month-olds' eye-movements as they watched a moving object disappear behind a screen. As soon as the object disappears, the babies look to the other side of the screen as if predicting its reappearance – once again suggesting that they know it to exist whilst out of sight.

But Bower is not completely satisfied with this interpretation. He argues that infant looking behaviour, if not their surprise, could be generated in other ways. For example, maybe babies cannot stop their heads from turning once they have started to track the moving object. Bower tested out this explanation by showing babies a moving ball and then stopping it in full view. He found that babies did stop their heads turning, but only very briefly – their heads then continued to 'track' along the predicted path of the ball. Bower proposes that this behaviour is produced by babies' belief that a moving object which has stopped is a different kind of thing from what was in motion: for a baby, there are two kinds of thing, stationary and moving.

A further series of experiments supports this conclusion. Hence one can show babies moving objects which change radically in shape and colour as they move and the babies show no surprise. But if a moving object changes speed or direction as it moves, watching babies become upset and look hither and thither, apparently to find out whether they are watching two objects or only one. Similarly, Bower has argued that, provided objects are in different places, they must seem to be different objects to the baby. Here he makes use of a system of mirrors which show babies their mothers face-on in triplicate.

Babies of less than five months seem wholly undisturbed by this sight, smiling, cooing and crying at each mother in turn. After five months they are upset to find their mother has three heads. Bower argues this study to show that, below five months, babies think they have a multiplicity of mothers, whereas the older child thinks he or she has but one. After five months, identity is no longer defined by place and movement alone: the baby has begun to use a more detailed rule to determine what counts as an object ('an object is a bounded volume of space that can move from place to place'). With age, the baby's knowledge of objects becomes increasingly specific: first he or she begins to act as if two objects can exist inside or behind one another without losing their identities. Finally the baby works out that, under some circumstances, two objects can share each others' movements (one being 'inside' the other).

The most obvious difference between Piaget's and Bower's view of early development is that Bower believes children have an idea of what an object is from birth whereas Piaget argues that the newborn baby takes almost a year to develop the capacity to form such an idea.

Problems with the View that Development is Based on Reason

The characteristic feature of the orientations to the development of thinking discussed in this chapter is that the keys to its description are exclusively taken to be problems which themselves have a logical form. In Piaget, the baby must come to understand that all objects have an existence which is permanent and independent from their perceivers. Or, in Bower, that no two objects can exist in the same place at the same time. This kind of description can be questioned on a number of counts.

First, it is a matter of opinion whether the kinds of logical proposition supposed by Piaget and post-Piagetians to underlie scientific knowledge are universally true. For example, modern physicists argue that no observation of sub-atomic particles can stand independently of the technical means used to make that observation. And cross-cultural and historical research shows people in other cultures and other eras to believe the 'foundations' of psychological processes to be very different from those assumed in our own culture. Likewise, ecologists argue that all organisms must be considered as having a complex and interdependent relationship of mutual influence with their environments. Certainly, in psychological experiments of the kind reported by Bower, Piaget, Spelke and others, the 'objects' which supposedly 'exist independently' of the babies are, in fact, specifically used to test their reactions. Whilst they are supposed by scientists to exist independently of the babies, their presentation and disappearance are certainly not independent of the relationship between baby and adult. In the final analysis, it is just this relationship which endows with significance both the objects and the babies' reactions to them.

Another kind of criticism directed at the kind of experimental work reviewed in this chapter focuses on the ambiguity of infant behaviours in science. Very few if any infant behaviours have an unequivocal meaning. A good example is looking. In this chapter we have seen that a baby's look may be seen as a consequence of a search for novelty (Spelke) or as a product of a search for sameness (Bower). Other interpretations are that babies look at one thing to avoid looking at another, because it reminds them of something or simply because they like it. Likewise smiling, which might be thought to be the most unambiguous of signals, has been variously interpreted by different scientists: as a sign of sympathy (as by Darwin; see p. 20 above) or as an asocial response to a fulfilled expectation that a particular action or event will have a predictable consequence, as shown in Papousek's experiments (see chapter 3) and in babies smiling and cooing at mobiles they can control.[32]

Scientists who assume that a baby's behaviours have a meaning which can simply be read off from their results without interpretive debate are at risk of confusing the significance of the observed behaviours to themselves, as psychologists, and the part these behaviours play within the system of meanings which make up the mental world of the child. As was argued by William James's friend, the American child psychologist J. M. Baldwin (1861–1934), it is just this system of meanings which is the developmentalist's proper object of study, a system which, according to Baldwin, is shaped by a changing aesthetic-cum-affective logic that runs deeper than and governs the practical and conceptual intelligence of problem-solving.[33]

For example, scientists must beware of concluding that babies 'do not know hidden objects exist' from observations that eight-month-olds do not search for reachable food which is covered by a cloth as they watch. We must recognize that such disappearances are likely to have different significances to babies than to the psychologists who codify them as exemplars of apparent physical absence. Babies may have their own reasons for not wishing to discover what happens when something disappears. Maybe the aesthetic value of food which disappears is changed: from ambrosia to poison, for example, from delectable to ugly and abhorrent. Similarly, we cannot be sure what an infant's expression of surprise or consternation at an object's reappearance means in terms of his or her thought-processes until we know what other events produce the same expression.[34]

One of the strengths of Piaget's early research on infancy was his use of a variety of different kinds of observation to support his proposition that babies develop an 'object concept' towards the end of their first year of life. Piaget's approach to studying the thinking of young children was akin to that adopted by psycho-analysts: anything might prove relevant to understanding why children thought as they did, from dribbling and accidental discoveries in babies to private rituals surrounding masturbation or their beliefs about the man in the moon in older children.[34] It was for this reason that Piaget argued that two years of training in the methods of interviewing children would be needed before a student could be trusted to explore a young child's understanding of the world.

Piaget's theory of infancy was different from Freud's but his findings were produced in similar and, Piaget later argued, theoretically compatible way.[35] In accordance with Baldwin's methodological warning, Piaget was careful to distinguish between the abstract propositional form of adult thinking and the sensori-motor form of infant intelligence. But neither Piaget's varied and broad-based interpretive approach to infancy nor his distinction between different kinds of intelligence have been adopted by the 'post-Piagetian' researchers into infant thinking discussed in this chapter.

Such researchers do not pay heed to the peculiarities of individual thinking before drawing general conclusions. The baby's consciousness is simply described in propositional terms as if these terms fitted babies' mental operations perfectly, just as they would fit the thinking of a logician. Hence, one scientist tells us that, from a few weeks of age, an infant 'distinguishes the category of people from the category of things'.[36] Another tells us that a baby 'begins the process of forming relationship with distinct and separate notions of self and other'.[37] A third concludes that five-month-olds 'know' 'that an object is a bounded volume of space that can go into spatial relations with another object, both retaining their identity'.[38] In this way words such as *know, distinguish, category, notion, intention, concept* are applied to infants as if their mental processes were indistinguishable from that of the scientists who study them. Such an approach to early mental growth falls foul of a serious confusion between the scientist's own standpoint and that of the infant being investigated.

If the baby's mental life were treated by its scientific interpreters as a distinct whole, changes in babies' reactions to objects could not be explained solely as the consequence of growing logical abilities. Emotional factors also play a part in the genesis of object-directed behaviour. Just as some things may have special 'sentimental' values for adults, so some inanimate objects may acquire a unique emotional significance in early childhood.

The psycho-analyst Donald Winnicott points out that many babies form strong emotional attachments to a cuddly toy, a piece of cloth or some other small object.[39] He suggests that, during the second year of life, the presence of these objects may be more important for calming the anxieties of babies than the presence of a parent. A teddy bear may be the baby's closest companion, being loved, nuzzled, bitten or thrown away at different points of the baby's daily emotional career. It would clearly be an incomplete picture of the baby's relationship to the physical world which failed to foreground these treasured toys. Yet there seems little room in information-processing schemes of development for the idea that intellectual life a has close link with emotional life.

Piaget and those critics whose work I have illustrated in this chapter assume that the most important skills for young children to develop are related to the basic physical structure of the world. Babies have to develop an awareness of the permanent existence of objects which disappear and reappear. They must understand time and space and causality. Only then can they begin to understand that special class of physical beings which we call people. Piaget argued that babies do not distinguish people from things until eight or nine months of age. Only then do they begin to sense that objects have a permanent existence and can therefore understand that some objects differ from others in having feelings and other states of mind.

A contrasting point of view is that nearly every major 'physical' change in a baby's world is marked or shaped by the responses of others, by social laws and conventions. Certain toys are deemed to be the baby's, others belong to the baby's brothers and sisters. Food appears only at regulated times and under socially controlled conditions. If the weather is cold the baby is wrapped up in more clothes than when it is warm. Fathers respond to the baby's cries in a different manner when drunk than when sober. And every day, around sunset, the baby goes through a series of complicated rituals which prepare her or him for bed.

Rather than assuming that babies first understand the physical world and only then become aware of people, it might be better to say that development is led by the growth of socio-emotional understanding. For example, the Russian experimentalist and critic of Piaget, L. S. Vygotsky (1896–1934) wrote that every function in the child's higher mental development appears twice:

> first, on the social level, and later, on the individual level; first, *between* people (*interpsychological*), and then *inside* the child (*intra-psychological*). This applies equally to voluntary attention, to logical memory, and to the formation of concepts. All the higher functions originate as actual relations between human individuals.[40]

If this is so, then the basic structure and details of the baby's early social relationships must be understood before we can explain what cognitive psychologists interested in perception see as development.

The idea of babies as intellectuals, who 'know', follow rules, and have intentions and concepts is linked to a false 'logocentric' assumption in developmental explanations.[41] This is the assumption that a knowledge of particulars and of concepts is logically, and must therefore be temporally, prior to a knowledge of propositions or, more generally, to participation in discourse and social life. A substantial movement in contemporary philosophy suggests that a more fruitful way of viewing the growth of knowledge is a consequence, not the foundation, of the individual's involvement with others.[42]

For example, Sellars draws a distinction between awareness-as-discriminative-behaviour and awareness 'in the logical space of reasons, of justifying and being able to justify what one says'.[43] Awareness in the first sense is manifested equally by amoebas, record-changers, birds and babies. Awareness in the second sense is justified true belief or 'knowledge' and is shown only by beings able to utter sentences with the intention of justifying the utterance of other sentences. In this sense: 'Thought is not merely expressed in words; it comes into existence through them.'[44] The next two chapters consider ways in which babies come to participate in communal life without *a priori* knowledge about the world or other people.

Summary

Current interest in the origins of the child's abilities to think and reason was stirred up by the debate prompted by Chomsky's work on language. But it also formed part of a more sweeping change in the scientific approach to the mind taking place in the 1950s and 1960s, known as the 'cognitive revolution'. A reference point for considering the origin of thinking was the work of Piaget, which had been conducted in the 1930s but was only translated into English in the 1950s.

Piaget's observations of infants were mainly used to explain how children came to be able to form internal representations of the external world, something which is crucial to the use of words as symbols for absent objects. The observations themselves were mainly of Piaget's own children, being very detailed and concerning a broad range of behaviours, from dribbling to searching for hidden toys. Most famous are Piaget's observations on the acquisition of 'the object concept', the birth of the child's understanding that invisible objects can continue to exist. But Piaget also described how, through a sequence of stages, babies begin to act intentionally and play or imitate in ways showing that, for them, out of sight is not necessarily out of mind.

Piaget's research on babies contrasts in many ways with contemporary research on infant thought. Recent experimenters have often challenged

Piaget's findings, claiming for example that babies know about the continuous existence of invisible objects months before Piaget said they did. The observational methods of these critics are generally based in the laboratory, not the home, as were Piaget's. And modern researchers tend to focus on a much narrower range of behaviours than did Piaget. Furthermore, the vocabulary used to describe the results of contemporary research suggests that babies think in a way very similar to adults, rather than having a completely different kind of intelligence, as Piaget proposed ('sensori-motor' versus logical). These differences of approach suggest that modern researchers may be imposing an inappropriate framework of interpretation on the mental lives of babies.

Furthermore, like his modern critics, even Piaget excluded many kinds of action from his picture of the baby's mental life, particularly social relationships and emotions. Hence, neither he nor his critics have been in a position to consider whether how babies treat things may be governed by more general socio-emotional processes (or 'social cognition') which are seen to best advantage in their dealings with other people. Research which casts light on these processes is reviewed in the next two chapters.

Further Reading

The Psychology of the Child by J. Piaget and B. Inhelder (Routledge & Kegan Paul, London, 1966) gives a concise introduction to Piaget's theory of intellectual development, providing a context for his observations on infancy.

Development in Infancy by T. G. R. Bower (Freeman, San Francisco, 1982, 2nd edn) gives a detailed account of Bower's reworking of the Piagetian approach to the psychology of infancy. A simpler and chattier introduction is to be found in Bower's *A Primer of Infant Development* (Freeman, San Francisco, 1979).

Children's Minds by M. Donaldson (Fontana/Open Books, Glasgow, 1978) is a fascinating and clearly written extension of research suggesting that Piaget, like Chomsky, fails to take sufficient account of the way in which small children understand others in picturing children's minds. This book is already a landmark in the description of intellectual development.

7

First Emotions

The works of psychologists such as Bower and linguists like Chomsky fascinate by virtue of their very improbability. Who would have thought that newborn babies had the slighest interest in understanding the abstract principles of reason or the formal rules of grammar? In contrast, no one who has heard babies crying can doubt that from birth their mental lives are dominated by powerful emotions. Amidst the storm of their passions and sensations, many scientists assume that the baby's first haven and anchorage is the growth of a love-bond to an adult upon whom the tiny child can depend for security. This chapter discusses scientific views of the baby's early emotional life.

Perhaps the most influential vision of the baby's first love affair is psycho-analytic. In chapter 4 we saw how Freud supposed that, at first, human babies have little sense of reality. Their mental lives are dominated by fantasy. Melanie Klein described in detail the structure of these early fantasies, beginning with a split between the good and the bad mother. Yet both Freud and Klein argue that whatever fantasies fill the infant's mind, early development is inevitably based on the child's real and lasting love for her or his mother. Freud describes the importance of this infant–mother relationship as 'unique and without parallel' in human life.[1]

A Biological Affair

In Freud's view, the first emotional bond grows out of the baby's dependence on the mother for food and comfort. Our first love is 'cupboard love'. But, as we have seen, psycho-analysts' interests in infancy are therapeutic rather than observational. A more easily verifiable version of the psycho-analytic view was that adopted by Watson and the behaviourists. Like Freud, Watson argued that the young child's emotional life was organized by an inherited tendency to seek pleasure and avoid pain. Watson also concluded that the child's early attachment to other people, and particularly the mother, was a product of the repeated association between her presence and supplies of food. As learning theory became more sophisticated, the child's emotional life was seen to be the product of processes in addition to classical conditioning. By the generalization of associations, learning from observation and imitation, babies will be led from pleasure at feeding to pleasure at the sight of the person who feeds them to pleasure in doing what the feeder does. According to behaviourists, the child's emotional life will take place in an increasingly variegated land-scape of objects and events which gain meaning from their associations with pleasures and pains in the past.

The theoretical simplicity and apparent common sense of the associationist account of early emotional development guarantees it considerable appeal. But in the 1940s and 1950s different researchers working on both animals and infants produced evidence which has been taken by some scientists to undermine the 'cupboard love' theory of early social life. One such line of research was pioneered in Europe by Konrad Lorenz before the Second World War.

Lorenz was a biologist who lived in Germany amongst a menagerie of tamed and hand-reared animals, including dogs, geese and jackdaws.[2] His observations led him to propose that evolution has endowed all species of animals with inherited behavioural systems which automatically adapt them to their natural environments. These fixed patterns of inherited action are much more elaborate than the simple reflexes which are all that Piaget and the behaviourists credit young babies with at birth. In particular Lorenz described how baby ducks and geese will, as soon as they hatch, follow the first moving thing they see. Most often, this means they start life by following one of their parents, though Lorenz's goslings followed him. Within a day or two, this peculiar magnetic response to movement disappears. From this time on, the goslings will only follow their chosen leader.[3]

Lorenz pointed out that this following behaviour, which he called 'imprinting', is obviously advantageous for a newly hatched bird that needs to survive in a hostile world. It ensures that it will always be within sight of a parent who is likely to know much more than the chick about the delights and dangers of the environment in which they live. This finding challenged learning theory because it showed that young animals may inherit relatively complex behaviours and predispositions which will have a profound influence on later development, provided that they experience

Plate 7.1 A duckling following a duck in the manner described as 'imprinting' by Konrad Lorenz. But only a minority of birds have young who can leave the nest soon after hatching and behave in this way. Most nestlings are, more like humans, born featherless and immobile.
Source: Author.

the right kind of environmental stimulation at the right time (during the 'critical period' for imprinting).

Another challenge to the behaviourist account of early development arose from an American study of captive monkeys by Harry Harlow in 1948.[4] Harlow devised a situation in which baby monkeys were reared in isolation in cages which contained two kinds of 'surrogate mother'. One surrogate was made of wire-mesh but carried a teat which fed the baby milk. The other was covered with soft cloth but provided no food. Harlow showed that babies formed a much stronger 'attachment' to the cloth-mother than the wire-mother. This was shown by the fact that the babies would spend much more time clinging to the cloth-mother than the wire-mother. And they would run to the cloth-mother rather than the wire one when frightened. Harlow concluded that young monkeys are born with a much clearer idea of what a parent should be than learning theory suggests. They were less interested in food than in finding a secure and furry base from which to explore the comfortless world in which they had been placed.

Perhaps the most important set of insights deemed to contradict the behaviourist view of emotional development was drawn from studies of babies' and young children's responses to separation from their parents upon their admission to hospitals. The most famous of these was conducted by René Spitz and his colleagues in two institutions outside

Vienna, a residential Nursery and a Foundling Home.[5] The Nursery was a penal institution to which delinquent girls were committed if pregnant. The babies were looked after in the Nursery by their mothers. The Foundling Home was filled with the babies of abandoned mothers and of married parents who for one reason or another could not care for their children. Spitz noted a number of illnesses in the children in these institutions, some of which occurred as a consequence of separations from mothers during the first year of life.

In both places children were breast-fed by their mothers for their first three months. In the Nursery, mothers usually continued to care for their children throughout the first year. When mothers and babies were separated for weeks or months, Spitz noted that babies typically became depressed. If the pair were reunited within a period of three to five months, no lasting consequences for the baby could be observed. But when separations lasted longer than five months there were very serious consequences.

In the Foundling Home mother and child were always separated after three months. The babies were well looked after in every bodily respect. Food, hygiene, medical care and medication were as good as, or even superior to that of the Nursery. But the Home was understaffed so that one nurse had to look after an average of ten babies. The babies were, in Spitz's words, 'emotionally starved'. As month followed month, the babies declined from depression to become completely passive.

> They lay supine in their cots. They did not achieve the stage of motor control necessary to turn into the prone position. The face becomes vacuous, eye coordination defective, the expression often imbecile. . . In our tests these children showed a progressive decline of the developmental quotient. By the end of the second year, the average of their developmental quotients stands at 45 per cent of the normal. This would be the level of the idiot. By the age of four years, with a few exceptions, these children cannot sit, stand, walk or talk.[6]

Spitz found that twenty-seven of the ninety-one babies he observed in the Foundling Home died in their first year of life. At least seven more died in their second year. In the Nursery a far smaller proportion (four) of the two hundred and twenty children died. Spitz concluded:

> This shows convincingly that institutionalization itself does not generate high mortality rates in infants, but that a specific factor within the institutions is responsible. There is one major difference between the Nursery and the Foundling Home: in the Nursery the infants had mothering, in the Foundling Home they did not.[7]

Spitz's work suggested that the physical 'rewards' of food and warmth were not enough to ensure healthy emotional development. Babies have a deep-seated biological need to form a secure emotional relationship and it is this relationship which, in Spitz's view, lays the foundation for physical, social and intellectual development. Alternatively, the absence of an adequate mother–child relationship in the first year of life forms a scar which predisposes the child to later mental illness.

Not long after Spitz conducted this study, doctors in Britain had become concerned about the less extreme but disturbing emotional reactions of young children who were forced to spend a period of weeks undergoing treatment for illnesses in hospital.[8] It seemed that two- and three-year-olds who had relatively short periods of separation from their parents and home generally went through a cycle of severe emotional upsets which amounted to a trauma. Over the first few days of the separation they became increasingly upset until they became listless and depressed, withdrawing from all the overtures of those who tried to help them. Eventually they would re-involve themselves with nurses and other children in a low-keyed way. When they were reunited with their parents, they showed acute ambivalence, clinging desperately to their mother as if wishing never to be removed from her, whilst simultaneously hitting her, biting her, avoiding her eye or refusing to answer her questions. A three-week separation might produce months of upset in which children 'regressed' to infantile behaviour that they had seemingly grown out of years before – reverting to baby language, wetting their bed, refusing to eat with a spoon or throwing temper tantrums.

Attachment Theory

In the 1950s these various kinds of evidence from studies of animals and early parent–child separations were drawn together as support for a theory of early social development by the British paediatrician and psycho-analyst John Bowlby.[9] According to its author, the idea inspiring 'attachment theory' was that 'human beings are happiest and able to deploy their talents to best advantage when they are confident that standing behind them there are one or more trusted persons who will come to their aid should difficulties arise.'[10] Bowlby proposed that this form of dependence had evolutionary origins which had left their mark on the behaviours and needs of all human infants.

It is generally recognized that young human beings are more helpless, and helpless for a much longer time, than other young mammals. Bowlby argued that there must therefore have been strong evolutionary pressures for the selection of infant behaviours which promoted parental protection during this period – especially protection from predators. He argued further that this evolutionary endowment would have important psychological consequences – amongst which would be universal dependence on trusted persons in times of difficulty.

Bowlby contrasted this view with social-learning theories of development. These did not assume that babies were, or would naturally become, social – as Bowlby was suggesting. They argued rather that children were made social by those who brought them up: children were 'socialized'.

In marshalling evidence to support his view, Bowlby gave particular attention to the first and second years of life. He argued that young humans, like other primates, are biologically endowed with a number of behaviour-patterns which, like the 'imprinting' behaviours observed by Lorenz, naturally promote a protective proximity between baby and mother. These 'attachment behaviours' are crying, sucking, clinging, smiling, grasping, eye-to-eye contact, calling and following. Most of these behaviours are present at birth. Bowlby proposed that, during the first year of life, these behaviours are slowly incorporated into a sophisticated behavioural 'system' which has as its goal the maintenance of proximity between mother and infant. He distinguished a number of developmental phases during the first year: familiarization with main caretakers (0–4 months), discrimination of the mother from others (around 7 months) and, following Piaget, recognition of the mother's (or mother-surrogate's) continued existence even when not immediately available to the senses (9 months). By this time, under normal conditions, the child's movements will be based around the location of the mother, much as an imprinted duckling bases itself on the whereabouts of the duck or drake. When relaxed the mobile baby may wander some distance from the mother, led on by her or his curiosity and wish to explore. But when frightened the behavioural 'control system' will reassert itself and the baby's goal will be to return swiftly to the haven of its mother's protection.

In proposing this timetable, Bowlby was drawing on one of the most striking findings about emotional development: the onset of 'stranger anxiety'. Up until seven or eight months of age, babies will smile at and interact with more or less anyone they meet. But around nine months, they are beginning to show unexpected fright and suspicion of people with whom they are unfamiliar. Under experimental conditions, they often cry or turn away from the stranger to bury their face in their parent's body, only later tentatively peeping out and shyly starting to make or receive overtures of friendship. Fear of strangers is taken by Bowlby as concrete evidence that a tie or 'attachment' has been successfully formed between mother and child. It is this attachment which is broken when young children are separated from their mothers. Partly as a result of Bowlby's work, many children's hospitals now prefer parents to accompany, to visit frequently or even to sleep in the same room as children undergoing treatment. This is to minimize the trauma of separation.

Attachment theory gained appeal from the explanation it gave to a number of far-reaching conclusions about social development that Bowlby and others had published in the 1940s and early 1950s. The main force of these conclusions concerned the crucial importance of experiencing a warm and continuous relationship with a minder during early childhood as a basis for maturing into a sane and healthy adult.

Before the Second World War, Bowlby had been trained as a psycho-analyst (partly under the supervision of Melanie Klein). During the war he undertook a study of forty-four juvenile thieves which focused on the conditions in which they had spent their first years of life. From an analysis of each case, Bowlby concluded: 'There is a very strong case indeed for believing that prolonged separation of a child from his mother (or mother-surrogate) during the first five years of life stands foremost among the causes of delinquent character development and persistent misbehaviour.'[11] His next major study was a review of scientific research on the needs of children who had lost their parents in the war with respect to mental health. This study – commissioned by the World Health Organization – came to a more emphatic conclusion: 'that when deprived of maternal care, a child's development is almost always retarded – physically, intellectually and socially – and symptoms of physical and mental illness may appear.'[12]

During and after the 1939–45 war, the BBC broadcast a series of programmes by leading experts on childhood, including Bowlby and D. W. Winnicott.[13] Their central thesis was that during the early years of life children need the continuous and undivided care of their mothers if they are to develop normally. This was at odds with the British government's policy *during* the war, when women were encouraged to work – a policy supported by the provision of public nurseries to provide substitute care for their children. Mothers could then take up places in the labour-force which had been vacated by men who had joined the Allied forces. But Bowlby's broadcasts fitted in with a general change in public opinion after 1945 that accompanied the closing-down of the 'war nurseries', the withdrawal of hundreds of thousands of women from the paid labour-force to make way for the returning soldiers and what the historian Denise Riley has called the rise of 'pro-natalism': persuading women to stay at home and increase the population by rearing normal babies 'for Britain'.[14]

It says much for the basic attractiveness of pro-natalism and the idea of attachment that attachment theory has been modified rather than abandoned as a result of the wide-ranging research it has provoked. This reception has not all been critical. Indeed, it has been said that there is 'near unanimity among theorists that infants are capable of attachments'.

Much confirming evidence has been collected. For example, a deduction from attachment theory was that what Piagetians called the 'object concept' was formed for emotional reasons, not logical ones. A baby's understanding that an object X still exists when not in place Y would have as its base not an advance in thinking, but the development and generalization of an *emotional* relationship to a particular person who thenceforth is felt by the baby to have a permanent place in the world. In this case, the behaviour that led Piaget to believe that the child understood the object concept would be an outcome of a more basic emotional change.

This coincidence of chronology between 'socio-emotional' and 'cognitive' development was turned to the attachment theorists' advantage in a study by Silvia Bell (1969) in the USA.[15] Bell showed that babies generally understood 'person permanence' (that their mother-figure continued to exist even whilst hidden) more than a month before they succeeded in Piaget's toy-hiding task which defines the first sensori-motor understanding of object permanence. (This finding was obviously compatible with the Vygotskyan idea that a person-based socio-emotional development precedes and even conducts the thing-based cognitive growth studied by Piaget and his followers).

Critiques of Attachment Theory

One of the first foci for criticism of attachment theory was on Bowlby's claim that babies are innately 'monotropic' – that they are predisposed to form a relationship with one person above all others and that this person will be the one who spent most time caring for them (usually their mother). Observations and mothers' reports collected by Rudolf Schaffer and Peggy Emerson of sixty babies over the first year of their life in Glasgow, Scotland, showed that babies begin their social life by developing a variety of important relationships (or 'indiscriminate attachments'), relationships which varied in intensity from person to person and day to day.[16] By the start of the second year these babies might be bonded to two or three people more or less equally, where circumstances allowed it – which they usually didn't. By this age the sole principal attachment was to the main child-minder (the mother) in only one half of the children studied. Nearly a third of the children were mainly attached to their fathers. This was despite the fact that mothers were always the parent chiefly responsible for child-care in this study. In short, babies are not all drawn to love only one person where there are alternatives. Babies are not monotropic.

The Glasgow study also showed that the formation of attachments did not simply depend on the development of a few innate 'fixed action patterns' into a control system with proximity to the main parent as its goal. When Schaffer and Emerson analysed their data it seemed that the varying sensitivities and responsiveness of adults to the babies' needs were amongst the most important factors which determined who the child would become attached to. A father who played regularly with his child might well be preferred to a mother who only spent time feeding and caring for her baby's physical needs. These findings led to a transformation of attachment theory, a transformation in which adult responses to the baby became as important a factor in accounting for the baby's emotional development as the patterns of contact-promoting behaviour with which babies are born.

A classic study supporting this point of view was published in the early 1970s by Silvia Bell and Mary Ainsworth.[17] Bell and Ainsworth studied a group of mother–baby pairs at three-monthly intervals over their first year of life. They were interested in causal relationship between how much babies cried and how mothers responded to their crying. The trend which stood out for them was that mothers who were sensitive and responsive to their babies' cries – picking them up and comforting them soon after they began to complain – tended to have babies who cried less and less as the first year progressed, whereas the babies of mothers who were less responsive continued to cry at a significantly higher level. This finding seemed to disprove any simple version of learning theory, which would have predicted exactly the opposite result: if every time a baby cries it is 'rewarded' by being picked up then it should cry more and more, not less, as time goes on. Rather, it suggested that if mothers were constantly available and attentive to their children during the early years, their children would naturally grow into obedient and healthy members of society. If mothers were *not* responsive, their children would be more likely to become 'anti-social and a menace'.[18] In this way, Schaffer and Emerson's critique can be re-understood in terms of attachment theory (babies turn to their fathers when their mothers behave unnaturally).

During the 1970s attachment theory came in for further constructive criticism. It was pointed out that the use of a reconstructed evolutionary past and animal examples was an unsatisfactory speculative rationale for the theory. After all, there are many animals which do not 'imprint' on their parents – why should it be ducklings which most accurately reflect the biological heritage of humans?

The behavioural evidence for attachment theory from observations of human infants also came under attack. It was pointed out that the behavioural equipment of newborn babies was much more complex and variable than was represented in attachment theory. The so-called 'fixed action patterns' of smiling, crying, clinging and so on were far from fixed, there being a whole gradation of smiles and cries, from low-intensity and short duration to high-intensity and continuous.[19] Moreover, attachment theory had nothing to say about what happened between infant and adult once proximity had been attained. Bowlby and Ainsworth could not predict how babies' responses to their parents' attentions might subsequently affect early social relationships. For example, did *how* babies cried in the Bell and Ainsworth study affect their mothers' responsiveness? Bell and Ainsworth only reported 'crying' as if it were a uniform behaviour unaccompanied by other behaviours and events – and so were unlikely to find any evidence that babies had effects on the adults who cared for them, not just vice versa.[20] Possibly some babies cry less 'seriously' or more annoyingly than others, and hence are picked up less. Alternatively the connection between maternal unresponsiveness and high levels of crying may both have had a common but independent cause – high levels of domestic tension, for example. Certainly attempts to reproduce Bell and Ainsworth's findings have failed.[21]

Criticisms have also been levelled at findings of 'stranger fear'.[22] These findings are usually produced in studies artificially conducted under controlled conditions. The 'stranger' is told to approach the baby in a series of pre-set stages rather than naturally and spontaneously trying to relate to the baby. When these procedural details are changed – when, for example, the 'stranger' exchanges pleasantries with the mother before looking at the baby, so that the baby can take a cue from the mother's response, or the introduction takes place in familiar surroundings at home – 'stranger fear' is rare: the vast majority of nine-month-olds make friendly rather than frightened responses to newcomers.

Finally, research has also questioned Bowlby's claim that 'deprivations' of parental care have far-reaching effects on the development of character and 'may entirely cripple' the capacity to make relationships with other people. The effects of long-term separations seem to depend on the social circumstances in which they occur and the child's understanding of the separation. Michael Rutter reports a study which shows that a single separation from both parents only causes an increased tendency to anti-social behaviour (in boys) if the boy comes from a 'poor marriage'.[23] If long separations are repeated, then they do predict greater anti-sociability in both 'good' and 'bad' marriages. But even complete deprivation of a mother-figure does not necessarily result in social failure. For example, in studies of children from broken homes, a distinction can be drawn between those broken by accidental death and those broken by divorce or separation. As Rutter reports, it is only the children of marital breakdown who are at more than average risk of getting into trouble as 'delinquent' following the separation.

As for repeated short separations from parents, studies of children in day-care compared with those reared at home show that both groups of children develop emotional bonds in much the same way and at much the same time. Moreover, day-care children develop their main bonds with their parents, not with the staff of the day-care centre, even when babies have been in day-care from the first weeks of life.[23]

These findings militate against the idea that children do not develop well unless they are in more or less continuous contact with their mothers from birth. On the other hand, as Spitz's study showed, babies in institutions may sometimes be severely affected or die if they do not receive frequent doses of affectionate contact with other human beings. And babies may be badly upset by separations from their care-givers under 'poor' family circumstances. So is it true that, as attachment theorists propose, babies are born with a set of fixed patterns of action which has a tendency to promote proximity to their primary caretaker that naturally produce 'love' (a synonym of 'attachment' according to Ainsworth) at nine months of age?[24]

The reasons why this question must be answered in the negative are well condensed in considering what a baby's life must be like *before* nine months of age. Is stranger anxiety the first anxiety? Is the first nine months normally a paradise, without worries, a kind of external 'life in the womb'? Does the baby not experience the profundities of terror or affection before nine months?

Rediscovering the Central Importance of Anxiety and Misery

Until the 1980s attachment theorists have not been in a good position to answer these questions. The first nine months is called by them a period of 'indiscriminate attachments', a stage of social promiscuity. It is a period in which the baby may easily depend on many people to soothe its fears and fulfil its needs. But it is a period of which, as Bowlby admitted when he first formulated it in 1958, attachment theory only deals with 'the positive aspects'.[25] *Why* babies cry to be picked up is not of interest in Bowlby's attachment theory. Attachment theory begins at the point when the baby *is* picked up. A cry is merely one amongst a number of 'attachment behaviours' which have proximity as a 'predictable outcome'. Proximity may be the only outcome of interest to attachment theorists, but to the baby the care of others will not be wholly predictable, in either frequency or quality. It is precisely this unpredictability, along with facts such as that young babies cry a great deal but don't laugh, that gives us some idea of how great an omission it is to leave the 'negative aspects' of the child's emotional tie to the world out of one's theory of early emotional development.[26]

If a central problem with attachment theory is that its advocates assume without evidence that anxiety begins with the formation of a distance-controlling love-bond around nine months of age, what is the alternative? It seems at least equally likely that the opposite is true: babies first begin to stick close to a minder or minders as a consequence of their continued sense of vulnerability, social anxiety or isolation. In this case, the primary driving force of emotional development would not be the growth of love but the transcendence of fear and anxiety, an idea which conforms closely to the vision of infancy put forward in psycho-analytic debates about the roots of the Oedipus complex. In particular, Lacan suggested that, humans are drawn to speak and otherwise to participate in the symbolic order of language, socially organized rituals and conventions, as an indirect way of gaining a sense of unity and control over a world in which they feel fragmented and impotent. His viewpoint has been adapted to the study of babies by Cathy Urwin, who has marshalled evidence to illustrate how important a theme the search for control over others may be in the early emergence of language.[27] For example:

> Roger (aged 16 months) and his mother are positioned around the play table. Roger picks up the receiver of the toy telephone, 'speaks' into it, and hands it to his mother indicating that she should do likewise. He then demands it back again. He directs his mother to get another, identical telephone from the side, and smiles when she obliges. The mother engages in a mock conversation with Roger, which he breaks by demanding the mother's phone. She concedes. Roger sits down on one of the two small chairs, gets off, and indicates to his mother that she is to sit on it. He gets on the other himself. He points to one of the telephones, indicating that they are to play telephones again. The mother does as bid, commenting 'Gosh, you are a little tyrant'.[28]

Elsewhere, research is accumulating which bears out the possibility that many of the infant's early achievements, including not only language acquisition and the formation of attachments but the development of cognitive schemata and the growth of humour, may result from efforts to transcend anxiety.[29]

Take humour for example. Attachment theory treats smiling and laughter as unequivocally proximity-promoting 'attachment behaviours'. But, through careful experimental testing, Alan Sroufe and his colleagues have shown that there is a close relationship between the events producing fear in babies and the events producing laughter. A mother putting on a mask will make her one-year-old laugh but a stranger putting on the same mask will make the same baby cry. Likewise, tossing the baby in the air, jiggling the baby, tickling or playing boisterous looming and sound games are all clearly events which are potentially upsetting as well as humorous. Scroufe argues that laughter and avoidance are two sides of the same coin. When an incongruous or unexpected event occurs:

> Tension is produced. If the infant's 'interpretation' of the event is negative, because of context and possible prepotent aspects of the stimulus situation, he will *cry and engage in avoidance behaviour*. If his interpretation is positive, he will smile or, depending on context and the amount of tension produced, *laugh and engage in approach behaviour*.[30]

Both these responses can be seen as attempts to gain control over stimulation, either by rejecting it or, through laughter and approach, 'by an ever more active involvement in producing the stimulus itself'.[31]

This analysis illustrates how a baby might become involved in social life without a predisposition to know or love other people. Such involvement would have three foundations: the fact that the basic denominator of the infant's waking life is misery, the fundamental asymmetry of power and knowledge between babies and their care-givers, and the fact, illustrated by Scroufe, that babies act in order to control anxiety.

Basic misery

Research shows that, even in the world's most privileged populations of children, babies spend an average of between 95 and 180 minutes a day crying or 'fussing' during the first three months of life. That is, young babies are miserable for between a quarter and a half of the time they are 'up' (not asleep or lying quietly in their cots). So, if we accept that infant crying is a good index of subjective distress, we must also accept that a most important factor colouring the behaviour of both infants and their care-givers is the baby's basic propensity for misery.[32] Hence, whilst it is traditional to construe parental behaviour as 'instinctive' or based on love, such behaviour is more simply explained as the consequence of an adult's repeated attempts to deal with this basic misery, whether by feeding, comforting, entertaining or otherwise diverting (not to mention battering) the baby. This means that one of the baby's most common waking experiences will be of involvement in repeated patterns of activity (feeding, rocking, nappy-changing, being picked up, bathed, carried, 'put down', played with, talked to, etc.), which either succeed or fail to ward off distress.

Infant–adult asymmetry

Bound up with the infant's basic misery is the baby's relative impotence to effect changes in its life-conditions relative to the power of adults.[33] This is a fact of which the infant will have repeated experience. Such experience will partly be based on adult care-givers' inevitably incomplete success in keeping the baby happy (that is, the baby is very often in a condition which may *or may not* be changed for the better by its elders). But infants also experience the adult's power over them directly every time their body is physically manipulated against or without their will. Their faces are wiped, their arms and legs are forced into and out of clothes for no apparent reason, they are put in water and taken out, spoons and bottles are thrust into their mouths, medicines are dropped into their eyes, nose or ears or injected into their thighs, attractive objects are wrested out of their hands, nappies are changed, they are strapped into car-seats, high-chairs, back-packs, they are picked up, put down, tossed in the air, held upside down, 'experimented' on, shaken, 'punished', and so on, day after day. This means that, if infants are at all capable of learning causal connections between the events that are salient to themselves and their own (re)actions, which of course they are (see pp. 41–2 above), they will soon come to associate adult practices with the onset and cessation of their own distress.

Acting to Control Anxiety

The idea that the mental life of babies is dominated by a principle of 'avoiding unpleasure' through movement is to be found in Freud. Freud argued that an attempt at such avoidance was the origin of the infant's kicking and screaming.[34] Likewise, the whole edifice of behaviourism and learning-theory is built on the assumption that humans form habits to minimize distress.

Recent research on babies extends this idea. A number of studies have shown a close link between involvement in different forms of action and the expression of anxiety. Sroufe's work on humour is a case in point. Another study shows directly that action can dispel anxiety in infants by demonstrating that one-year-olds who could control the movements of a toy by hitting a panel manifested less fear of an unpredictable toy than did infants who had no control over the toy's movement.[35] And Jerome Kagan has concluded from a voluminous review of contemporary data that early actions, emotions and cognitions are motivated by the infant's efforts to gain control over conditions that create a feeling of uncertainty: the baby's active involvement in the world grows at the edge where anxiety is transformed.[36]

In the next chapter we will see that observations of infant–adult interactions in the early months of life show that, far from being innately predisposed to 'converse with' an attentive adult, as some psychologists claim, babies will often pointedly ignore their 'attachment figures'.[37] Indeed it seems, as with Sroufe's analysis of smiling and laughter, that both babies' involvement in and avoidance of face-to-face interactions with adults are based on a desire to control the practices which incorporate them.

Even such seemingly peaceful activities as sleeping and playing are often marked by patterns of action which suggest that the baby's relationship to them is ambivalent. Hence six-month-olds may not sleep unless they are previously sung to, rocked, fed or patted in the same way every night. Or they may develop their own rituals involving a treasured object, a favourite place or a game repeatedly staging disappearance and return by burying the head in a quilt and then turning to look out again.[38] Day-time games may play on similar themes (for example Peek-a-boo) or reveal the fragility of the infant's mastery of its anxiety in other ways. For example, an infant robustly playing a 'banging' game with a plastic fish accidentally smashes the fish and immediately bursts into inconsolable tears. Even the cute 'wide-eyed' curiosity and playful seeking after adventure of children, their 'energy', suggests that apprehension is of their essence.[39]

So, we must accept that babies will swiftly recognize a link between the onset and cessation of their own basic misery and the practices of adults. And we admit evidence suggesting that babies transcend the anxiety associated with their relative impotence and vulnerability to distress by engaging in activity, preferably activity likely to give them some control over the practices to which they are subject. It only remains to conclude that babies must inevitably learn that the best way to gain a sense of control over the booming, buzzing confusion of stimulation which assaults them is to become actively involved in the practices of adults.[40] It is this involvement which would lead the child to love and to know, not vice versa.

As adult practices are largely discursive, with all that implies in terms of temporal patterning, the inevitability of the baby's involvement in them is undoubtedly increased by the newborn's ready senses of timing and cause–effect relations.[41] Timing and cause–effect relations are of course the features of social behaviour which adults typically exaggerate when dealing with babies.[42]

Summary

The early years of life are typically taken to be the period most dominated by emotions in the human life-span. In the psychology of infancy, babies' emotions are generally assumed to centre on the relationship with the mother. The importance of this relationship has most often been emphasized by showing what happens when babies are deprived of maternal care, as in the work of Spitz, Harlow and Robertson.

In the late 1950s, insights from work on maternal deprivation, combined with other research on animals, babies and psycho-analytic patients, were combined by Bowlby into a general theory of early emotional development called 'attachment theory'. Bowlby's basic assumption was that babies are born pre-adapted to become social without training. Provided that they are brought up in a 'natural' environment, where the mother is more or less continuously attentive and responds sensitively to the baby's signals and needs, babies will automatically form a deep love-bond to the mother during the first year of life. Bowlby supposed this bond to lay the foundation for all subsequent social, emotional, physical and intellectual developments.

Attachment theory is still widely subscribed to by professional psychologists. Nevertheless, it has been considerably modified by the research it has provoked. It now seems unlikely that babies seek only one love-relationship during the first year of life. If more than one adult is available to them, they are likely to form more than one emotional bond. It also seems that children who are professionally cared for (e.g. in day-care centres), even from the first few months of life, form bonds to their parents and otherwise develop just like babies who are brought up by their mothers at home. Moreover, the way in which babies are 'pre-adapted' as social beings has been called into question. Bowlby described their pre-adaptations in behavioural terms: they are equipped with such socially efficacious behaviours as smiling, looking, clinging, sucking, following and so on. More recent research has suggested that the crucial factors in emotional development arise from the quality, not the mere existence, of interactions between babies and adults. For instance, babies may have preferences for particular kinds of interaction with others, preferences that need investigating in their own right (see next chapter).

Perhaps the most serious fault of attachment theory is its failure to consider the 'negative aspects' of the baby's tie to others. Attachment theorists generally assume that the only important social behaviours with which infants are born tend to promote proximity with others. This assumption simultaneously ignores the possibilities that babies may at times want to avoid interaction with others and that parents may 'naturally' experience ambivalence about their babies' demands on them. It is doubtful whether a theory of emotional development which concentrates only on the infant's proximity-promoting behaviours, ignoring the grounds of that promotion in the adult's relationship to the child, what goes on once proximity between baby and minder has been gained and how proximity is broken, can ever be adequate to account for the complexities of the growth of human mental life. Recent research has produced evidence supporting an 'anxiety-centred' account of the baby's involvement in social life which contradicts attachment theory.

By analysing in detail the debate surrounding attachment theory, this chapter has illustrated the importance of considering babies' emotional behaviour in forming a rounded vision of infancy. But criticisms of attachment theory suggest scientists need to consider further both the affective range of early infant behaviour in social situations and the basis of adults' responses to babies. Both these lines of enquiry have served to promote a body of recent research involving detailed observational studies of early infant–adult interactions based on the fine-grained analysis of films and video-tapes. These studies are discussed in the next chapter.

Further Reading

Attachment and Loss. vol. I: *Attachment* by J. Bowlby (Penguin, Harmondsworth, 1969) is the seminal formulation of attachment theory and gives good accounts of the work by Spitz, Harlow and others which led Bowlby to claim an evolutionary basis for his theory.

Infant–Mother Attachment: The Origins and Developmental Significance of Individual Differences in Strange Situation Behaviour by M. E. Lamb, R. A. Thompson, W. Gardner, E. L. Charnov and J. P. Connell (Erlbaum, Hillsdale, NJ, 1985) is an up-to-date account of research on attachment theory relating to the key experimental situation used to assess attachments in clinical work – the 'strange situation'.

Maternal Deprivation Reassessed by M. Rutter (Penguin, Harmondsworth, 1981, 2nd edn) is a comprehensive review of the literature concerning recent research on the basic contention of attachment theory: that maternal deprivation impairs child development. Rutter is generally critical of Bowlby's theory, suggesting, for example, that provided people are kind of babies, they may be satisfactorily reared from birth onwards by more than one minder, as in day-care.

War in the Nursery: Theories of Mother and Child by D. Riley (Virago, London, 1983) puts the proposals of attachment theory in a historical perspective, suggesting that they partly reflect general changes in the social atmosphere surrounding children following the Second World War in Great Britain, changes which led to a widespread promotion of maternal domesticity or 'pro-natalism'.

Quality in Child Care: What Does the Research Tell Us?, edited by D. A. Phillips (NAEYC, Washington, DC, 1987), summarizes a number of large American studies of child care, stressing the importance of quality in debates about the effects of early non-parental care on infants.

8

Motives for Self-expression

In 1623 the Czech philosopher Comenius expressed what must already have been a well-worn idea, the idea that even very young infants 'know what a wrinkled and what an unwrinkled brow means'.[1] The belief that babies are born with the ability to understand the expressions of others has proved of continuing interest to philosophers and scientists. It is to be found in the writings of the Scottish 'common-sense' philosopher Dugald Stewart (1753–1828).[2] And, as we have seen, it was also advanced by Charles Darwin: 'An infant understands to a certain extent, and as I believe at a very early period, the meaning or feeling of those who tend him, by the expression of their features.'[3]

The Need to Analyse Early Interactions

In recent years a new urgency has attached to the search for observational evidence to support this belief. As we saw in the last chapter, researchers studying early emotional development have been led to question Freud's argument that the child's early years are dominated by anxiety, conflict and guilt, which, though repressed, continue to affect us throughout life. Many scientists now believe that babies simply attach themselves to their parents, thereby building a secure basis for adult happiness. But this theory is based on a fairly crude portrait of the infant's behaviour in the earliest months. When analysed in more detail, does the infant's attitude during this period support the view that humans are born predisposed to form a love-relationship based on the realistic recognition of the other as a trustworthy and caring person? Or are babies' first relationships with others the fruits of anxiety and fantasy, as Freud and his followers have suggested?

The roots of rational thought

In research on the infant's progress towards rationality, questions about the extent of babies' understanding of other people has also become increasingly topical. As Piaget's notion that babies are born unable to recognize any difference between their own perceptions of the world and the world itself has been increasingly questioned, an alternative point of view has been developed: namely, that the main motivation for the child's cognitive development is a search for 'the conditions for realizing the joy of interhuman communication'.[4] The child is deemed to be born peculiarly well-adapted for understanding other people and it is only Piaget's preoccupation with the logic of the physical world that has blinded him to this obvious insight.

An example quoted by Margaret Donaldson to make this point it taken from a reworking of a classic Piagetian experiment by Martin Hughes.[5] In Piaget's experiment children are put in front of a papier mâché model of three mountains and then asked to choose from a range of pictures to show what the mountains would look like from a side-on view. Children younger than seven years generally fail this test, leading Piaget to conclude that children of six and less are unable to take the viewpoint of someone else or are 'egocentric'.[6]

In Hughes's experiment, children are shown a model of two intersecting walls, creating four hiding-places. A toy policeman is placed so that he can 'see into' two of the spaces, but not the other two. Children are then asked to hide a doll representing a little boy so that the policeman can't see him. When children show they do understand this task, a second policeman is placed so that, between them, the policemen can see into three of the four hiding-places made by the walls. Children are then asked to hide the boy again, though now there is only one safe place. Hughes found that children as young as three years old passed this test.[7] Donaldson argues this finding to show that, contrary to Piaget, children are very good at reading the intentions and plans of other people, provided they are tested in situations which are familiar enough to make 'human sense' to the child.[8]

Further evidence to support this point of view comes from Judy Dunn's detailed observations of the relationships which grow up between brothers and sisters in the home.[9] She reports incidents which show that even one-year-olds have sufficient understanding of their older siblings both to comfort and to annoy them. If concerned about their sibling's distress they may stroke them or go to fetch their favourite teddy bear. On the other side of the balance are examples such as this:

Anne, three years old, is playing with her teddy bear, her favourite comfort-object. She is making a 'tent' for him in the kitchen with a chair and a cloth. Eric, her younger brother, watches. Five minutes later both children are in the front room, and they have a fight over the possession of a toy car. Anne wins the fight. Eric is angry. He runs back to the kitchen, pulls Anne's 'tent' to pieces and hurls the teddy across the room. Anne bursts into tears.[10]

The work of Donaldson, Hughes and Dunn leads us to ask what are the roots of the infant's ability to make human sense of other's actions? Are babies born with innate ability to recognize and understand others' states of minds? Or do these observations of infant sense-making have their basis in the acquisition of a recognizable (to adults) language of self-expression, a set of behaviours which is more a vehicle for the indirect elaboration of the child's own motives and feelings than evidence for an understanding of others? An analysis of the roots of communication in infancy is of pressing importance to answer these questions.

The basis of speech

The study of early language development has also increasingly raised questions about the possibility and importance of communication in early infancy.[11] As we saw in chapter 5, research on parental babytalk has forced a substantial revaluation of the adult's contribution to language acquisition. Contrary to Chomsky's belief, the baby is from birth surrounded by language which is regular and highly structured. In the 1970s a number of researchers suggested that the baby's ability to speak was built upon the development of pre-verbal routines between adult and child such as games and the routines surrounding bathing, feeding, bedtime and nappy-changing. These familiar formats for co-operative action create a common context in which particular sounds and gestures can take on word-like or sentence-like functions.[12] In a game of Peek-a-boo, a baby may become used to announcing its reappearance from behind a chair with the sound 'Ah!'. In feeding, a sound such as 'Mm' may come to mean 'I want'. And when bathing, an effort to grasp a particular toy may eventually be transformed into pointing. In time, words will take the place of these sounds and gestures. Instead of pointing, the child will learn to say 'duck' or 'boat'. Instead of 'Mm' she will say 'juice'. Instead of raising her arms as a signal to be picked up, she will simply say 'Up'.[13]

In this light, the interpretive role played by mothers and other care-givers in the development of communication becomes crucial. The steady

Plate 8.1 The social routines with which babies become familiar as they grow up are thought by some scientists to be the basis of intelligence and language later in life.
Source: UNICEF/Abigail Heyman.

sophistication of the routines which provide scaffolding for the construction of language depends as much or more on the minder's intelligence as on what is going on in the head of the baby. Here, for example, is Vygotsky's analysis of the development of pointing:

> Initially, this gesture is nothing more than an unsuccessful attempt to grasp something, a movement aimed at a certain object which designates forthcoming activity. The child attempts to grasp an

object placed beyond his reach; his hand, stretched toward that object, remains poised in the air. His fingers make grasping movements. At this initial stage pointing is represented by the child's movement, which seems to be pointing to an object – that and nothing more.

When the mother comes to the child's aid and realizes his movement indicates something, the situation changes fundamentally [cf. Skinner p. 69 above]. Pointing becomes a gesture for others. The child's unsuccessful attempt engenders a reaction not from the object he seeks but *from another person*. Consequently, the primary meaning of that unsuccessful grasping movement is established by others. Only later, when the child can link his unsuccessful grasping movement to the objective situation as a whole, does he begin to understand this movement as pointing. At this juncture there occurs a change in that movement's function: from an object-oriented movement it becomes a movement aimed at another person, a means of establishing relations. *The grasping movement changes to the act of pointing.* As a result of this change, the movement itself is then physically simplified, and what results is the form of pointing that we may call a true gesture. It becomes a true gesture only after it objectively manifests all the functions of pointing for others and is understood by others as such a gesture. Its meaning and functions are created at first by an objective situation and then by people who surround the child.[14]

Vygotsky's analysis shows the development of pointing to have three stages: the observable expression of a desire by the child (grasping for an object); its interpretation and fulfilment by adults (treatment of the gesture as pointing); and the child's subsequent recognition that his or her gesture has acquired a new meaning for others.

This view of language as an outcome of the growth of sophisticated non-verbal routines involving both adult and child leads us to ask what is the psychological basis for early infant–adult interaction? Are babies born pre-adapted to decode the meaning of others' responses to themselves? Or do they simply learn that their behaviour has new consequences and therefore can be used in new ways, without reference to the mental states of those who rear them? Scientists are still debating these questions. The ensuing discussion is intended more to give a flavour of their debate than to settle it.

The Study of Babies as Communicators

At the beginning of the 1970s, scientists were rarely prepared to argue that young babies reacted to people as anything more than very complex inanimate stimuli. Babies apparently preferred to look at schematic faces rather than at other patterns and to watch moving things rather than still ones. But their interest in people was seen as nothing more than a result of the fact that people combined a number of features to which babies were pre-programmed to be attracted. According to this argument, one should be able to design a non-human stimulus that satisfies babies as much or more than people do by combining pattern, contrast, movement, rhythm and so on in an ideal way. Thus in 1971, Schaffer concluded that 'At birth an infant is essentially an asocial being. . . Other people, he [the baby] soon finds out are fascinating things to watch and feel and listen to, but as yet they do not constitute a class of stimuli distinct from the inanimate world.'[15]

During the 1970s research of various kinds challenged this conclusion. Much of this research was based on the fine-grained analysis of films and video-tapes of young infants in interaction with adults. Thus by 1975, Jerome Bruner felt he was in a position to publish a direct contradiction of Schaffer's claim that young babies cannot distinguish people from things. He argued that the child has an innate capacity to construct ways of interpreting people, basing his argument on 'ample' evidence that: 'The child in his [or her] responses from a few weeks of age distinguishes the category of people from the category of things.'[16]

As evidence, some psychologists have enthusiastically pointed out that babies show an enormous range of interpretable expressions. Their eye-movements, cries, coos, postural changes, gesticulations and facial expressions bear eloquent testimony to many shades of mental state. Surely such astonishingly complex expressive behaviours can only have evolved for one purpose, the purpose of communicating with others?

For example, attention was drawn to the infant's facial expressions. Anatomical studies of the adult face have shown that humans possess forty-two different blocks of muscle specifically adapted to emotional expression. In combination, these muscles allow an extraordinarily rich variety of facial displays. Nevertheless six easily identifiable expressions have been picked out as a basis for analysis, the so-called 'pure' expressions of joy, disgust, anger, fear, surprise and sadness.[17] These are the labels about which there is most consensus when people from many different cultures are asked to rate photographs of different expressions. (Photographs of actors specially trained to pose 'blends' made up of components of various 'pure' expressions, e.g. disgust plus anger plus surprise, prove more difficult to judge.)

When researchers familiar with adult facial expressions focused on the faces of babies, they found that at least forty of the forty-two expressive muscle-groups are active in the first days after birth.[18] Moreover, despite the presence of some diffuse, low-level expressive activity, the facial muscle actions of young infants are often well-defined and easy to see, even when these are complex blends of the 'pure' expressions. Particularly interesting, the combinations of these elementary expressive muscle-movements are not random. For example, smiling in infants as young as four weeks of age is a facial behaviour which simultaneously involves a relaxation of the brows and changes in the lower face, often being preceded by a period when the brows are lowered as if in concentration. New observations continually add to these glimpses of pattern in early expressive behaviour, observations which suggest that human babies have complex and variable subjective lives from birth onwards. Might not such innate comprehensibility to others betoken an innate comprehension of others in babies?

Similarly, when adults talk to each other intimately, films show that they not only discuss the same things, they join in a non-verbal and usually unconscious dance together. If one person crosses her legs, the other may cross his. Two people will tend to lean forward almost simultaneously when the conversation becomes engrossing, and simultaneously move apart when it loses its grip. Even the smallest bodily movements take place in concert – movements of the hands and fingers share the same rhythm, as do adjustments of posture.[19] Indeed some have suggested that body-movements have a grammar reflecting spoken language – large movements occurring at change of topic, smaller ones at the ends of sentences and tiny motions accompanying words and phrases. In 1973 two scientists from the United States had the idea of applying conversational motion-analysis to the movements of newborn babies as they listened to tape recordings of adult speech. In a paper which stirred up great interest, they published their findings that a two-day-old baby moved in synchrony with an adult saying 'Come over and see who's over here.' Taking all the baby's visible motions, of the head, eyes, hands, feet, arms, legs, shoulder and hips, they found a large proportion of these motions began or ended at boundaries between units of speech: syllables or words. They suggested that this ability to participate in the way the actions of those around them were organized would give babies immediate access to the non-verbal, bodily aspects of their immediate local culture and language.[20] Surely such mutuality of *physical* action, such dancing together must be matched, if only briefly, by a mutuality of *mental* action?

And then there are the baby's eyes! For the first few weeks of life, babies's eyes appear unfocused. A very young baby seems to look through people rather than at them. But around the sixth week, at almost the same time that she or he first smiles directly at particular people, a baby will begin really to look others in the eye. This is a potent turn-on. Parents who are asked to describe their early feelings about their babies often say that the baby's first eye-to-eye look makes her or him seem like a person for the first time.[21] And young babies, for their part, generally seem to prefer looking to human faces and listening to human voices than any other naturally occurring stimulus.[22] Why would this be if baby and mother and others did not wish to understand and be understood by each other?

Further evidence that babies can follow and adapt to the behaviours of others has been drawn from studies of imitation. Against Piaget's belief that true imitation does not appear until the second half of a baby's first year was set evidence that babies can imitate adult facial expressions as early as two and three days of age. In 1977, in the USA, Andrew Meltzoff and Keith Moore published findings showing that, if an adult models behaviours such as poking out the tongue, opening the mouth and protruding the lips, a three-week-old is likely to copy these expressions, often with surprising accuracy.[23] In 1983, Meltzoff and Moore reported a similar experiment on forty babies less than three days old. Once again they found that babies copied tongue-protrusion and mouth-opening so frequently that there was less than one chance in a thousand of their results being a fluke.[24] Surely, to imitate an adult's action a baby must first understand the action?

Also in support of this general argument a number of researchers have reported studies showing that, if infant–adult interactions are experimentally disrupted, babies show characteristic patterns of distress. For example, in the midst of a face-to-face interaction, mothers may be asked to stop talking and freeze their expressions for one or two minutes. Under these circumstances, babies will typically look puzzled and upset, turning away from their mother to stare at their own hands or clothes.[25] Surely these patterns show that, as babies can be offended or affronted by experimental insults, they must be born knowing how infant–adult communication *should* be conducted?

Finally, under optimal conditions of infant–adult interaction, two-month-olds show a characteristic pattern of communicative behaviour involving swift and delicate movements of the lips and tongue which are associated with gesticulations. The occurrence of this behaviour in an appropriate context is claimed to be evidence of an evolutionary human pre-adaptation to speaking with others and has been called 'prespeech'.

Prespeech

One of the most consistent exponents of this point of view has been the New Zealander Colwyn Trevarthen. In the late 1960s Trevarthen worked with Jerome Bruner at Harvard, along with Tom Bower, Martin Richards, Berry Brazelton, Hanus Papousek and others. It was Trevarthen,

Brazelton and Richards who in 1968 undertook the study which had convinced Bruner that from the first weeks of life, babies distinguish the category of people from the category of things. Since 1970 Trevarthen has continued to work on infancy in Scotland. During the later 1970s he became increasingly convinced that human babies are born with

> mysterious but very powerful psychological mechanisms that ensure interpersonal and social cooperation in human intelligence. This last function, social cooperation, is of course the most special feature of human intelligence. It gives humans adaptive domination over all other forms of life, and unlimited power to acquire and transmit techniques for mastery of the environment.[26]

His conclusions is not unlike Chomsky's, discussed in chapter 5. But rather than being born with a 'Language Acquisition Device', human babies have a device for generating *social co-operation* which is located in the brain at birth. If allowed to communicate freely, this mechanism leads two-month-old babies to engage adults (especially mothers) in 'highly-regular, conversation-like exchanges in which it is clear that the infant exercises the primary control of events.'[27]

According to Trevarthen's vision of early development, two months is the first peak of mother–infant communication. After three months babies become less interested in 'conversing' with others and more interested in reaching for and grasping objects, and in playing games. These early games generally involve simple rhythmical noises made by the baby-minder, who simultaneously makes repeated physical contact with the baby (e.g. poking the baby's stomach or shaking the baby's feet). Trevarthen calls them 'person–person' games.[28] Their appearance coincides with the first infant laughter (around four months).[29] As the baby's ability to manipulate objects improves, games involving objects become increasingly popular: the baby laughing more at objects animated by the minder than at the minder herself.

According to this vision, the next major change in communication occurs around nine months of age with the emergence of 'truly cooperative activity'.[28] Babies become interested not simply in objects as objects and people as people but in what people do with objects. Objects begin to have a symbolic potential in the baby's mind: a ball is something to be given or withheld from others. And others' uses of objects may now be imitated. It is this general transformation of communication which Trevarthen believes to underlie – amongst other developments – a new interest in the way adults make objects disappear (as discussed by Piaget); the use of vocalizations to refer to things and events (as noted by Bates); spontaneous giving to others (as discussed by Klein); and a willingness to be instructed. But all these abilities are built up by a brain process which endows even very young infants with the ability to share states of mind with those who look after them.[30]

Part of the appeal of Trevarthen's analysis comes from his insistence that babies are extremely active in their own development. Development is at least partly the result of cognition and 'the deeper processes by which individual voluntary action grows'.[31] Trevarthen is committed to the view that the infant has a very active subjective life which is the main contributor to developmental progress. Contrary to associationist, behaviourist or 'peripheralist' explanations of psychological development,[32] Trevarthen argues that his

> detailed observations are quite inconsistent with the view that the child's learning ability and voluntary communications are fabricated from without by the mothers. Indeed we think it more correct to say that the pupil role grows in the infant and that this causes the teacher role of the mother who is, no doubt, adapted to become a teacher in and of herself.[33]

Controversy

Whilst ideas similar to or based upon Trevarthen's have found expression in writings on infancy by psychologists, psycholinguists and clinicians on both sides of the Atlantic, they have also aroused considerable controversy amongst experimentalists interested in infancy.[34] This controversy centres on what seems to be an unnecessarily bold step in reasoning of the kind we have been discussing. We may be quite happy to accept that babies have very active subjective lives. But this does not mean that babies have easy access to the subjective lives of others. For example, babies certainly do have a wide range of quickly variable expressions which make vivid sense to adults. But to assume these expressions are expressions *which demonstrate an understanding of others* is to put beyond doubt the question that is at the heart of research on infant–adult communication; namely, whether the baby is able to share understandings with the adult. Surely a baby 'in conversation' with an adult could have a view of the world, and express it in a manner that scientists could satisfactorily interpret, without that view being a genuine understanding of the adult with whom the baby was interacting?

Evidence supporting an affirmative answer to this question has come from a number of directions. In the first half of the 1980s, Bruner's claim that babies distinguish categorically between people and things was seen to rest on too slender a basis of evidence. In one experiment, video-tapes of babies interacting with people, things and animated things were found to produce very similar reactions in three-month-old infants.[35] The only behavioural difference obvious to lay observers was in the reactions of babies to animate versus inanimate stimuli. The babies' responses to people were not seen as different from those directed at moving things. Thus, if babies do 'see the difference' between any two categories of stimuli from birth, this is less likely to be a difference between people and things than between animate and inanimate objects.

Later work shows that young babies certainly manifest different modes of action in dealing with the world, including object-directed reaching, smiling and cooing, 'prespeech' (see below), sleep and complaint. But these are not confined to any one kind of stimuli. Babies may coo and smile at an inanimate mask or a golf club just as they may reach to grasp a living eye or a tooth.[36] This suggests that a baby's initial approach to the world is not based upon a categorical distinction between people and things.

Likewise, early imitation is undoubtedly evidence for an interesting kind of magnetic involvement by babies in adult behaviour. But babies not only stick their tongues out at people who poke tongues at them but at pencils which are poked at them too.[37] Early imitation may show babies have a sense of what it feels like to make a particular kind of movement or grimace. But this does not mean that they *understand* any more about the movement they imitate than a parrot does about human speech it picks up. Nevertheless Tom Bower and Jennifer Wishart argue imitation to prove that babies are born with an abstract understanding which enables them to recognize the 'humanness' of others.[38] And Andrew Meltzoff argues imitation as evidence that babies are born with the basis for social 'attunement' which enables them to build bridges between self and other.[39]

The argument that calculated disruptions of early infant–adult interactions show that babies innately know what to expect from adults in communication has drawn two kinds of criticism. In the first place, it can be argued that, given the swift learning capacities of newborn babies, it is not surprising that after one or two months babies start to 'know what to expect' when an adult talks to them.[40] For example, Aidan MacFarlane has shown that babies can learn to distinguish their mothers from other women by smell in the first week of life.[41] Thus, if two months later an experimentalist arranges for that baby's mother to freeze her face for two minutes in the midst of an otherwise usual interaction, it is not surprising that the baby becomes upset. This finding certainly shows the baby to have a subjective life which the actions of adults affect. But it does not show that the baby *understands* the adult's more usual actions. Only that they are familiar, and hence pleasanter, than stony silence.

A Test Case

The most convincing evidence for an innate understanding of others comes from the fine-grained analysis of films recording mothers chatting with their two-month-olds face-to-face. Trevarthen argues such films to show that not only do mothers attend closely and respond to subtle changes in mood of their babies, but the babies themselves 'perceive and interpret the mother's personality'.[42] The expression of the babies in these films are claimed to show that the babies perceive the mental states, intentions and feelings which inspire and give significance to their mothers' expressions. For example, a mother who is emotionally distressed will produce distress in her baby. Alternatively, a mother who deals affectionately and sensitively with her baby will find that her baby responds to her with attempts at communication (prespeech), positive expressions and, later on, facetious clowning and play. In fact, Trevarthen finds on the two-month-old's behalf 'subtle modification to the form of her actions, proving that the baby can perceive the mother's unique personal attributes.'[43]

An illustration of the kind of evidence that supports this conclusion follows. It is a description of the first seventy seconds of filmed interaction between a mother, Mary, and her nine-week-old daughter, Jude.[44] The interaction can be divided into seven successive events:

Event 1 Jude is sitting alone in the recording-studio. Having been instructed to 'chat' with her daughter, Mary comes in and sits down in front of Jude, and then leans forward, imitating Jude's rather gormless expression and uttering an ape-like 'Oo! Oo! Oo! Oo!' Jude's face blossoms into a broad and happy smile lasting six seconds.

Event 2 Mary laughs at the success of her tease and greets Jude enthusiastically: 'Hello. Hello. Are you going to have a talk today? Are you going to have a talk?' As if in answer to Mary's questions, Jude's face becomes more serious and she starts to make what looks like a series of finely articulated but soundless remarks, her lips and tongue rapidly forming speech-like movements and her hands animatedly waving and gesticulating ('prespeech').

Event 3 At this burst of 'talkativeness' in Jude, Mary interrupts herself and begins to comment understandingly: 'Aha! Aha! Aha! You've had a busy day? You've had a busy day? Yes you have. Yes you have. You've had a busy day, my darling.' A little later, the experimenter enters the recording-studio behind Mary, and Mary turns swiftly to see what is going on. Jude, who has been 'talking' to Mary contentedly up to this point, registers dismay. Her face falls and her 'prespeech' ceases.

Plate 8.2.1–3 Jude responds to her mother's teasing expression with a broad smile.
Source: Author.

Plate 8.3.1–3 Jude manifests 'prespeech'.
Source: Author.

Plate 8.4.1–3 Jude's face falls as Mary turns away from her.
Source: Author.

Plate 8.5.1–3 Jude turns away from her mother.
Source: Author.

Event 4 Mary turns back to Jude, but without her former animation. The experimenter is still adjusting equipment behind her and it seems that she is waiting for him to go. She leans back in her chair, away from Jude, mutters a few of the phrases which she had been using before the interruption and again glances away from Jude to see what is happening behind her. Jude makes a brief burst of 'prespeech' to Mary but, looking increasingly despondent at Mary's continued lack of interest in her, turns away from her mother to stare at the floor away on her left.

Event 5 The experimenter leaves the studio and Mary draws closer to Jude, greeting her and teasing her, as in Event 1: 'Hello. Hello Judy. What do you see? Boo-Boo-Boo'. Jude turns back to Mary and begins to look more cheerful. Her right hand rises and she starts to make further speech-like motions and gesticulations.

Event 6 Mary immediately responds to Jude's prespeech: 'Are we going to have a *big* talk about it!' Mary starts talking with intense animation, more loudly than she had previously and with an exaggerated expression of surprise on her face. It seems that she is compensating or over-compensating for the lapse of her interest in Jude, due to their interruption. Jude begins to look puzzled and a little angry. Her 'prespeech' behaviour subsides and she starts to turn away again from Mary.

Event 7 Mary suddenly changes her manner. Her face once again becomes attentive and enquiring. Her tone of voice drops from loud to an almost conspiratorial intimacy. She says: 'You're clever, aren't you! You're clever. You're a clever girl!' Jude turns back to her with renewed interest. Her face registers pleasure and surprise and, once again, she becomes 'talkative'. (This filmed sequence continues for a further four minutes.)

Does this sequence show that Jude understood or shared mental states with Mary? Or does it show that Jude enjoyed expressing herself as long as Mary preserved a sensitive and restrained demeanour, acting as a gentle foil for Jude's complex expressive actions? For in the latter case, there is no need to claim that Jude understands Mary, only that Mary can provide what Jude wants.

Jude is happily expressive for as long as her mother imitates, supports and otherwise mirrors her own feelings. But as soon as Mary's attention is diverted, becomes exaggerated or depressed, Jude is upset and withdraws from her mother. Most importantly, Jude shows no interest in what has diverted or is preoccupying Mary. She does not follow Mary's gaze to look at the intruding experimenter. She does not sit back, like her mother, and wait for the intruder to depart. Neither does she wait understandingly for her mother to 'have her say' after the experimenter has gone. The form of

Plate 8.6.1–3 Jude smiles at her mother as Mary greets her after the interruption.
Source: Author.

Plate 8.7.1–3 Jude's reaction to her mother's exaggerated expressions. *Source*: Author.

Plate 8.8.1–3 Jude's re-involvement in the interaction after her mother's change of expressive style.
Source: Author.

the interaction seems to hinge on Mary's willingness to subordinate her own feelings and preoccupations to supportively complementing her daughter's fragile overtures and changing expressions of feeling.

Alternatives to the Hypothesis of Innate Mental Sharing

Clearly it is possible that early expressive behaviour does bear witness to babies understanding the adults with whom they interact. Certainly they seem to depend heavily upon the kind of response they get from adults in these early 'conversations'. But the existing evidence is also compatible with the hypothesis that babies are deeply interested in and affected by adults but do not understand them. Thus even the most specialized of the expressive behaviours deemed to evince understanding of others, prespeech, may be more simply explained as the product of the same magnetic processes which produce the pressure to imitate.

What are these processes? Two formulations have been suggested. The first is that the desire for attunement with another seen in early imitation and prespeech is the same desire that produces the fascination with mirrors noted by Lacan. The pressure to become involved in the expressions of others is what psycho-analysis call the pressure to *identify* with others. As discussed in the previous chapter, it comes about as a defence against and transformation of the anxious and fearful feelings of disintegration which are supposed by Freud, Klein and Lacan to typify the early months.[45] Alternatively, prespeech has been linked to the phenomena called by ethologists (biologists who study animal behaviour in the wild) *social facilitation*: 'the performance of a pattern of behaviour already in the performer's repertoire, as a consequence of the performance of the same behaviour by other individuals'.[46]

Just as one person yawning enhances the likelihood that watchers will yawn, so an adult's speech in face-to-face interaction raises the likelihood that babies will perform similar facial and oral actions. Judy Dunn suggests that such facilitation is unlikely to occur without a prior coincidence of calm, attentive, expressive moods in adult and infant.[47] But once it occurs, once the child begins to appear to 'chat' with the adult, the well-documented human propensity to interpret the actions of infants as meaningful will lead to an amplification of the adult's conversational efforts and the kind of interaction recorded above will result.

Negative responses

Part of the evidence against the view that prespeech is the product of a brain mechanism which generates human co-operation comes from studies

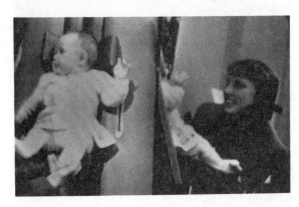

Plate 8.9.1–3 A mother who has been trying to catch her four-month-old daughter's eye, turns away to see what can be attracting the baby's attention. As soon as the mother looks away, the baby sneaks a darting look at her face. But by the time the mother looks back at the baby, the baby has turned away again to stare at the wall.
Source: Author.

showing that even very young infants from the earliest weeks of life, will often avoid contact with a friendly but familiar adult.[48] Why should this be, if babies are overwhelmingly motivated to co-operate with and comprehend others? Similarly, observations of children interacting with same-aged friends or close siblings show teasing and aggression to be common from the first year of life onwards.[49]

The fact that infants spontaneously show negative states of mind in conditions which might be expected to produce social interchange and mutual delight fits with an image of the infant's initial orientation to others as being anxious and narcissistic: that is, veering between forms of action which accentuate the likenesses between self and other (imitation, prespeech in response to maternal 'Echoing', repetitive game-playing) and intense frustration with and rejection of the other (cf. Narcissus rejecting his own image after discovering it was a reflection in the Greek myth).

Ogden has recently suggested that the child's consciousness may arise from just this kind of oscillation of mood. For the creation of consciousness is essentially a process of selection involving the affirmation of some aspects of experience at the expense of others. This becomes possible and necessary only as a result of conflicting desires leading to the need to maintain two different modes of representing or experiencing the same event at the same time.[50]

As stated in the last chapter, any theory of social development must account for the genesis of intrinsic negative emotional states as it accounts for positive ones. Theories of early development which stress the communicative precocity of little babies generally ascribe a secondary status to negativity. It is said that, under optimal or 'natural' observational conditions, young babies will communicate happily with their mothers. When negative forms of behaviour are recorded, they are not described as generated by the child, being caused 'by the partner being either too insistent in responding or not responsive enough. The former type of insensitivity produces avoidance, the latter exaggerated soliciting, depressed withdrawal or distress'.[51] But a correlation between maternal insensitivity and infant avoidance is not evidence for a causal relationship. Maternal insensitivity may be produced by infant anxiety or both kinds of negativity may be produced by some third factor such as a catching anxiety in the recording-studio or lack of sleep.

Self-expression as a search for support or as the transcendence of anxiety

Whilst no one can deny a place to the infant's complex drive to self-expression in any account of development, it may be that this expressiveness bears witness to a mental life that is dominated by babies' search for support to their own motivations, or the need to transcend their basic misery, rather than an interest in the motivations of others. It may be this need, rather than an understanding of others' intentions, that leads young children to use expressions and gestures which become increasingly language-like with age.

Thus, when we reconsider Donaldson's interpretation of the success of a three-year-old girl in Hughes's 'hide a boy' test, we should ask, whose intentions and feelings is the girl understanding? Both boy and policemen are toys made of plastic. They have neither feelings nor intentions. If anything the successful child is demonstrating to the experimenter that she can comply with his commands by showing that she knows what the word 'hide' means. The experimental situation itself is carefully contrived for ulterior purposes to which she can have no clue. Likewise, when a one-year-old gives his crying sister his own teddy bear, is he copying behaviour he has seen often before? Is he simply trying to stop her making an unpleasant noise? Is he experimenting with ideas of cause and effect? Does he confuse what she needs with what he would need if upset? Or does he genuinely understand that she needs comforting and how this is best to be achieved?

The science of babies cannot yet give a decisive answer to these questions. But, when faced with scientific statements which suggest babies are inherently understanding and co-operative, it is important to remember that a bleaker vision of infancy also fits the facts. For, given the undoubted irrationalities, self-centredness and misunderstandings which plague communication between adults, these two different visions of infancy suggest contrasting pictures of the developmental process. The rosy vision of babies suggests that something must go wrong during childhood to produce an adult world which is riven by strife. The darker vision of infancy suggests that development is a continuing struggle to overcome a nature which is neither intrinsically happy nor harmonious nor benign. In the next chapter I colour in the contrast between these contrasting visions of infancy.

Summary

For many of today's scientists interested in babies, the most telling test of infants' mental capacities is their reaction to other people. After all, babies almost always meet the world through the agency of their elders, whether this be in love or violence, verbal play, the manipulation of objects such as bottles, balls and spoons, reward and punishment, or in psychological laboratories. Hence, how babies understand adults is crucial to the interpretation both of scientific observations of infancy and to the general interpretation of early mental life.

This chapter suggests two ways of understanding the infant's early reactions to others: firstly, as based on an inborn orientation towards understanding others' states of mind and, secondly, as based on the use of others to reflect and extend or overcome the baby's own state of mind. Which of these interpretations one accepts depends on the sense one makes of the subtle and unsubtle behaviours young babies manifest when observed in interaction with adults. These behaviours include misery, imitation, varied emotional expressions, gesticulations and oral movements, bashing, locomotion, and a preference for sensitively supportive maternal behaviour over exaggerated or uninterested styles of response.

The relative merits of other oriented and self-seeking interpretations of early expressive behaviours were assessed through the discussion of a detailed description of an animated interaction between a nine-week-old girl and her mother. Whilst we do not as yet, and may never, possess the kind of evidence which could resolve the ambiguity of infants' behaviours with others *in general*, I argue that the self-seeking or 'narcissistic' reading of infant expressions is simpler, demanding a smaller leap of the imagination, and fits the facts reported here better than the idea that babies are born with an innate understanding of others. The self-seeking reading of early infancy implies a very different, and darker, vision of the infant's developmental task from that implied by the other-directed reading, in which human co-operation and understanding is something continually to be striven for, not biologically guaranteed.

Further Reading

The First Relationship: Infant and Mother by D. N. Stern (Fontana/Open Books, Glasgow, 1977) is an engaging summary of research into early interactions between mothers and babies by one of the leading contemporary investigators in the field. A more extensive and up-to-date account is to be found in Stern's *The Interpersonal World of the Infant* (Basic Books, New York, 1985). Stern is generally sympathetic to the view that babies attune themselves to others from early in life.

The Mental and Social Life of Babies: How Parents Create Persons by K. Kaye (Harvester, Brighton, 1982) gives a good account of the way in which babies, although not able to understand others early in life, become able to share mental states towards the end of the first year.

'Psychology of Infants' by C. B. Trevarthen, L. Murray and P. Hubley is a chapter in the *Scientific Foundations of Paediatrics*, ed. J. Davis and J. Dobbing

(Heinemann, London, 1981, 2nd edn) which persuasively marshals evidence for the view that babies are born with a faculty for understanding other people.
Social Perception in Infants edited by T. M. Field and N. A. Fox (Ablex, Norwood, NJ, 1985), is a representative series of recent research projects probing the infant's responses to and understandings of people.
The Child's Entry into a Social World by H. R. Schaffer (Academic, London, 1984) presents a clearly written critical review of research on early infant–adult interaction. Schaffer questions the idea that young babies are born as social beings.

9

Infancy and Paradise

In the preceding chapters I have made links between different kinds of scientific observation about babyhood and the particular theoretical preoccupations of the researchers who made those observations. Thus an interest in making plausible the theory of evolution by natural selection led Darwin to remark on early abilities which could serve as a platform for the natural development of such human faculties as reasoning and language. Alternatively, an interest in the possibility of widespread social change led associationists and behaviourists to emphasize the ease with which little babies learn from experience. Piaget's preoccupation with rationality led to a different description of infant behaviour than did the interests in the origin of love or in the growth of communication. But in this chapter I want to stand back from considering particular approaches to the study of infancy with a view to asking more general questions. These questions concern the discursive context in which scientific statements about infancy are placed.

So far, the history I have told has been of a double eclipse in psychological discussions of the progressive associationism subscribed to in different ways by Hartley, Bentham, the Darwins, Freud and his followers (e.g. Watson). The first phase of this eclipse was the denial of the relevance of mental states to theories of human development. The second phase was the introduction of embryological and 'instinctive' accounts of infancy by such writers as Charles Darwin, Piaget, Bowlby and Chomsky. As shown in chapter 4, a consequence of subscribing to the associationist perspective I have been trying to resurrect is that statements of psychologists about babies can no longer be taken as simply being 'about babies'. Such statements need interpreting as much as babies do.

A venerable method of interpretation, used for centuries in Biblical criticism and advocacy, is circular, from evidence to meaning, or meaning to evidence, and back again, until an interpretation of the action or text in question is arrived at (the 'hermeneutic circle'). In recent decades, this method has been combined by social scientists with the view that human action is 'plurivocal' or radically ambiguous. This means that the origin of an interpretation is never to be sought 'in the nature of the evidence', whether written on the rocks or etched into early human expressive behaviour. Rather, a conclusion must always partly be determined by the interpreter's own cultural presuppositions, personal prejudices or framework of analysis.

Hence any general scientific conclusion supported by evidence of particular events will involve a 'symptomatic' reading of those events, pointing to a meaning beyond them. Interpretation always 'thickens' data to embody the analyst's vision. 'What we call our data are really our own constructions of other people's constructions of what they and their compatriots are up to.'[1] This is as true of the data of experimental scientists as it is of interpretive ones. But experimental science obscures this fact because most of what we need to comprehend a particular event, observation, or whatever, is insinuated as background information before the thing itself is directly examined. Hence: 'If you want to understand what a science is, you should look in the first instance not at its theories or its findings, and certainly not at what its apologists say about it; you should look at what the practitioners of it do.'

Modern understanding of what is 'symptomatic' in a text stands in debt to the techniques of clinical inference used in psycho-analysis. Thus Freud's work on dreams illustrates a variety of different interpretive techniques which can help to explain the creation of symptoms. For example, the manifest content of a dream often omits direct reference to its central meaning. Hence all dream-images and symptoms should be interpreted independently from their apparent verbal context or rationale. In fact the *prima facie* narrative of a dream may be of little value in its ultimate interpretation, being a consequence of what Freud calls 'secondary elaboration', and often self-contradictory. This implies that, at least initially, an analyst may seem guilty of willful misinterpretation to the person being analysed. Hence dream-analysts should interpret a variety of symptoms not just one, only later turning to see if the symptoms can be used to tell a coherent tale. Finally, symptoms may be 'overdetermined' or make sense in more than one, apparently unrelated, way.

What would happen if these tenets were to be applied to contemporary scientific texts discussing the psychology of infancy?

This chapter tries to answer this question in a provisional way by exploring how current scientific research might unrealistically *idealize* infancy as a period of harmony, a kind of paradise – a criticism recently voiced by a number of commentators.[2] I argue that, whilst such an idealization is certainly not the stated aim of any contemporary researcher, it is likely to remain a latent meaning of research on babies until developmental psychology changes in three ways. First, to redress its tendency towards the eternal 'postponement' of questions linking the study of children to needs for political action. Secondly, to recognize that its prime concern should not be the theoretical problem of what is 'in the child', but the practical problems of promoting *care* or sympathy, including not only the care of children but the care of the people who look after children, not to mention care of the weak, the poor and the otherwise woebegone. And finally, to recognize the inadequacy of appeals to biological evolution as 'guaranteeing' any one vision of infancy.

The Baby as Scientist in Small

When God created Adam, 'in his own image created He him'.[3] A cultural stereotype of the ideal scientist would have to include the following features. The scientist would be male, and as a 'normal' Western adult, heterosexual and monogamous. This means he would be supported by a traditional wife whose job it was to attend to his practical and domestic needs. As this is an ideal portrait, he would be profoundly in love with this woman. He would be clever and an intellectual. This means he would learn fast and think clearly and conceptually, the distinctions he made mapping real differences in the external world. He would have an intuitive grasp of the universal principles governing nature and he would be successful in gaining control over the events that interested him. He would be able to differentiate his own point of view from that of others. But he would be a compassionate man, able to understand and empathize with those around him. Might a review of the hypotheses, findings and 'artistic handwriting' of contemporary scientists studying infancy show that these features of the ideal scientist are to be found in psychological discussions of babies?[4]

   Certainly generic 'he's' are nowhere more entrenched than in child psychology.[5] And a central tenet of Bowlby's theory of attachment, which he has clung to in the face of much evidence to the contrary is that babies are 'monotropic' (cf. 'monogamous'): 'there is a strong bias for attachment behaviour to become directed mainly towards one particular person and for a child to become strongly possessive of that person.'[6] This person is typically the mother. The baby's attachment to the mother is described by Ainsworth as synonymous with 'love' and Bowlby quotes with approval Freud's statement that the baby's relationship to the mother is 'unique, without parallel . . . the prototype of all later love-relations'.[7] The 'mother' is a woman who, in attachment theory, is seen as naturally responsive and sensitive to the baby's demands, accepting of and co-operative with the baby and more or less continuously available to care for 'him'.[8] Of course, this image of the mother's 'natural' role (cf. the wife) is not only to be found in attachment theory (see for example Klaus and Kennell on 'bonding', Winnicott on 'primary maternal preoccupation', and the discussion of 'symbiosis' below).[9]

Concerning the baby's abilities, we are warned by Bower that these are ever in danger of being underestimated. The newborn 'begins life as an extremely competent social organism, an extremely competent learning organism, an extremely competent perceiving organism.'[10] And Lipsitt concludes that the newborn baby's ability to learn is without rival in the animal kingdom.[11] But recent research suggests that babies are not simply quick learners, they are, 'intellectuals'.[12] Two decades of demonstrating how Piaget underestimated the intelligence of infants mean that the baby is now deemed to be able to conceptualize in the womb, if not the gene.[13] Babies are also talked of as being able to 'follow rules' and 'distinguish categories' from birth.[14] Moreover, babies' 'knowledge' is not illusory or culturally relative: their concepts and categories map 'the' difference between people and things, the 'essential nature' of objects.[15] And the baby is not simply an intellectual but a 'rational agent', capable of formulating and carrying out 'intentions' within 'an extraordinarily brief period' after birth.[16] This means that, at least in normal conversational settings, 'the infant exercizes the primary control of events'.[17] Babies are born with a basic capacity to distinguish 'self' from 'other'.[18] And they are capable of understanding or sharing others' states of mind and of empathy early in the first year of life.[19]

How might such a vision come about? In the first place, we might point out that, since many scientists have adopted models of the mind which exclude how babies experience the world from their studies, – the babies are viewed as 'pure' cognitive systems – the kind of evidence which would challenge views of infancy as bliss, namely the analysis of suffering versus pleasure, is automatically left out of the analysis.

Secondly, as I argued earlier, the idea of babies as intellectuals, who 'know', follow rules, and have intentions and concepts is related to a false 'logocentric' assumption in developmental explanations. This is the assumption that a knowledge of particulars and of concepts is logically, and must therefore be temporally, prior to a knowledge of propositions or, more generally, to participation in discourse and social life. The problem with this assumption is that it denies both historical and cross-cultural evidence that a knowledge-based view of individual functioning is peculiar to our own culture and era. A substantial movement in contemporary philosophy suggests that a more fruitful way of viewing the growth of knowledge is as a consequence, not the foundation, of the individual's involvement in discourse and social life.

'Logocentric' assumptions mean scientists overestimate the similarities between infants and adults by using adult terms which are technically inappropriate for the study of babies. Take, for example, the claim that young babies 'have intentions'. Much of Piaget's book *The Origins of Intelligence* is taken up with explaining why he believed that it took ten months or so before babies were capable of *intending*.[20] Subsequent investigations have challenged this view, not by questioning the terms of Piaget's argument, but by suggesting these terms can be applied to much younger children than Piaget thought. Writers such as Bruner, Kaye and Bower see any behaviour – animal or human – as intentional if it shows adjustment to, and ceases upon the attainment of, an obvious goal.[21]

But the concept of intention is important in philosophy and law because it is related to the moral problems of individual freedom, consciousness and responsibility. Stuart Hampshire writes: 'For human beings, to be conscious is to have active intentions.'[22] Linguistic philosophers such as Hampshire and Elizabeth Anscombe argue that the most important criterion for describing an action as intentional is the agent's use of language – something which infants lack (by definition). Indeed Anscombe suggests that 'the term "intentional" has reference *to a form of description of events* [her emphasis].'[23] Thus the same action may be intentional under some descriptions and unintentional under others.

Because infants and animals are not able to base their actions upon linguistic descriptions, they cannot be deemed to intend in the same way as adults do. When scientists and others ascribe intentions to non-verbal creatures, this shows more about how adults like to use (or over-extend) a particular linguistic form than it reveals about the subjective lives of infants.[24] Such over-extensions should not draw attention away from the analysis of the dynamics that lead adults to intend to do the things they do – and don't do.

The Baby's Life: 'And, Behold, it was Very Good'

As noted in chapter 7, young babies spend a large proportion of their waking life fussing and crying. But until recently child psychologists have managed to avoid discussing the ordinary misery of babies as having prime theoretical significance.

The most common method of avoidance, given the current hegemony of 'cognitive psychology', is simply by treating babies as what Norman calls 'pure cognitive systems', systems which have no structural links to the emotions.[25] Hence Chomsky's 'Language Acquisition Device' allows babies to acquire language without sweat or tears. The split between cognition and affect is also sanctioned by Piaget, who argued that affectivity is 'like gasoline, which activates the motor of an automobile but does not modify its structure'.[26] Hence, even some recent explanations of early cognitive development do not incorporate the infant's emotional life at all, although using such emotional expressions as surprise, curiosity or pleasure in mastery as measures of intelligence.[27]

A vision of infancy as a time of progressive achievement may further be promoted by editorial practices favouring the publication of 'positive' results in psychological journals. This would make papers showing that babies do not understand the events affecting them, do not make obvious distinctions, are confused, irrational, unpredictable, unskilled or unhappy, far less likely to be written, let alone published, than attention-grabbing results demonstrating that babies *do* precociously understand, act or think in 'advanced' ways.

The scientific concentration on the positive as normal in studies of infancy can be illustrated by an instructive conceptual slippage in the historical elaboration of attachment theory. As noted in chapter 7, when Bowlby first formulated his theory of the child's tie to 'his' mother, he explicitly proposed it only as a theory 'of the *positive aspects* of the child's tie' (my emphasis).[28] But, as attachment theory became more influential, its selectiveness was increasingly forgotten. 'Attachment' and 'the infant–mother relationship' were soon taken to be synonyms, even though the theory's sole concentration on 'proximity-promoting' behaviours remained unchanged.[29] Hence, the possibility that babies' negative or proximity-avoidant behaviours might have significance for understanding their socio-emotional development plays no part in the theory. It is this slippage that leads to the questionable interpretation of infant crying as unequivocally 'proximity-promoting' rather than as ambiguous or aversive and the interpretation of infant anxiety as the consequence rather than as a possible cause of attachment-formation.

Common experimental procedures may also contribute to the idealization of infant development. For example, studies of early infant–adult interactions are generally set up in such a way that interactions which are not harmonious are automatically excluded from analysis. The exercise of recording specific infant behaviours is much like fishing. Very often one does not catch what one wants. For this reason, mothers are often asked to bring their infants into the experimenter's laboratory when the baby is likely to be 'in a good mood', well fed, comfortable, healthy, not tired, etc.[30] And if the baby does get upset whilst under observation, recording is often halted until the baby cheers up or a more tractable subject can be found.[31] For example, experiments on infant perception may have drop-out rates of anything from 30 to 125 per cent.[32] So when one reads that the 'goal' of mother–infant interaction is 'mutual delight', or that the first year of life is 'bliss', one must ask how representative the data are upon which this conclusion is based.[33] This question is particularly pertinent when data are collected in micro-analytic film studies which are so labour-intensive that only brief vignettes from single cases can be reported in detail.[34]

The Baby's World as a Garden of Eden

The book of Genesis tells us that, when God had breathed life into his clay-Adam, He put him in a garden, full of exquisite and nutritious plants, 'pleasant to the sight'.[35]

The normal backcloth of infancy is often viewed as no obstacle to delight in the writings of developmentalists. Three errors can be thought to contribute to this misperception: a misapprehension of evolutionary theory; a failure to recognize the importance of the difference between laboratory conditions in universities and the usual conditions of infant life; and, finally, a general neglect of the fact that developmentalists, and the majority of their subjects, live in a state of affluence to which most of the world's population can only aspire (40 per cent of human beings live 'below the poverty line'.)[36]

1 The majority of developmentalists subscribe to the view that their findings are compatible with evolutionary theory. But they also assume that to have evolved is to be adapted. Thus Piaget's central tenet is that the growth of intelligence must be seen as a biological adaptation which fits the organism increasingly effectively and harmoniously with the environment: 'there is no organizing function, at whatever level, that does not harmonize with the environment'.[37] Likewise, Bowlby and Ainsworth see attachments as a set of successful biological adaptations to the problem of rearing the almost helpless human infant. Similar arguments are legion in the developmental literature. For example, the Gibsons' theory of affordances depends on the notion of an evolutionarily assured 'dovetailing' of perceiver with the world.[38] Or consider Klaus and Kennell's rationale for the existence of 'bonding' (see below).[39]

These arguments may be taken to imply both that the form of all biological features is determined by natural selection *and* that natural selection inevitably ensures a harmonious fit between organism and environment. This implication is mistaken. Darwin himself insisted that survival of the fittest was only one amongst a number of selective principles. In his view, many biological features appear maladaptive or irrelevant in terms of fit between phenotype and surroundings (e.g. the panda's thumb). It was this maladaptiveness that led him to pay so much attention to sexual selection (e.g. the pheasant's tail). He also pointed out that some of the most remarkable biological adaptations are far from optimal in design.[40] Since Darwin's time, other non-adaptive principles of selection have been documented, in particular, genetic drift.

Gould and Lewontin make these points and another, which has particular reference to the human brain. They argue that natural selection may produce a feature such as a large brain for only one adaptive reason (e.g. the promotion of bipedalism). But that single change may have a variety of 'non-adaptive sequelae' – such as foreknowledge of death or a heightened susceptibility to anxiety. There is thus no guarantee that all features of mentality are adaptive.

Furthermore, there is the problem of environmental changes outstripping previously adaptive behaviours, as presumably happened to all extinct species and is maybe happening to humanity. That evolution does not naturally guarantee psychological harmony has been empirically shown in studies of rejections within infant–mother pairs of rhesus monkeys.[41] Thus *it is an error to suppose that infants must, as a consequence of evolution, normally live in harmony with their minders and environment or that any particular behaviour or feature of mental life must be adaptive.*

2 Much experimental work on infancy takes place *in vitro* – on the social equivalent of a desert island.[42] Whilst the subjects' relations with experimenters and to the laboratory are crucial in determining how mothers and infants behave in experiments, these transient relations can only bear tangentially on the factors governing normal social conditions. Different adults apparently behave in similar ways in the laboratory (e.g. producing the same kind of babytalk – what Kaye calls 'all pretty words and no sense'), yet there is no way for most studies to represent the different anxieties, responsibilities, standards of living, demands of other children, interpersonal relationships and work commitments which usually shape the lives of parents, and hence of their children. Many studies focus only on well-educated, middle-class mothers with small families. Yet when consistencies in behavioural development are sought, the economic or educational status of families accounts for almost all the consistencies over time that can be found in the behaviours of different infant–mother pairs (see pp. 163–6 below). This suggests that the important factors in child development are the ones which operate *outside* the laboratory.

An illustration of the difficulties implied by these findings can be taken from Kaye's work. In comparing father–infant with mother–infant interaction, Kaye writes that 'the principal conclusion from a

Plate 9.1 The impact of sexism on development. The babies in this picture are two-year-old twins, both raised at home. The picture was taken in a nutritional rehabilitation centre in southern India. The difference in their condition is entirely due to the fact that the boy was nursed and fed first, his sister getting what was left over. Even here in the clinic, it is the crying boy, not the apathetic little girl, who gets all the attention.
Source: UNICEF/Photo/Balcomb.

large number of studies is that fathers interact with babies pretty much as mothers do.'[43] But when field-work is done it is found that men have considerably less to do with babies than mothers, one study showing that working fathers take outright responsibility for their children for only one hour per week on average whereas the corresponding figure for working mothers is forty hours.[44] And, per unit time of child-care, fathers are considerably less involved with nappy-changing and feeding whilst playing more and being more violent to their babies than mothers.[45] Yet factors relating to these differences do not show up in any of the laboratory-based studies that Kaye reviews.

3 The final criticism of the 'pleasant garden' vision of infants' environments is obvious. Infant and maternal mortality in many countries is still at a level worse than that of Victorian England at its worst (15 per cent of babies dying in their first year).[46] Disease, poverty and starvation are rife in three continents. Forty-one per cent of all children under fifteen do not have access to clean water.[47] Even in highly developed countries such as the USA and the UK, infant mortality and the poverty in which children live is currently increasing.[48] For example, over the last decade in Australia, the 'lucky country', the number of children living below the poverty line has doubled.[49] But these are only the most obvious indices. Domestic violence continues, marriages break up, war's rage on, prescriptions for tranquillizers and stress-related diseases run at record levels. This is not to mention the symptoms of smaller-scale tensions and disagreements which are a feature of any social arrangement and which colour the life-patterns of all children.

Whilst it is true that a great deal of work has been done on such topics as the relation between infant malnutrition and psychological development, the physical and sexual abuse of children, parental depression and early interaction and on family dynamics and development, this work is seldom considered as relevant to the kind of scientific theories discussed in this book.[50] The assumption is that *normally* all goes well. Hence general theories of infancy are constructed which glibly forget the political and psychological dynamics which routinely produce depression, poverty, war, parental frustration and irrationality as these affect little children.

Mothers as Secondary

The Bible tells us that God created Adam. Only later did he conceive Eve. Babies too may well be wrapped up at first in their own worlds and only later establish a love-relationship with 'the mother'. But this does not mean that we should follow the assumptions of contemporary cognitive psychology of infancy where the baby is considered to be of primary importance in the explanation of its own development.

In Chomsky, the mother's babytalk to the child is 'degenerate' and of little help to the child for constructing grammatical utterances. In the work of post-Piagetians, the idiosyncratic aims of the 'others' interacting with babies throughout any given experiment are given no place in subsequent descriptions of development: psychologists have literally pared the social environment out of existence when analysing the passage of exchanges between themselves and their infant subjects which makes up each study. For Piaget, this neglect of personal processes might be justifiable on theoretical grounds in the case of the infant, who is supposed to be unable to distinguish people from things until nine months. But it can hardly be justified on grounds of the mother, nor on methodological grounds, grounds of which the 'counter-transference' (the researchers' attitude to their subjects) is always a crucial part.

This neglect of the social environment in describing infant development is in a peculiar way even sanctioned by those scientists of infancy who do discuss the environment in the shape of 'the mother'. For scientists have generally assumed that they *already* know how to explain what it is to be a mother. Motherly devotion is simply instinctive for women when they bear children, something guaranteed by evolution.

The case of 'bonding'

A recent version of this idea is the 'bonding' hypothesis, advanced by two American paediatricians Marshall Klaus and John Kennell in 1976.[39] Drawing on an analogy with certain herd-living animals, such as elk and goats, they have suggested that there is a very short sensitive period after birth during which mothers are in a special state which makes them more than usually ready to fall in love with their child. They argued that if the mother was not given skin-to-skin contact with her baby during this period, the mother would remain distant from her child and dire consequences would follow: physical abuse, abandonment and 'failure to thrive' in the baby. Their argument was of particular concern because it was common practice in many hospitals to separate babies from their mothers for a number of hours after birth, at precisely the time when bonding is supposed to take place. Klaus and Kennell reported research which they claimed to support the idea of bonding.

But when mothers who had had a chance to bond with their babies were compared with mothers who had not had such a chance, observers who did not know which type of mother was which (Klaus & Kennell neglected the importance of this control) could distinguish no consistent differences in the attitudes of the two groups to their babies.[51] The bonding hypothesis is hence a myth, though a myth that fully accords with tendencies for men to argue that women are better fitted than themselves to rear small babies, and to see a lack of mother-love as the main cause of children's problems.

The case of 'symbiosis'

Versions of the same myth abound in current scientific literature. Researchers do not refer to care and deprivation but to 'maternal' care and 'maternal' deprivation.[52] Indeed there is a long-standing tradition that treats this merging as a fact of life. Thus, just as Eve is supposed to have been created as a helpmate for Adam, so many scientists describe the early relationship between baby and mother as one of psychological 'symbiosis', or in terms which suggest that the mother's mentality is essentially subordinate to the needs of her child.

Symbiosis is a term which biologists use to describe an association of organisms which live attached to each other and contribute to each other's support. An example is the arrangement between life-cycles of *Rhizobia*, nitrogen-fixing bacteria, and certain leguminous, pea-bearing plants. These little creatures infect the hairs on the roots of the pea and form nodules, supported by carbohydrates in the plant's circulatory system. Simultaneously, the plant flourishes because *Rhizobia* absorb nitrogen gas from the air and turn it into forms of ammonia that become the nitrates essential for plant-growth.[53] Similarly, we human beings support bacteria in our guts which in return help us to break down and absorb what we eat. René Spitz extends the metaphor of symbiosis as follows:

> When the infant experiences a need, it will provoke in him an affect that will lead to behavioural changes, which in their turn provoke an affective response and its concomitant attitude in the mother; she behaves 'as if she understood' what particular need of the infant causes his affective manifestation.[54]

Spitz described the relationship between infant and mother as 'reciprocal' on this score. Following him, John Shotter writes that mother–infant interactions have the character of a *mutuality* in which: 'one individual responds in an immediate and unconsidered manner as a result of the way he [*sic*] apprehends the immediate and unconsidered reaction of the other individual to him.'[55] (A similar idea is implied in Bowlby's and Ainsworth's attachment theories).

Such scientists believe that early symbiosis is all-important for the development of independence: what is first managed by mother and baby together (the gratification of needs, the avoidance of danger, the observance of social regulations, the use of objects) must later be achieved by the child alone.

There are two problems with notions like psychological symbiosis as a representation of maternal thinking. First, the idea that mothers respond to babies in an 'immediate and unconsidered manner' is clearly not true. Picture, for example, a mother who is woken by her baby crying.[56] Such a mother will doubtlessly consider, however briefly, whether or not she should go to her child. Is the crying serious? Should it be ignored? Is the baby hungry? Should the father do the honours? What does Dr Spock or Penelope Leach say? Whatever the mother's response is, it will not be immediate from an analytic point of view.

Secondly the idea that the mother–infant relationship is *reciprocal*, which is central to the biological definition of symbiosis, stands no scrutiny. Babies depend on their adult minders in a way which is wholly absent in the adult relationship to the baby. Adults nurse babies. Babies cannot nurse adults. Indeed, if we wanted to find a biological parallel for the mother–infant bond, a better image would be of the baby as a parasite: 'an animal or plant which lives in or upon another organism and draws its nutrient directly from it'.[57]

The case of 'mirroring'

An extension of the idea of 'psychological symbiosis' in scientific discussion about mothers and babies is when the mother is seen as the *mirror* of her baby's development. A popular expression of this idea was published in English in 1967 by D. W. Winnicott.[58]

Winnicott set off from a literal 'chronological' reading of Lacan's famous paper on the Mirror Stage of consciousness. How, he asked, are we to understand the normal emotional development of the blind if it is mirrors *as such* that play the crucial role in early mental growth? Surely it is the mother herself who adopts a 'mirror-role' in interacting with the newborn baby so that her face, her voice and her actions reflect back the baby's own expressions and mental states?

Whilst it may seem improbable that adults could ever immediately and unconsciously tune in to babies' demands, Winnicott argued that such a response in matters was normally ensured by nature. During the late stages of pregnancy, mothers enter a state like a temporary mental illness which Winnicott called 'primary maternal preoccupation'.[59] The mother's concern for her baby will have gradually developed since conception and by birth become a state of heightened sensitivity through identification with the baby which lasts in its most acute form a month or more after the baby is born. This

> gives the mother her special ability to do the right thing. She knows what the baby could be feeling like. No one else knows. Doctors and nurses may know a lot about psychology, and of course they know all about body health and disease. But they do not know what a baby feels like from minute to minute because they are outside this area of experience.[60]

Whenever the mother has mentally identified with the baby, she becomes merged with it, her expressions reflect back the baby's mood to the baby: 'What does the baby see when he or she looks at the mother's face? I am suggesting that, ordinarily, what the baby sees is himself or herself. In other words the mother is looking at the baby and *what she looks like is related to what she sees there.*'[61] The same kind of maternal concern can be reflected in the way she talks to, holds, handles and otherwise presents the world to her baby.

Winnicott's equation between mother and mirror has been enthusiastically taken up in studies of maternal speech during early language learning.[62] A variety of researchers have shown that so-called 'motherese' is far from being disorganized or the 'degenerate input' which Chomsky imagined to inundate the child. Thus, whilst apparently talking nonsense, the baby's elders both verbally and non-verbally interpret their child's moods and behaviours in a way which is made regular for the child. For example, statements like 'You're not looking very happy', 'What a nice smile', or 'You've got your hand in the air' may be accompanied by a pantomime of gestures and intonation which mirror the most recent actions of the child. When the verbal content of mothers' speech to two-month-olds is analysed, as many as four words out of five may refer to the baby's name, body or mental state.

Such other-centredness as observed in the laboratory cannot be taken to typify the whole mother–child relation or to be naturally true of all mothers. That the way babies are spoken to by their elders can be socially shaped is shown by cross-cultural research.

In Western Samoa, for example, babies are primarily looked after by an elder sibling, not the mother. This arrangement means that Samoan babies do not experience the same kind of mother's speech as found in the USA:

> A child exhibiting some distress – wet diapers, hunger, thirst, etc. – may express this information to her mother. However, typically the mother does not then respond directly to the child. Rather, the mother will turn to an older sibling of the child who is responsible

for active care and will direct that sibling to respond to the child's distress. At that point the sibling responds verbally or non-verbally directly to the child. . . Samoan children usually do not expect a direct verbal response to a notification of their needs. Indeed, under certain circumstances, such as when the mother is talking to another adult, the child learns to expect no response at all from the mother.[63]

To sum up, 'mirroring', 'symbiosis', 'bonding' and 'maternal instinct' are all ways of imagining that the baby's and the mother's aims are the same after birth. They are concepts that allow scientists to banish mothers' own experiences of difficulties in understanding and looking after babies from the analysis of infancy.[64] Shotter has recently elevated this banishment to be a methodological principle in infant research:

> the scientist's task is *not to render the actual experience of mothers explicit*, but to give an account (a) of how 'things-are-thought-to-be' for the proper development of a child in our community, *and* (b) of how 'things-must-be-if-personhood-is-to-be-achieved'.[65] [Shotter's emphasis]

For example, in discussing a mother who slaps her child, it is possible for psychologists 'to give a much fuller account (than the mother) of why she laid her hand violently upon the flesh of her child – *the* reason for *her* reason in fact [Shotter's emphasis]'.[66] (This attitude to mothers is strangely at odds with his general stance: 'as professional academics our task is . . . to produce accounts of how persons account to themselves for themselves.[67])

Blaming the Mother

To remove feminine experience from the primary description of infancy is to open the door to what have been called mother-blaming (*mal de mère*) accounts of individual development. Thus, just as God created Adam and then a woman helper whose actions led to his exile from paradise, so the mother is at first excluded from the description of infancy, to be brought in at a later date. As with Eve, it is usually only when early development goes wrong that mothers become the centre of psychological and medical attention (see p. 144 above). The assumption is that mothers naturally devote themselves to their babies eight days a week. A mother who does not so devote herself is unnatural, unloving or otherwise 'disturbed'.

A hint of this view is to be found in Winnicott's discussion of babies' excretions:

> Perhaps there is a whimpering sound by which the mother knows that if she comes quickly she may be able to attend personally to a

motion which otherwise becomes just a wasted mess. This is the very beginning of co-operation and social sense, and is worth all the trouble it involves. How many children who wet the bed for some years after they could get up, and save a lot of washing, are going back in the night to their infancy, trying to go over their experience again, trying to find and correct something that was missing. The thing missing in that case was the mother's sensitive attention to signals of excitement or distress which would have enabled her to make personal and good what otherwise had to be wasted, because there was no one to participate in what happened.[68]

In this quotation Winnicott's image of a mother is the familiar one of a 'symbiotic' woman who should be attentive night and day to her child's every sound and movement. But this image is combined with the assumption that most 'difficult' children owe their difficulties to the way in which they have been cared for by their mothers. That such 'mother-blaming' is general in child psychology is confirmed by surveys of leading psychological journals which discuss case-studies of individual children with problems.[69]

But ideas that mothers *cause* the problems of their children would only be tenable if there were strong evidence to show that early traumas have predictable effects later in life. Researchers seeking such effects have generally failed to produce this evidence.

As discussed in chapter 7, much of the appeal of attachment theory is based on the belief that it explains why insufficient maternal care leads to delinquency, deviance and other developmental difficulties later in life. Likewise, the proponents of mother–infant bonding argue that an early interruption of what they see as the process that emotionally cements mother to child has dire consequences for later mental growth. Subsequent research has only supported these claims, however, where the supposedly detrimental events occur against a background of continuously inadequate rearing conditions. Other researchers have encountered similar difficulties in finding any definite developmental consequences of differences in early infant–mother interaction which are not to be explained by general differences in social class, educational level of parents or ethnic member-ship.[70]

These difficulties lead us to a general problem which is fundamental to research on babies. For, from Darwin and Freud onwards, the earliest period of life has been assumed to be the most vulnerable to experience which will fix the subsequent shape of an individual's psychological growth. But a great variety of research on developmental effects shows that early experience may predispose an infant to later problems, but it is what is broadly called 'the caretaking environment' which determines the eventual outcome. For example, even babies having the most obvious of early traumas, such as being born substantially pre-term or suffering quite serious neonatal illness, have very different developmental outcomes depending on home circumstances. It is only a short step from this kind of finding to the conclusion that it is the care-giver's position, rather than the baby's mental make-up, that is central to any explanation of early development. This implies that the study of children must be premissed upon a prior understanding of the adults who control their upbringing. As Wundt said: 'It is an error to hold, as is sometimes held, that the mental life of adults can never be understood except through analysis of the child's mind. The exact opposite is the case.'[71]

As Wundt's remark suggests most researchers into infant cognition fail to base their formulations on a careful enough empirical investigation of the normal dynamics of maternal experience and the ways in which housing conditions, sexual relationships, wealth and other social vectors impinge upon the lives of those who look after babies. Psychologists such as Winnicott, Bowlby, Ainsworth, Klaus and Kennell simply *assume* that mothers are naturally and primarily devoted to their children.

Yet, when the necessary empirical work is done, mothers are found to have a very ambivalent relationship with their young. For example, Ann Oakley reports interviews with fifty-five first-time mothers, finding that the birth of a child often meant a deterioration in the relationship between the child's parents (which may have effects on the child) and that most mothers felt that the losses were far greater than the gains in early motherhood.[72] Brown and Harris's (1978) study of women in inner London found that the three best predictors of depression were marriage,

Table 9.1 Loss versus gain in early maternal care

Mothers' reactions	% of sample
Not interested in in the baby at birth	70
Disappointed with baby's sex	25
Babycare harder work than expected	77
Felt angry/violent towards baby	70
Cannot get enough sleep	100
Feeding problems	73
Felt very anxious about baby	45

$N = 55$.

This table shows responses of 55 first-time mothers to questions about the impact of childbirth.
Source: Ann Oakley, *Women Confined*.

low socio-economic status and primary responsibility for children under the age of five. Of people who fulfilled all three criteria, one fifth were seriously or 'clinically' depressed.[73]

Studies of those who are yet to bear children show that the aims of would-be parents are also diverse and confused. When asked, the men and women interviewed by Joan Busfield said that their aims in having children were as often to do with making their own marriage work as with any intrinsic pleasure expected from child-rearing.[74] When the motives and plans of potential mothers are investigated at length, deep contradictions are revealed in their attitudes to family life.

For the female academic researchers studied by Jane Selby, family-life posed a dreaded curtailment of independence and opportunity as well as an attractive alternative to the stresses of, for example, being the only woman in a laboratory of unsympathetic men or an isolated worker in a library.[75] For the working-class sixteen-year-old girls interviewed by Shirley Prendergast and Alan Prout, there was a clear conflict between a realistic vision of their mothers as leading unenviable, depressed, unrewarded lives and the public, sentimental vision of motherhood as the woman's only fulfilling vocation.[76] And the working-class eight-year-old girls, whose fascinating story *The Tidy House* and related discussions are analysed by Carolyn Steedman, reveal a similar awareness of the contradictions of motherhood, 'the getting and regretting of children'.[77]

In this light 'symbiosis', 'bonding' or 'mirroring' are certainly not sufficient characterizations of normal women's relationships with infants. Far from being the 'natural' consequence of evolution, a self-denying attention to babies, as witnessed by doctors or specifically in the infant–mother interactions filmed by psychologists, may be an anxious reaction on the mother's part, either short-term or long-standing, to the immediate circumstances of the mother's life: an attempt to convince herself or those who are watching her that motherhood is worthwhile or that she is good at it. And, by calling parental devotion 'natural', its status as an achievement itself standing in need of explanation is lost.

Feminist research puts in perspective any idea that babies recognize and share the goals and intentions of the women who look after them. The kinds of intention at issue in most psychological research on mental sharing are filling in a simple jig-saw puzzle or naming a doggie in a picture-book. To describe these tiny pieces of the mosaic that makes up a mother's psychic life as intrinsic to the woman's main goals is both to belittle and to misunderstand that life. Far more likely the game-playing and indulgent verbal nonsense by which psychologists characterize 'normal mothering', when they do occur at home, are parts of maternal management strategies with complex motivations of which the baby can have even less idea than psycholoigists seem to.

Plate 9.2 Shared mental states? The naive smile of a child shows that it is oblivious of the despair shown in its mother's face and her surroundings of abject poverty in Bangladesh.
Source: UNICEF/Bernard P. Wolff.

Sara Ruddick's exploratory essay 'Maternal Thinking' investigates these strategies. Amongst those most relevant to the 'mirroring' behaviour scientists see in experiments on early infant–mother interactions is her description of a humble or obedient maternal attitude she identifies with a 'cheery denial' of the woman's own desires and thoughts. She argues that the mental processes of mothers are thus quite different from those of scientists, for whom prediction and control are central aims.[78]

The 'Innocence' of Science

The aim of this chapter has been to show that, whilst seeming at most marginal, the equation between infancy and Eden may be linked to a powerful logic in scientific research on babies. The Genesis stories of Adam and Eve do indeed parallel scientific stories of infancy: accentuating the positive side of babyhood at the expense of the negative, treating the mental states of babies as if they were much like those of the scientists who study them, ignoring the impoverished conditions in which most babies are reared when devising theories of infancy, and relegating the conditions and experience of women to a secondary place in the analysis of babyhood – except where women are deemed to be at fault for the difficulties of their children.

It is important to note that there are large numbers of psychologists and other scientists who have spent much effort in criticizing the kind of theory criticized here or in demonstrating the importance of the kinds of behaviour and circumstance which these theories ignore. Nevertheless it is clearly also important to recognize that such major post-war investigators of infancy as Piaget, Chomsky and Bowlby, not to mention many lesser lights, have advanced ideas about babies which accord in one way or another with the beatific vision.[79]

Why should this, be? Two kinds of answer seem appropriate. First, historians have suggested that the modern interest in babies is at least partly structured by social conditions, the rise of a 'language of pronatalism' or of increased 'cultural despair' since the Second World War.[80] Secondly, and not incompatible with such historical conditioning, the thinking of scientists which lets us see infancy as paradise must be afflicted by a kind of irrationality which allows them to think as they do – and, presumably afflicts us too.[81] A critical analysis of this blighted kind of reasoning was made by William Blake towards the end of the eighteenth century.

Blake's analysis

In this connection, Blake published a now famous book of illustrated poems, *Songs of Innocence* in 1789.[82] The poems were about animals and young children. Despite their simplicity, these songs were not naive. They were written to parody and reveal a hidden 'state of the human soul'. For Blake, the state of 'innocence' is one in which the existence of pain and cruelty are denied, in which everything ends 'happily ever after'. The 'innocent' adult retreats from confronting the harsh realities of life. So, in *Songs of Innocence*, we are given a series of apparently happy verses in which the world seems at peace with itself, in which children are surrounded by sympathy, in which the lessons of religion are true and infancy is bliss. But these images are not quite what they seem. Witness Blake's song called 'The Blossom':[83]

> Merry, Merry Sparrow!
> Under leaves so green
> A happy Blossom

Sees you swift as arrow
Seeks your cradle narrow
Near my Bosom.

Pretty, Pretty Robin!
Under leaves so green
A happy Blossom
Hears you sobbing, sobbing
Pretty, Pretty Robin,
Near my Bosom.

The scene is delightful and tenderly described. But the sobbing of the robin goes on, despite the joys of the self-deceiving blossom and the nearness of the singer's bosom.

The sequel to *Songs of Innocence* was published in 1795. *Songs of Experience* illustrate a very different 'state of the soul'. Here the singer is only too well aware of the ills which surround him: the hypocrisy of the church, child prostitution, the heartlessness of fathers, sickness and poverty. Here infancy is not a time of joy but of sorrow and when the nurse remembers the days of her youth, her face 'turns green and pale'.

But Blake's analysis goes beyond this bitter evaluation. He is concerned to transcend the social, sexual and spiritual conditions which produce the ills of the world in which he lives. And, as his late work *For the Sexes: the Gates of Paradise* (1819) makes clear, he believed that the first barrier to such transcendence is innocence of what he calls 'thy mother's grief'.

The etching illustrating the first key to the *Gates of Paradise* depicts a sleeping baby in a chrysalis on a white leaf above which hangs another leaf, a black leaf, hiding a caterpillar. The chrysalis symbolizes the possibility of spiritual transformation – the soul being traditionally represented as a butterfly. Of the parasitic caterpillar-worm which diminishes the life of the plant that supports it, Blake writes:

> The Caterpillar on the Leaf
> Reminds thee of thy Mother's Grief.[84]

In Blake's terms, the attitude to infancy that this chapter has sketched is 'innocent'. But to move beyond innocence it is not sufficient simply to stress the negativities of early childhood and of mothering, although these must clearly be acknowledged. Rather it is necessary to imagine a different kind of developmental science, what Ault has called in his commentary on Blake, a 'visionary physics' of the human spirit.[85] The primary aim of this physics would not be to find out about babies and how they develop. It would be to develop and transform the lives, the understanding, the visions, of those who care to ask questions about babies. This aim, which we saw in chapter 4 to have been shadowed forth

Figure 9.1 Blake's etching from *The Gates of Paradise*.
Source: Tate Gallery.

in Lacan's reading of Freud, has been taken up during the past decade by psychologists interested not simply in how humans behave, but in how humans interpret the meaning of others' behaviours, adopting the *hermeneutic* or interpretative method. This method defines the 'new paradigm' in psychology, to which we will return in the final chapter.[86]

Summary

One of the most common debates amongst those who comment on academic life concerns the scientific status of psychology. Can psychology be a science, like physics or biology? Can psychologists overcome the apparent contradiction in studying subjective things like emotions and beliefs in an objective way, without expressing their own emotions and beliefs, by adopting carefully controlled methods of observation? Can facts about mental life 'speak for themselves', without being coloured by the outlook of those who collect them? Or must psychology always be a subjective discipline, like literary criticism or law, where the investigator always uses evidence to advocate a particular point of view, a particular vision of the events under discussion, a vision selected from a range of possible visions?

Answers to these questions are usually given on logical grounds and in general philosophical terms. On one side it is argued that psychology will only make a genuine contribution to knowledge if human actions are viewed simply as physical phenomena, as movements which can be measured, counted and controlled. Any appeal to the mental states supposedly inspiring these movements, wants, choices, beliefs, fantasies or plans, is not only unscientific but irrelevant to the explanation of human behaviour (e.g. behaviourism). Others reply that unless psychologists find a way of studying mental states as such, of recognizing that the proper topic of psychology is mental life or states of consciousness, then their work cannot be called psychology. And the only way of studying mental states is subjectively, because humans can only discover the mental states of others by comparing them with and using their own perceptions.

This chapter goes a step beyond these arguments in principle. It shows that even when scientists do control their observations of babies with the utmost care, their findings favour one amongst many possible moral perceptions of infancy. My aim has not been to question particular findings about babies, to cast doubt on the existence of the behaviours that babies are reported to exhibit. My aim has been to show that when the details of 'objective' research on babies are reviewed, they may form themselves into a value-laden picture of the beginnings of human life, albeit without the conscious design of the investigators themselves. At the heart of this picture is an image of innocence, the harmonious image of madonna and child, 'meek and mild', as in a Christmas card.

I argue that the vision of infancy as bliss can only be maintained if scientists condone a selective blindness to the negative aspects of babyhood, aspects which emerge all too quickly once one considers as a whole the daily life of babies and those who look after them. I make this argument in order to sketch an alternative vision of infancy – as a struggle to transcend ambivalence. But I do not want to stop at this point, implying simply that the vision of infancy as a struggle is true whereas the paradisal image is false. My aim has been to demonstrate that *whatever* facts about babies one chooses to discuss, these facts will always imply a subjective evaluation of infancy.

I am concerned to tackle the bias of scientific research on infancy because the vision of human development I draw out undermines the serious consideration by scientists and politicians of the need to improve provisions for child-care. If infancy, in the average expectable environment, is naturally guaranteed to be bliss, what need is there for subsidized creches and kindergartens? And if, for certain individuals, infancy turns out to be hellish, then that must be the result of individual abnormalities, a case for special treatment, not symptomatic of a general malaise.

Finally, this chapter questions the way in which scientific research on babies (and, by extension, on any group of human beings) should be read. When we read, for example, that humans are capable of communication at eight weeks of age or have formed their most profound love-relationship by nine months or spend the earliest period of infancy in a state of psychological symbiosis with their mothers, we should not only ask 'Do the behaviours reported in this study support the stated conclusion?' but also, 'What vision of infancy and of child care does this conclusion imply?' In this respect, the science of babies is no different from any other form of literature about children. For the science of babies does not exist in a moral vacuum and research on infancy is always coloured by moral concerns.[87]

Further Reading

War in the Nursery: Theories of the Child and Mother by D. Riley (Virago, London, 1983) places research on infancy from the 1880s to the present day in the context of political and intellectual debates about child care. Riley focuses particularly on changing opinions and practices surrounding child-care before, during and after the Second World War and their links with the rise of 'academic' theories of early development such as attachment theory.

Women Confined: Towards a Sociology of Childbirth by A. Oakley (Robertson, Oxford, 1980) is a pioneering investigation of fifty-five women's responses to the birth of their first children. Oakley's work explicitly questions assumptions that mothers naturally form an unambivalent attachment to babies.

The Image of Childhood by P. Coveney (Penguin, Harmondsworth, 1967) surveys the ways in which the child has been portrayed in literature through a wide range of authors, from Blake and Wordsworth to Woolf and Joyce. Coveney suggests that authors' attitudes to children are inseparable from their attitude to life in general and from the literary sensibility of their age.

Centuries of Childhood by P. Aries (Penguin, Harmondsworth, 1973) argues that modern conceptions of children would be completely foreign to people living in the sixteenth century. Whilst Aries's book has been challenged on historical grounds, it has encouraged modern readers to recognize that contemporary ideas of childhood may be largely constituted by the spirit of the age in which we live.

The Child and Other Cultural Inventions edited by F. S. Keisel and A. W. Siegel (Praeger, New York, 1983) is a collection of papers from a symposium debating the hypothesis that the way in which adults, including child psychologists, conceive of 'the child' is socially constructed. The papers consider a wide range of uses, including methodology, cultural and historical differences, theory-construction, the moral dimension of psychological research and fathering. Verbatim transcriptions of the symposium's discussions add a lively and humorous dimension to the book.

Critical Theories of Psychological Development edited by J. M. Broughton (Plenum, New York, 1987) contains a variety of chapters questioning the way in which psychologists construe development. Particularly relevant are the editor's introduction, Adrienne Harris's chapter on 'The rationalization of infancy' and David Ingleby's exploration of the connection between 'Psycho-analysis and ideology'.

10

Psychology as Advocacy

The behaviour of the infant is so ambiguous it is easy for the culture's beliefs about human nature to influence observers' interpretations of what they think they see.

Jerome Kagan, *The Nature of the Child*

The legendary poet Simonides is said once to have been the sole survivor of a sumptuous banquet held in Thessaly. Having incurred the wrath of the gods, Scopas, the host, and the other guests were all crushed when the roof collapsed on them. Their corpses were so unrecognizably mangled that Simonides was asked by the bereaved kin if he could tell them who was who. This he did by remembering the places at which everyone had been sitting. As a result, he discovered that orderly arrangement in space is essential to good memory.[1]

In later times an art of remembering grew up which was based on Simonides' discovery. This art is known to have been used in the training of Roman orators. Students of oratory were taught to get to know an imposing temple, mansion or theatre in which they selected a sequence of stations – an altar, a window, stairs, and so on. The students were then taught to form vivid images representing the things they wished to recall; a burning child on the altar, an ebony urn thrown through the window, a purple dog leaping up the stairs; each image being assigned to a place in the well-known building. When holding forth, orators would walk through the building in their mind's eye, remembering in order the images which denoted the things they wished to say. As Cicero described it, the places were like a waxen writing-tablet, and the images were like letters scratched on the wax.

More recently, parallels between the genesis of mental activity and writing came to be drawn in a rather different 'longitudinal' way. In Cicero, the metaphor of writing on wax was used to characterize a trained act of the imagination necessary for oratory. But, by 1596 (after the invention of the printing press), philosophical theologians were arguing as follows:

> Angels already have full and complete knowledge in the highest degree that can be imparted into them; men, if we view them in their spring, are at the first without understanding or knowledge at all. Nevertheless from this utter vacuity they grow by degrees, till they come at length to be even as the Angels themselves are. . . The soul of man being therefore at first as a book, wherein nothing is and yet all things may be imprinted.[2]

Or, more laconically, a hundred years later: 'The Mind of Man is, at first (if you will pardon the Expression) like a *Tabula rasa*; or like Wax, which while it is soft, is capable of any Impression, until Time hath hardened it.'[3]

One consequence of this generalization of the *tabula rasa* metaphor to the process of mental formation as occurring across the individual's biological life span is that the importance of temporal planning and active imagination has its place taken by a more passive, hidden, almost mechanical stamping of experience by/from the world on to the mind of a single growing individual.[4] No longer is it the orator who is taught to write on wax; now the wax is the mind and 'things' are passively imprinted in it.

It is this more general, passive sense of the metaphor that has been taken up in modern texts introducing students to the study of child development. Hence, in the so-called 'nature–nurture' controversy, the champions of nurture argue that children develop through the influence of the external environment on the blank mind of an 'infinitely receptive student'.[5] This is often taken to be the view of behaviourists such as Watson and Skinner. Against them, 'nativists' such as Chomsky and Bower argue that the individual's most important characteristics vis-à-vis the analysis of intelligence or language result from a chemically-endowed inheritance laid down at the marriage of sperm with egg, without reference to external imprinting or personal experience.

Neither the 'nature' nor the 'nurture' view fits well into the study of child development. In by-passing the need to describe personal states of consciousness (or experience) in their explanation of human faculties, nativists ignore what James calls the most fundamental of all the postulates of psychology, that psychology is the study of states of consciousness.[6] And to call the child an 'infinitely receptive student' or utterly empty is clearly at odds with the common experience of teachers and children. Indeed, when read carefully, no scientist, not even the most passionate believer in the shaping power of environmental influences, can be said to claim that a baby's behaviour or mental condition is a *tabula rasa* at birth. At the very least, the infant's world is of significance to itself in ways no scientist can dismiss – for example, in that hunger or pain is distressing.

On the other hand, *from the scientist's point of view*, infancy is very much an empty book or memory theatre in which a great and conflicting variety of things may be said about the basis of human nature. To use the words of Clarke-Stewart, infancy gives us a 'natural museum' in which a multitude of scientific exhibits can be mounted (see p. 11). Babies provide scientists with what is almost a *carte blanche* to speechify about the fundamentals of psychological change.

So, what kind of speech is that of the science which speaks of babies? It is speech that looks for a beginning, an origin of the faculties of the mind. It is speech claiming to report a practice of observation which produces evidence that the mind begins as the scientist says it begins and so seems to verify the plausibility of a certain way of thinking about the mind. Yet there is no consensus about how to think about babies. The only agreement is that the discussion of infancy is somehow crucial in order to give theoretical speculations about adulthood a firm basis in fact. Tacitly, scientists agree to differ. A common 'factual basis' is more apparent than real, each scientist drawing upon different and sometimes conflicting findings. The scientific value of observing babies is *rhetorical*. It allows scientists to draw conclusions that they would not otherwise be able to draw.

The question must be asked whether observations of babies can ever lead us to understand the psychological origin of the relationship between human individuals and their world. Is the kind of developmental history which the study of children implies, taking as its model the biological life-cycle, the kind of history which answers fundamental questions about adult consciousness and experience? Most of the scientists whose work has been reviewed in this book would answer 'yes' to both these questions.

Yet there is another approach to the study of human experience which can represent the temporality of consciousness without necessary recourse to the study of childhood. In this new 'hermeneutical' paradigm of the discipline, consciousness is not deemed to have its definitive beginning in infancy. Although it is true that young children must 'become conscious', they do not become conscious of themselves or of the world in any one permanent way, and the way in which they attain consciousness is not fundamentally different from the way in which adults become conscious of things and issues in their world.

This recognition has the effect of reversing the way in which scientific investigations of infancy are read. The science of babies is no longer to be seen as 'discovering' the ways in which babies become conscious of the world. The science of babies reveals first and foremost the way in which scientists become conscious of babies. This is to recognize that science is a form of literature and its language does not transparently 'report' facts about the world but actively constitutes and interprets understandings of reality. As Heidegger remarks, 'Language is the house of Being'. And the language of the science of babies primarily houses the Being of those who devise and use it, namely scientists, not the Being of those whom that language is ostensibly 'about' (namely babies).[7]

Hence, this book questions what the study of infants can tell us about human development. It discusses contributors to developmental psychology who, by any standards, would be considered leading figures in their field. But it consistently draws links between what key scientists have said about babies and their broader intellectual concerns, to underline the rhetorical quality of the science of babies. It also suggests that there is an intrinsic, albeit often unacknowledged, ambiguity in infant behaviour: 'the facts' about babies do not come painted with ready-made significances.[8] Hence, in order to formulate general statements about early development, a certain amount of violence must be done to reduce ambiguity to order. The examination in chapter 9 of the scientific vision of infancy as paradise was an exploration into this kind of interpretive violence.

What I have wanted to make clear is that the study of human development, as epitomized by the science of babies, is the result of a choice about how to view child psychology as a discipline. Most researchers have chosen to see human development as a natural process, much like the growth of an animal or plant. Just as an apple grows into a tree or a tadpole becomes a frog, so babies grow into mature human beings. Under this conception, each species will have its own peculiarities and be governed by its own laws of growth: the developmental psychologist's job is to observe humans growing and deduce the laws governing our development. According to this view, the scientist's own preoccupations and states of mind should be kept altogether out of the investigation in order to preserve her or his objectivity in recording what she or he sees.

Set against the view of developmental psychology as a branch of biology are those who argue the ethical issues bound up with research on children are crucial to the psychological analysis of human development.[9] In this view, the meaning of behaviour cannot simply be *seen*, for behaviour is ambiguous and needs interpretation. It would be a contradiction in terms to say that human researchers should not become personally involved in their research. On the contrary, it is precisely this involvement that gives their research its sense and direction, enabling them to divine the meaning and importance of their subject-matter. The main point of this second kind of research is that it should lead both the experimenter and those with whom he or she communicates to develop with increasing clarity their visions of human action, the better to criticize human deficiencies and foster human potentials.[10]

It is implicit in this second view of developmental psychology that any attempt to banish scientists' own experience or subjectivity from their studies will rebound by subverting the authenticity of their evidence. Chapter 9 showed how the discoveries of scientists adopting a biological approach to infancy are liable to be subverted by an unrealistic glorification of babyhood. I suggest that their defects are a consequence of the scientific attempt to study and explain human development without reference to that all-important if troublesome category in psychology – states of mind, experience or inner life – whether it be of mothers, babies or the scientists themselves.

Viewed in this light, the research considered in this book has a double significance: if developmental studies are inevitably subjective, then even the work of those who espouse the scientific ideals of natural history should have both an ethical and an evidential moment. Thus Darwin's use of observations about babies was to illustrate a general theory about our own evolutionary origins. In this way, babies become not just found objects but means to convince sceptical adults that their ultimate origins were not divine but bestial, thereby forcing people to reassess the sources of their own beliefs and experience. On the other hand, Charles Darwin's relative lack of interest in the study of subjectivity in advancing his evolutionary theory, together with his emphasis on instincts, have led many of his followers to believe that the keys of biochemical genetics and neurophysiology could themselves unlock the mysteries of psycho-genesis. As I argued in chapter 2, this is implicitly to underrate the importance of mental life in explaining human change.

In chapter 3 we saw that the work of those opposed to the idea that mental qualities are simply inherited or instinctive has a similar ambiguity for those interested in the study and development of human experience. On the one hand, by reviewing the work of modern behaviourists alongside the early associationists, I showed how theories of infancy that are inspired by the idea that mental growth results from the cumulative effect of past events have generally been advanced to illustrate the need for social changes to cure serious ills in the human community. On the other hand, behaviourism is to be contrasted with early associationism in marking the modern shift towards denying any explanatory status to individual consciousness or inner life in psychology.

Chapter 4 perhaps developed the clearest contrast between the idea that the study of babies has an evidential significance *explaining* subsequent human development, of showing how 'the child is father to the man',[11] and the belief that references to infancy have an 'ethical' significance, being mainly valuable in revealing and reflecting back upon the thought-processes of the adults who make those references. We saw that Freud entertained two different kinds of hypothesis about early childhood. On the one hand his patients' reconstructed experiences were thought to *cause* adult neurosis, either directly, as in the seduction theory, or by affecting the normal sequence of early development in a way that constrained adult character-formation, as in his famous stage-theory of infantile sexuality. Alternatively the reconstruction of childhood experience in therapy was seen by Freud as a process which significantly enriches both patient's and analyst's communication about and understanding of the patient's current problems but casts no direct light on what really happened in the patient's first years of life.

Freud's statement about infantile sexuality had a similar function to the statements about infants by Darwin and learning theorists: to challenge current scientific conceptions of the mind. Freud's challenge is his assertion that human behaviour is constituted by sexuality in a way to which adult consciousness is predominantly blind. But by openly questioning the causal status of constructions of childhood in the dynamics of mental illness, Freud and his followers provoke scientists to ask whether the study of children is a diversion from rather than a source of privileged access to understanding the underpinnings of adult thinking. The question why and how adults use the study of children to explore their own minds then takes logical precedence over questions about the mental states of children. It is this question forces us to rethink the relationship between developmental theory and childhood.

I used the discussion of Freud, Klein and Lacan to draw out the centrality of the moral and psychological qualities of *language* in Freud's later conception of the therapeutic experience. As Bettelheim has argued, statements such as 'Wo es war, soll Ich werden' (literally: where it was, I shall become), which are often taken to be theoretical formulations (where id was, there the ego shall be), should be translated with full recognition of their existential implications as 'oughts' and 'ought nots'.[12] Hence, 'Wo es war, soll Ich werden' might be expanded to mean: We *should* become conscious of those parts of us of which we are unconscious.

But psycho-analysis is also a form of description of events which suggests that language reproduces itself by means of a process of *repetition* which is open to change through interpretation by adults, a process psycho-analytic case-studies are intended to illustrate. It is this process of moral repetition by adults, through what have loosely been called language 'games', that should become the first problem of developmental psychology, not the study of babies alone. An early landmark in this kind of developmental discipline was Kierkegaard's *Repetition: An Essay in Experimental Psychology* (1843). This essay favourably contrasts the love known through the will to repeat old experiences with the love known through recollection, set in the past, as is the infant's love for the mother when viewed by adults.[13] (In one sense, babies enforce this process of repetition on those who look after them, leading adults to relive and revise their own childhood experiences.)

Chapter 5 discussed a 'modern' approach to the relationship between infancy and language which is in marked contrast to that developed in chapter 4. Chomsky treated child language primarily as an object generated in the brain of the child, not as a vehicle of experience. As such, Chomsky's approach to infancy is primarily biological or logical, not hermeneutic. Nevertheless, as Chomsky's critique of Skinner makes plain, his statements about young children were made as much to wake behaviourists up to the complexity of language and the importance of accounting for 'internal operations' in the human sciences as to explain how language is acquired by babies.

Chapters 6 to 8 explored the grounds of response to Chomsky's account of language learning. They reviewed respectively theories of early cognition, early emotion and early social life as contributors to communicative development. Whilst indulging the modern scientific taste for treating different aspects of the baby's mental life separately from each other, these chapters are implicitly united by an attempt to draw a well-rounded picture of the infant's mental life. Noting that most modern theories of infancy fail to see negative states of mind as having equal status with babies' more happy and successful dealings with their worlds, I used discussion of empirical evidence, including frames from a film, to advance the idea that our initial state is one of narcissism, based in anxiety. This is not an original conclusion, being central to Piagetian and psycho-analytic conceptions of the origin of human intelligence, not to mention versions of feminism, existentialism and post-structuralism.[14] It contrasts with the idea that humans have an innate or very early understanding of others.

Chapter 9 explored how it is possible to use modern scientific evidence to construe infancy as paradise. I argued that we need to seek alternatives to this vision to reveal its partiality and to do justice to the diverse experience constituting infancy, both from the viewpoint of babies and their minders. I drew a parallel between contemporary scientific theories of infancy and the biblical story of Adam and Eve to suggest that there is an implicit misogyny in the vision of infancy as paradise.

Conclusion

This book has undertaken to show that there can be no 'empirical' observation of babies that does not imply an evaluative vision of infancy. This means that it is more than a matter of choice about 'technical matters' when we decide whether our method as psychologists is just to be 'up-to-date', 'scientific', 'experimental' – without further comment – or to be something more than a technique. Scrupulous researchers, and scrupulous readers, must go further to consider how different kinds of technique produce different kinds of 'finding' which differently reflect and refract the dominant debates about children in the body politic. Clearly, in a moral science of psychology, these reflections and refractions need to be 'for the best' – to promote human welfare.[15] Once this kind of moral or political consideration is an explicit and self-conscious part of the psychologist's method, the job psychologists do becomes more akin to advocacy than science.

Whilst this is no place to go in to the many parallels between the lot of the psychologist and that of the advocate, the equation between psychology and advocacy does remove an apparent contradiction between the two main themes in this book: that 'internal evidence', as well as historical and cross-cultural research, shows child psychology to be a cultural invention, and, that infancy is a time dominated by anxiety and the wish to transcend it.[16] For, if everything scientists say about babies is a social construction, how can it be any truer to say that infancy is hell than to call it bliss?

The answer to this question is that there is no answer to questions about infancy which can always and everywhere be taken as true.[17] Scientific questions about babies always emerge from particular circumstances for particular reasons. Hence, scientific 'answers' must be tuned to these circumstances and reasons. The circumstances which give the key to current scientific debates about the minds of babies are, I would suggest, two. An often muzzled communal debate about the quality of child-care, which has an ever-increasing urgency with the rising consciousness of the needs and oppression of women, and widespread starvation and misery. Hence I do not claim that the recognition of anxiety in infancy (both of babies and mothers) is simply 'an accurate picture of reality', as if this were the sole criterion of truth. My hypotheses are rendered as a plea for justice for those who cannot speak. My aim is to be a faithful advocate, one who envisions the truth as, in James's phrase, 'what it is better for us to believe'.[18] I conclude that it is truer, because it is *better*, for scientists in the West today to place infant anxiety and the problem of child-care at the heart of scientific concerns about infancy than to concentrate on the baby's cognitive 'advances' and downplay the position of women. The more hellish vision of infancy turns out, paradoxically, to be the nobler hypothesis.

Notes and References

Chapter 1 Looking at Babies

1 V. Walkerdine, 'Developmental psychology and the child-centred pedagogy: the insertion of Piaget into early education', in *Changing the Subject: Psychology, Social Regulation and Subjectivity*, ed. J. Henriques, W. Hollway, C. Urwin, C. Venn and V. Walkerdine (Methuen, London, 1984).
2 The 'new paradigm' in psychology is well outlined in K. J. Gergen, *Toward Transformation in Social Knowledge* (Springer-Verlag, New York, 1982). Versions of its hermeneutical subdivision are described in M. J. Packer, 'Hermeneutic inquiry in the study of human conduct', *American Psychologist*, 40 (1985), 1081–93; J. A. Beshai, 'Is psychology a hermeneutic science?', *Journal of Phenomenological Psychology*, 5 (1975), 425–40. See also: J. Shotter, *Images of Man in Psychological Research* (Methuen, London, 1975); A. Gauld and J. Shotter, *Human Action and its Psychological Investigation* (Routledge & Kegan Paul, London, 1977). For more general reading on hermeneutics, see: R. E. Palmer, *Hermeneutics: Interpretation Theory in Schleiermacher, Dilthey, Heidegger and Gadamer* (Northwestern University Press, Evanston, Ill., 1969).
3 See J. Shotter, *Social Accountability and Selfhood* (Blackwell, Oxford, 1984).
4 Gauld and Shotter, *Human Action*, p. 199.
5 J. Shotter and S. Gregory, 'On first gaining the idea of oneself as a person', in *Life Sentences*, ed. R. Harré (Wiley, Chichester, 1976).
6 G. H. Mead, *Mind, Self and Society* (Chicago University Press, Chicago, 1934).
7 S. Kvale, 'The qualitative research interview: a phenomenological and a hermeneutical mode of understanding', *Journal of Phenomenological Psychology*, 14 (1983), 171–96; M. H. Honey, 'The interview as text: hermeneutics considered as a model for analyzing the clinically-informed research interview', *Human Development*, 30 (1987) 69–82.
8 C. R. Darwin, *The Expression of the Emotions in Man and Animals* (Murray,

London, 1872), esp. ch. 6; C. R. Darwin, 'A biographical sketch of an infant', *Mind*, 2 (1877), 285–94.

9 J. B. Watson, 'John Broadus Watson', in *A History of Psychology in Autobiography*, vol. III ed. C. Murchison (Russell & Russell, New York, 1936/ 1961), p. 274.

10 B. F. Skinner, *Verbal Behavior* (Prentice-Hall, Englewood Cliffs, NJ, 1957); N. Chomsky, Review of Skinner's *Verbal Behavior*, *Language*, 35 (1959), 26–58.

11 P. J. Caplan and I. Hall-McCorquodale, 'Mother-blaming in major clinical journals', *American Journal of Orthopsychiatry*, 55 (1985), 345–55; W. Kersen, 'The American child and other cultural inventions', *American Psychologist*, 34 (1979), 815–20; S. Chess, 'The "blame the mother" ideology', *International Journal of Mental Health*, 11 (1982), 37–47.

Chapter 2 The Question of Genesis

Epigraph. A. Clarke-Stewart, S. Friedman and J. Koch, *Child Development: A Topical Approach* (Wiley, New York, 1985).

1 A. Moorehead, *Darwin and the Beagle* (Hamilton, London, 1969).

2 ibid., p. 14.

3 C. R. Darwin and T. H. Huxley, *Autobiographies*, ed. G. de Beer (Oxford University Press, London, 1974), p. 34.

4 H. E. Gruber and P. H. Barrett, *Darwin on Man: A Psychological Study of Scientific Creativity* (Wildwood, London, 1974), ch. 10.

5 ibid.

6 R. M. Young, 'The idea of psychology in Darwin's thought', in *Darwin's Metaphor: Nature's Place in Victorian Culture* (Cambridge University Press, Cambridge, 1985); C. R. Darwin, *The Descent of Man and Selection in Relation to Sex* (Murray, London, 1871).

7 I owe my appreciation of the importance of Darwin's discussions with other naturalists during this formative period to Monica McCallum, Dept. of the History and Philosophy of Science, University of Melbourne.

8 E. Darwin, *Zoonomia or the Laws of Organic Life* (Johnson, London, 1794–6); E. Darwin, *The Temple of Nature or the Origin of Society: A Poem with Philosophical Notes* (Johnson, London, 1803).

9 C. R. Darwin, 'Autobiographical Fragment', in Darwin and Huxley, *Autobiographies*.

10 C. R. Darwin, Notebook M, in Gruber and Barrett, *Darwin on Man*, p. 297.

11 Darwin, *Temple of Nature*, p. 77.

12 C. R. Darwin, Notebook on Child Development, Cambridge University Library (unpublished).

13 Darwin and Huxley, *Autobiographies*, p. 45.

14 Darwin, Notebook on Child Development, p. 6.

15 ibid., p. 12.

16 ibid., p. 19.

17 C. R. Darwin, 'A biographical sketch of an infant', *Developmental Medicine and Child Neurology*, 13 (1971), supplement 24, 1–8, p. 6. (First published in *Mind*, 2 (1877), 285–94.)

18 Darwin, Notebook on Child Development, p. 26.

19 e.g. M. D. Klinnert, 'The regulation of infant behaviour by maternal facial expression', *Infant Behaviour and Development*, 7 (1985), 447–65.

20 C. R. Darwin, *The Expression of the Emotions in Man and Animals* (Murray, London, 1872/1921).

21 ibid., pp. 14–15.

22 ibid., p. 149.

23 ibid., p. 176.

24 ibid., p. 179.

25 ibid., p. 381.

26 J. Taine, 'The acquisition of language by children', *Mind*, 2 (1877), 252–7.

27 Darwin, 'Biographical sketch of an infant', p. 8.

28 ibid.

29 ibid.

30 Comenius, *Orbis Sensualium Pictus*, tr. C. Hoole (Leacroft, London, 1632/1777, 12th edn), p. 3.

31 Darwin and Huxley, *Autobiographies*.

32 S. J. Gould and R. C. Lewontin, 'The spandrels of San Marco and the Panglossian paradigm: a critique of the adaptationist programme', *Proceedings of the Royal Society of London (Series B)*, 205 (1979), 581–98.

33 G. A. Miller, *Psychology: The Science of Mental Life* (Hutchinson, London, 1964); W. James, 'Does "consciousness" exist?', in *Essays in Radical Empiricism* (Harvard University Press, Cambridge, Mass., 1912/1976).

34 Darwin, *Descent of Man* and *Expression of the Emotions*.

35 Darwin, *Temple of Nature* (Additional Notes), p. 39.

36 ibid., p. 40.

37 R. A. Hinde, *The Biological Bases of Human Behavior* (McGraw-Hill, New York, 1974), p. 7.

38 ibid., p. 24.

39 J. Piaget, *The Origins of Intelligence in Children* (Routledge & Kegan Paul, London, 1953); S. Ferenczi, 'The birth of the intellect', in *Final Contributions to the Problems and Methods of Psycho-Analysis*, ed. M. Balint (Hogarth, London, 1931/1955); B. S. Bradley, The asymmetric involvement of infants in social life, *Revue Internationale de Psychologie Sociale* (in press).

40 W. James, *The Principles of Psychology* (Dover, New York, 1890/1950), vol. I, p. 196.

41 C. R. Darwin, *On the Origin of Species by Means of Natural Selection, or, The Preservation of Favoured Races in the Struggle for Life* (Watts, London, 1859/1950), pp. 413–14.

42 J. Huxley, *Evolution: The Modern Synthesis*, ed. J. R. Baker (Allen & Unwin, London, 1974, 3rd edn), p. 524.

43 R. F. Ewer, 'Natural selection and neoteny', *Acta Biotheoretica*, 13 (1960), 161.

44 E. Mayr, 'Evolution und Verhalten', *Verhandlungen der Deutschen Zooligischen Gessellschaft*, 64 (1970), 322.

45 Darwin, *Descent of Man*.
46 S. Rose, L. J. Kamin and R. C. Lewontin, *Not in Our Genes: Biology, Ideology and Human Nature* (Penguin, Harmondsworth, 1984).
47 James, *Principles*, ch. 6; D. Davidson, 'Psychology as philosophy', in *Essays on Actions and Events* (Clarendon, Oxford, 1974/1980). See also A. Gauld and J. Shotter, *Human Action and its Psychological Investigation* (Routledge & Kegan Paul, London, 1977).
48 S. Butler, *Evolution Old and New: or Theories of Buffon, Dr Erasmus Darwin, and Lamarck as compared with that of Mr Charles Darwin* (Hardwick & Brogue, London, 1879).
49 e.g. Thomas Reid (1710–96), *Thomas Reid's Inquiry and Essays*, ed. K. Lehrer and R. Beanblossom (Indianapolis, Bobbs-Merrill, 1975); Dugald Stewart (1753–1828), *Elements of the Philosophy of Human Mind*, ed. W. Hamilton (Edinburgh, Clark, 1877), vol. III; D. Tiedemann, 'Observations on the mental development of a child', in *Historical Readings in Development Psychology*, ed. W. Dennis (Appleton-Century-Crofts, New York, 1787/1972); Carolyn Steadman, in *The Tidy House: Little Girls Writing* (London, Virago 1982), reports that the archives of regional libraries in the UK are stuffed with unpublished notes by mothers on the behavioural development of their babies, dating from well before Charles Darwin set sail in HMS *Beagle*.

Chapter 3 From Associationism to Behaviourism

1 E. Darwin, *The Temple of Nature or the Origin of Society: A Poem with Philosophical Notes* (Johnson, London, 1803), pp. 100–1.
2 D. Hartley, *Observations on Man, His Frame, His Duty, and His Expectations* (Scholars' Facsimiles, Gainesville, Fla., 1749/1966).
3 ibid., p. 270.
4 Janusz Sysak, 'From empiricism to romanticism: a study of the views on psychology of David Hartley, Jeremy Bentham and Samuel Taylor Coleridge' (Master's thesis, Sorbonne Nouvelle, 1985). I am indebted to Janusz for many discussions about these issues; R. M. Young, 'Association of ideas', in *Dictionary of the History of Ideas*, ed. P. P. Wiener (Scribner's, New York, 1973), pp. 111–18.
5 J. Bentham, *An Introduction to the Principles of Morals and Legislation* (Blackwell, Oxford, 1789/1948).
6 Hartley, *Observations on Man*, p. 24 (quoted in Sysak, 'From empiricism to romanticism', p. 9).
7 E. Darwin, *Zoonomia or the Laws of Organic Life* (Johnson, London, 1794–6); Darwin, *Temple of Nature*.
8 Darwin, *Temple of Nature*, p. 151.
9 ibid., p. 12.
10 E. Darwin, *The Botanic Garden: A Poem in Two Parts with Philosophical Notes* (Moore, Dublin, 1793), Preface.
11 I. P. Pavlov, 'Experimental psychology and psychopathology in animals', in

Experimental Psychology and Other Essays (Philosophers' Library, New York, 1957), pp. 151–70.

12 ibid., p. 155. This unusual sentiment is echoed in Samuel Beckett's Pavlovian reading of Proust's *Remembrance of Things Past* (*Proust*, New York, Grove, 1931/1970, p. 46), when he writes: 'If neither [love nor friendship] can be realized because of the impenetrability (isolation) of all that is not "cosa mentale", at least the failure to possess may have the nobility of that which is tragic, whereas the attempt to communicate where no communication is possible is merely a simian vulgarity, or horribly comic, like the madness that holds a conversation with the furniture.'

13 J. B. Watson, 'Psychology as the behaviorist views it', *Psychological Review*, 20 (1913), 158–77.

14 J. B. Watson and R. Morgan, 'Emotional reactions and psychological experimentation', *American Journal of Psychology*, 28 (1917), 163–84.

15 J. B. Watson and R. Rayner, 'Conditioned emotional responses', *Journal of Experimental Psychology*, 3 (1920), 1–14.

16 ibid., p. 5.

17 ibid.

18 ibid., p. 11.

19 J. B. Watson, *Psychological Care of the Infant and Child* (Allen & Unwin, New York, 1928), p. 21.

20 ibid., pp. 81–2.

21 R. C. Hulsebus, 'Operant conditioning of infant behaviour: a review', in *Advances in Child Development and Behavior*, vol. 8, ed. H. W. Reese (Academic, New York, 1973), pp. 111–59.

22 B. F. Skinner, *Verbal Behavior* (Appleton-Century-Crofts, New York, 1957), p. 312.

23 B. F. Skinner, 'Baby in a box', in *Cumulative Record* (Appleton-Century-Crofts, New York, 1959), p. 420.

24 ibid., p. 422.

25 B. F. Skinner, *The Shaping of a Behaviorist* (Knopf, New York, 1979), p. 290.

26 ibid.

27 B. F. Skinner, *Walden Two* (Macmillan, New York, 1946).

28 H. D. Thoreau, 'Civil disobedience', in *Anti-Slavery and Reform Papers*, ed. H. S. Salt (Sonnenschein, London, 1845/1890).

29 A. Y. Davis, *Women, Race and Class* (Random House, New YOrk, 1981), ch. 13.

30 N. Chomsky, Review of Skinner's *Verbal Behavior*, *Language*, 35 (1959), 26–58; N. Chomsky, 'Psychology and ideology', in *For Reasons of State* (Random House, New York, 1973).

31 L. P. Lipsitt, 'Learning capacities of the human infant', in *Brain and Early Behavior*, ed. R. J. Robinson, (Academic, London, 1969); T. G. R. Bower, *A Primer of Infant Development* (Freeman, San Francisco, 1979).

32 H. Papousek, 'Individual variability in learned responses in human infants', in *Brain and Behaviour*, ed. R. J. Robinson (Academic, London, 1969), pp. 251–66.

33 Skinner, *Shaping of a Behaviorist*, p. 287.

Chapter 4 The Dynamics of Desire

1 P. Meisel, Introduction: 'Freud as literature', in *Freud: A Collection of Critical Essays*, ed. P. Meisel (Prentice-Hall, Englewood Cliffs, NJ, 1981), p. 1; S. Freud, *Moses and Monotheism* (Hogarth, London, 1939).
2 J. van Herik, *Freud on Femininity and Faith* (University of California Press, Berkeley, 1982); B. Bettelheim, *Freud and Man's Soul* (Chatto & Windus, London, 1983).
3 J. Swift, 'The difficulty of knowing one's self', in *Prose Works of Jonathan Swift*, vol. IX: *Irish Tracts and Sermons*, ed. T. Scott (Blackwell, Oxford, 1745/ 1948).
4 ibid., p. 295 Cf. 2 Kings 8 : 8 ff.
5 S. Freud, 'A special type of choice of object made by men', Penguin Freud Library, 7 (Penguin, Harmondsworth, 1977), pp. 231–42.
6 ibid., p. 235.
7 R. Graves, *Greek Myths* (Penguin, Harmondsworth, 1960).
8 S. Freud and J. Breuer, *Studies on Hysteria* (1895), Penguin Freud Library, 3 (Penguin, Harmondsworth, 1974), pp. 202–55.
9 J. M. Masson, *The Assault on Truth: Freud's Suppression of the Seduction Theory* (Faber, London, 1984); J. Malcolm, *In the Freud Archives* (Knopf, New York, 1984).
10 S. Freud, 'Screen memories' (1899), in *Collected Papers*, vol. V, ed. J. Strachey (Hogarth, London, 1957), pp. 47–69.
11 The problem with this hypothesis is the assumption that memories of sexual adventures in childhood are based in *children's* desires for such adventures, rather than the desires of the adult patient who remembers the events, see pp. 59–60 below.
12 S. Freud, *The Interpretation of Dreams* (1900) (Penguin, Harmondsworth, 1976).
13 S. Freud, 'Formulations on the two principles of mental functioning', (1911) Penguin Freud Library, 11 (Penguin, Harmondsworth, 1984), pp. 29–44.
14 Freud, *Interpretation of Dreams*, p. 720.
15 ibid., p. 721.
16 S. Freud, 'Infantile sexuality' (1905), in Penguin Freud Library, 7 (Penguin, Harmondsworth, 1977), pp. 88–126.
17 F. J. Sulloway, *Freud, Biologist of the Mind: Beyond the Psychoanalytic Legend* (Basic, London, 1979).
18 S. Freud, *Introductory Lectures on Psycho-Analysis* (1916–17), Standard Edition, 16 (Hogarth, London, 1963), p. 354. Quoted in Sulloway, *Freud*, p. 260.
19 Freud in Sulloway, *Freud*, p. 260.
20 Freud, 'Infantile sexuality', p. 98.
21 ibid., pp. 103–4.
22 S. Freud, 'Femininity', in *New Introductory Lectures on Psycho-Analysis* (1933) (Penguin, Harmondsworth, 1973), pp. 145–69.
23 S. Freud, 'Some psychical consequences of the anatomical distinction between

the sexes' (1925), Penguin Freud Library, 7 (Penguin, Harmondsworth, 1977), pp. 323–44.

24 J. M. Selby, 'Feminine identity and contradiction: women research students at Cambridge University' (D.Phil. thesis, Cambridge University), pp. 51–2. I am indebted to Dr Selby for the heart of this section.

25 S. Freud, 'On narcissism: an introduction' (1914), Penguin Freud Library, 11 (Penguin, Harmondsworth, 1984), pp. 59–98.

26 Graves, *Greek Myths*.

27 C. Lasch, *The Culture of Narcissism: American Life in an Age of Diminishing Expectations* (Norton, New York, 1979).

28 S. Freud, *Beyond the Pleasure Principle* (1920), Penguin Freud Library, 11 (Penguin, Harmondsworth, 1984), pp. 269–338.

29 M. Klein, 'The psycho-analytic play technique: its history and significance', in *Envy and Gratitude and Other Works 1946–1963* (Hogarth, London, 1955/ 1975), pp. 122–40.

30 M. Klein, 'Early stages of the Oedipus Complex', in *Love, Guilt and Reparation and Other Works 1921–1945* (Hogarth, London, 1928/1975), pp. 186–98.

31 M. Klein, 'Notes on some schizoid mechanisms' (1946), in *Envy and Gratitude*, pp. 1–24. Cf. pp. 129–31 below.

32 M. Klein, 'Some theoretical conclusions regarding the emotional life of the infant' (1952), in *Envy and Gratitude*, pp. 61–93.

33 ibid.

34 Freud, 'Screen memories', p. 69.

35 S. Freud, 'From the history of an infantile neurosis' (1918), Penguin Freud Library, 9 (Penguin, Harmondsworth, 1979), pp. 233–366.

36 S. Freud, 'Remembering, repeating and working-through' (1914), Standard Edition, 12 (Hogarth, London, 1958), p. 147.

37 J. Lacan, 'The function and field of speech and language in psycho-analysis' (1953), in *Écrits: A Selection*, tr. A. Sheridan (Tavistock, London, 1977), pp. 52–3.

38 J. Lacan, 'The mirror stage as formative of the function of the I' (1949), in *Écrits*, pp. 1–7.

39 ibid., p. 1.

40 Lacan, 'The function of language', p. 55.

41 J. Lacan, 'Aggressivity in psycho-analysis' (1948), in *Écrits*, p. 9–10. Note the similarity to Christ's statement that 'where two or three are gathered together in my name, there am I in the midst of them' (Matthew 18:20).

42 The English philosopher Richard Lindley is shortly to complete a book on this topic.

43 M. Eliade, *Myths, Rites, Symbols: a Mircea Eliade Reader* (Harper & Row, New York, 1975), quoted in R. A. Shweder, 'Rethinking culture and personality theory, III: From genesis and typology to hermeneutics and dynamics', *Ethos*, 8 (1980), 60–94.

Chapter 5 Before Grammar

1 C. R. Darwin, 'A biographical sketch of an infant', *Mind*, 2 (1877), 285–94; H. Taine, 'The acquisition of language by children', *Mind*, 2 (1877), 252–7.
2 W. F. Leopold, *Speech Development in a Bilingual Child: A Linguist's Record* (Northwestern University Press, Evanston, Ill., 1949).
3 L. Bloomfield, 'A set of postulates for the science of language', *Language*, 2 (1926), 153–164.
4 B. F. Skinner, *Verbal Behavior* (Appleton-Century-Crofts, New York, 1957); N. Chomsky, Review of *Verbal Behavior* by B. F. Skinner, *Language*, 35 (1959), 26–58.
5 Skinner, *Verbal Behavior*, p. 2.
6 ibid., p. 44.
7 ibid., p. 45.
8 ibid.
9 ibid., p. 3. See also B. F. Skinner, 'Walden Two revisited', in *Walden Two* (Macmillan, New York, 1946/1976) for Skinner's comments on the social responsibilities of the behavioural scientist in the age of nuclear war.
10 Chomsky, Review, paras. 3 and 4.
11 ibid., para. 5.
12 ibid.
13 ibid.
14 N. Chomsky, *Syntactic Structures* (Mouton, The Hague, 1957).
15 D. McNeill, Developmental psycholinguistics, in *The Genesis of Language*, ed. F. Smith and G. A. Miller (MIT Press, Cambridge, Mass., 1966); R. W. Brown, *A First Language: The Early Stages* (Allen & Unwin, London, 1973).
16 Brown, *First Language*.
17 L. Bloom, *Language Development: Form and Function in Emerging Grammars* (MIT Press, Cambridge, Mass., 1970).
18 A. N. Meltzoff, 'The roots of social and cognitive development: models of man's original nature', in *Social Perception in Infants*, ed. T. M. Field and N. A. Fox (Ablex, Norwood, 1985).
19 T. H. Leahey, *A History of Psychology* (Prentice-Hall, Englewood Cliffs, NJ, 1980), p. 347.
20 See Chomsky's Appendix to E. H. Lenneberg, *The Biological Foundations of Language* (Wiley, New York, 1967).
21 N. Chomsky, *Cartesian Linguistics: A Chapter in the History of Rationalist Thought* (Harper & Row, New York, 1966).
22 N. Chomsky, *Language and Mind* (Harcourt Brace Jovanovich, New York, 1972), pp. 83–4; R. Descartes, Reply to Objections V, in *Descartes's Philosophical Works*, ed. E. W. Haldane and G. R. T. Ross (Dover, New York, 1911/1955).
23 Chomsky, *Language and Mind*, p. 78.
24 ibid., p. 66.
25 E. V. Clark, 'What's in a word? On the child's acquisition of semantics in his

first language', in *Cognitive Development and the Acquisition of Language*, ed. T. E. Moore (Academic, New York, 1973).

26 K. Nelson, 'Structure and strategy in learning to talk', Monographs of the Society for Research in Child Development, 38 (Chicago: University of Chicago Press, 1973), pp. 1–137.

27 E. H. Rosch, 'On the internal structure of perceptual and semantic categories', in *Cognitive Development and the Acquisition of Language*, ed. T. E. Moore (Academic, New York, 1973).

28 A. J. Elliot, *Child Language* (Cambridge University Press, Cambridge, 1981).

29 L. B. Ames, 'Children's stories', Genetic Psychology Monographs, 73 (1966), pp. 337–96.

30 ibid., p. 345.

31 R. Weir, *Language in the Crib* (Mouton, The Hague, 1962), p. 138.

32 J. S. Bruner, with Rita Watson, *Child's Talk: Learning to Use Language* (Oxford University Press, Oxford, 1983).

33 C. E. Snow, 'Mothers' speech to children learning language', *Child Development*, 43 (1972), 549–65; C. E. Snow and C. A. Ferguson, *Talking to Children: Language Input and Acquisition* (Cambridge University Press, Cambridge, 1977); B. Sylvester-Bradley and C. B. Trevarthen, 'Babytalk as an adaptation to the infant's communication', in *The Development of Communication*, ed. N. Waterson and C. Snow (Wiley, Chichester, 1978).

Chapter 6 Babies as Thinkers

1 J. S. Bruner, *In Search of Mind: Essays in Autobiography* (Harper & Row, New York, 1984).

2 J. Macnamara, 'Cognitive basis for language learning in infants', *Psychological Review*, 79 (1972), 1–13.

3 J. Piaget, 'Jean Piaget', in *A History of Psychology in Autobiography*, vol. IV, ed. E. G. Boring, H. S. Langfeld, H. Werner and R. M. Yerkes (Clark University Press, Worcester, Mass., 1952).

4 J. Piaget, *The Essential Piaget*, ed. H. E. Gruber and J. J. Voneche (Routledge & Kegan Paul, London, 1977).

5 Piaget, 'Piaget', p. 244.

6 ibid., p. 245.

7 J. Piaget, *The Language and Thought of the Child* (Routledge & Kegan Paul, London, 1924/1954).

8 Piaget, 'Piaget', p. 238.

9 Piaget, *Language and Thought*, p. 9.

10 ibid., pp. 18–19.

11 ibid., p. 10.

12 L. S. Vygotsky, 'Thought and speech', *Psychiatry*, 2 (1939), 29–54.

13 J. Piaget, *The Origins of Intelligence in the Child* (Routledge & Kegan Paul, London, 1937/1953).

14 ibid., p. 90.

15 ibid., p. 167.

16 ibid., p. 215.

17 ibid., p. 301.

18 ibid., p. 338.

19 J. Piaget, *The Child's Construction of Reality* (Routledge & Kegan Paul, London, 1937/1953).

20 ibid., pp. 10–11.

21 ibid., pp. 36–7.

22 ibid., p. 53.

23 ibid., p. 79.

24 J. Piaget, *Play, Dreams and Imitation* (Routledge & Kegan Paul, London, 1945/ 1951).

25 ibid., p. 63.

26 E. Bates, L. Camaioni and V. Volterra, 'The acquisition of performatives prior to speech', *Merrill-Palmer Quarterly*, 21 (1975), 205–26.

27 ibid., p. 217.

28 M. B. Keating, B. E. McKenzie and R. H. Day, 'Spatial localization in infancy: position constancy in a square and circular room with and without a landmark', *Child Development*, 57 (1986), 115–24.

29 E. S. Spelke, 'Perceptual knowledge of objects in infancy', in *Perspectives on Mental Representation*, ed. J. Mehler, M. Garrett and E. WAlker (Erlbaum, Hillsdale, NJ, 1982).

30 T. G. R. Bower, *Development in Infancy* (Freeman, San Francisco, 1974); T. G. R. Bower, *A Primer of Infant Development* (Freeman, San Francisco, 1979).

31 J. H. van den Berg, *The Changing Nature of Man: Introduction to a Historical Psychology* (Norton, New York, 1961); K. J. Gergen, 'The social constructionist movement in modern psychology', *American Psychologist*, 40 (1985), 266–275.

32 J. S. Watson, 'Smiling, cooing and the game', *Merrill-Palmer Quarterly*, 18 (1972), 323–39.

33 J. M. Baldwin, 'James Mark Baldwin', in *A History of Psychology in Autobiography*, vol. I, ed. C. Murchison (Clark University Press, Worcester, Mass., 1930).

34 C. Urwin, 'Splitting the difference: psycho-analysis and developmental psychology', in *Children in Social Worlds*, ed. M. P. M. Richards and P. Light (Polity, Cambridge, 1986); J. Piaget, *The Child's Conception of the World* (Littlefield, Totowa, NJ, 1929/1975).

35 W. Mays, 'Piaget and Freud' (Piaget Memorial Lecture, Manchester Polytechnic, 1981).

36 J. S. Bruner, 'The ontogenesis of speech acts', *Journal of Child Language*, 2 (1975), 1–19.

37 D. N. Stern, 'The early development of schemas of self, other and "self with other"', in *Reflections on Self Psychology*, ed. J. D. Lichtenberg and S. Kaplan (Erlbaum, Hillsdale, NJ, 1983).

38 J. G. Wishart and T. G. R. Bower, 'A longitudinal study of the development of the object concept', *British Journal of Developmental Psychology*, 3 (1985), 243–58.

39 D. W. Winnicott, 'Transitional objects and transitional phenomena', in *Playing and Reality* (Penguin, Harmondsworth, 1971).

40 L. S. Vygotsky, *Mind in Society: The Development in Higher Psychological Processes* (Harvard University Press, Cambridge, Mass., 1978), p. 57.

41 J. Derrida, *Of Grammatology* (Baltimore, Johns Hopkins University Press, 1967/1974); B. S. Bradley, 'The asymmetric involvement of infants in social life: consequences for theory', *Revue Internationale de Psychologie Sociale* (in press).

42 R. Rorty, *Philosophy and the Mirror of Nature* (Princeton, Princeton University Press, 1979); J. Henriques, W. Hollway, C. Urwin, C. Venn and V. Walkerdine, *Changing the Subject: Psychology, Social Regulation and Subjectivity* (London, Methuen, 1984).

43 W. Sellars, *Science, Perception and Reality* (London, Routledge, 1963), p. 169.

44 L. S. Vygotsky, *Thought and Language* (Cambridge Mass., MIT Press, 1934/1962), p. 125.

Chapter 7 First Emotions

1 S. Freud, *An Outline of Psycho-analysis* (194), Standard Edition, 23 (Hogarth, London, 1964), p. 188.

2 K. Lorenz, *Studies in Animal Behavior*, vol. I (Harvard University Press, Cambridge, Mass., 1971).

3 W. Sluckin, *Imprinting and Early Learning* (Methuen, London, 1965).

4 H. F. Harlow, 'The nature of love', *American Psychologist*, 13 (1958), 673–85.

5 R. A. Spitz, *The First Year of Life* (International Universities Press, New York, 1965).

6 ibid., p. 278.

7 ibid., p. 281.

8 J. Robertson, 'Some responses of young children to loss of maternal care', *Nursing times*, 49 (1953), 382–386.

9 J. Bowlby, 'The nature of the child's tie to his mother', *International Journal of Psycho-Analysis*, 39 (1958), 350–73; J. Bowlby, *Attachment and Loss*, vol. I: *Attachment* (Hogarth, London, 1969).

10 J. Bowlby, 'Self-reliance and some conditions that promote it', in *The Making and Breaking of Affectional Bonds* (Tavistock, London, 1979), p. 103.

11 J. Bowlby, *Forty-Four Juvenile Thieves: Their Characters and Home-Life* (Baillière Tindall & London, 1946), quoted in L. Comer, *Wedlocked Women* (Feminist Books, Leeds, 1974), p. 142.

12 J. Bowlby, *Child Care and the Growth of Love* (Penguin, Harmondsworth, 1953).

13 D. W. Winnicott, *The Child, the Family and the Outside World* (Penguin, Harmondsworth, 1964); D. Riley, *War in the Nursery: Theories of the Child and Mother* (Virago, London, 1983).

14 Riley, *War in the Nursery*.

15 S. M. Bell, 'The development of the concept of object as related to infant-

mother attachment', *Child Development*, 41 (1970), 291–311. On the 'near unanimity' about the formation of attachments amongst developmental theorists see M. E. Lamb, 'Father–infant and mother–infant interaction in the first year of life', *Child Development*, 48 (1977), 167–81.

16 H. R. Schaffer and P. E. Emerson, 'The development of social attachments in infancy', Monographs of the Society for Research on Child Development, 29 (Chicago: University of Chicago Press, 1964), pp. 1–77.

17 S. M. Bell and M. D. S. Ainsworth, 'Infant crying and maternal responsiveness', *Child Development*, 43 (1972), 1171–90.

18 M. D. S. Ainsworth, S. M. Bell and D. J. Hogan, 'Infant–mother attachment and social development: "socialization" as a product of reciprocal responsiveness to signals', in *The Integration of a Child into a Social World*, ed. M. P. M. Richards (Cambridge University Press, Cambridge, 1974), p. 114.

19 C. Pratt, 'A study of infant crying behaviour in the home environment during the first year of life' (D.Phil thesis, Oxford University, 1977). See also B. Sylvester-Bradley, 'A study of young infants as social beings' (Ph.D. thesis, Edinburgh University, 1980).

20 R. Q. Bell, 'A reinterpretation of the direction of effects in studies of socialization', *Psychological Review*, 75 (1968), 81–95.

21 J. Dunn, *Distress and Comfort* (Fontana/Open Books, Glasgow, 1977); A. K. Clarke-Stewart, 'Interactions between mothers and their young children: characteristics and consequences', Monographs of the Society for Research in Child Development, 153 (Chicago: University of Chicago Press, 1973).

22 R. Solomon and T. G. Decarie, 'Fear of strangers: a developmental milestone or an overstudied phenomenon?', *Canadian Journal of Behavioural Science*, 8 (1976), 351–62; H. L. Rheingold and C. O. Eckerman, 'Fear of strangers: a critical examination', in *Advances in Child Development and Behaviour*, vol. VIII, ed. H. W. Reese (Academic, New York, 1973).

23 M. Rutter, *Maternal Deprivation Reassessed* (Penguin, Harmondsworth, 1981).

24 M. D. S. Ainsworth, 'The development of mother–infant attachment', in *Review of Child Development Research*, vol. III (University of Chicago Press, Chicago, 1973).

25 Bowlby, 'Nature of child's tie'.

26 M. Main, 'Avoidance in the service of attachment', in *Behavioural Development: Bielefeld Interdisciplinary Project*, ed. K. Immelman (Cambridge University Press, Cambridge, 1982).

27 C. Urwin, 'Power relations and the emergence of language', in *Changing the Subject: Psychology, Social Regulation and Subjectivity*, ed. J. Henriques, W. Hollway, C. Urwin, C. Venn and V. Walkerdine (Methuen, London, 1984).

28 ibid., p. 304.

29 The following account is a summary of an argument I have put forward in B. S. Bradley, 'The asymmetric involvement of infants in social life: consequences for theory', *Revue Internationale de Psychologie Sociale* (in press).

30 L. A. Sroufe and J. P. Wunsch, 'The development of laughter in the first year of life', *Child Development*, 43 (1972), 1340 (Sroufe and Wunsch's emphasis).

31 L. A. Sroufe and E. Waters, 'The onotgenesis of smiling and laughter: a

perspective on the organization of development in infancy', *Psychological Review*, 83 (1976), 179.

32 J. Bernal, 'Crying during the first ten days of life, and maternal responses', *Developmental Medicine and Child Neurology*, 14 (1972), 362–72; T. B. Brazelton, 'A clinical perspective on infant crying', in *Infant Crying: Theoretical and Research Perspectives*, ed. B. M. Lester and C. F. Z. Boukidis (New York, Plenum, 1985).

33 Cf. K. Nelson, 'Social cognition in a script framework' in *Social Cognitive Development: Frontiers and Possible Futures* (Cambridge, Cambridge University Press, 1981).

34 S. Freud, *The Interpretation of Dreams* (Harmondsworth, Penguin, 1976), p. 757.

35 M. R. Gunner, K. Leighton and R. Peleaux, 'The effects of temporal predictability on year-old infants' reactions to potentially frightening toys'. Paper given to the Society for Research in Child Development, Detroit, April 1983.

36 J. Kagan, *The Nature of the Child* (New York, Basic Books, 1984).

37 B. Sylvester-Bradley, 'Negativity in infant–adult exchanges and its developmental significance', in *Communication in Development*, ed. W. P. Robinson (London, Academic, 1981); B. S. Bradley, 'Visual avoidance of mothers at four months', (in preparation).

38 Peter Selby played this game at around six months of age. A similar but more elaborate game is discussed in S. Freud, *Beyond the Pleasure Principle*, in Penguin Freud Library, 11, ed. A. Richards (Penguin, Harmondsworth, 1984) pp. 283–7.

39 This point is made in S. Kierkegaard, *The Concept of Dread* (Princeton, Princeton University Press, 1844/1946).

40 The 'booming, buzzing confusion' is mentioned in W. James, *Principles of Psychology*, vol. 1 (Norton, New York, 1890), p. 488.

41 C. L. Miller and J. M. Byrne, 'The role of temporal cues in the development of language and communication', in *The Origins and Growth of Communication*, ed. L. Fegans, C. Garvey and R. Golinkoff (Ablex, Norwood, 1984).

42 K. Kaye and R. Charney, 'Conversational asymmetry between mothers and children', *Journal of Child Language*, 8 (1981), 35–50.

Chapter 8 Motives for Self-expression

1 Comenius, *The School for Infancy*, quoted in the translator's introduction to J. A. Komensky ('Comenius') *Orbis Pictus*, introduced by J. E. Sadler (Oxford University Press, Oxford, 1659/1968).

2 D. Stewart, 'Of language', in *Works* Vol. IV, ed. W. Hamilton (Smith, London, 1792/1877), p. 8: 'A child is able at a very early period to understand the meaning of smiles and frowns, of a threatening or a soothing tone of voice; long, at least, before it can be supposed capable of so much observation as to remark the connexion between a passion and its external effect.' This volume of

Stewart's work was republished in the same year as Darwin wrote his 'Biographical sketch', and Darwin's wording is at one point very close to Stewart's. We know that Darwin was a close adherent of Stewart from E. Manier, *The Young Darwin and His Cultural Circle* (Reidel, New York, 1978). Interestingly, Stewart explicitly opposed Erasmus Darwin's understanding of psycho-genesis, an orientation that may have endeared him to Charles Darwin if we are to believe the virulent indictment in S. Butler, *Unconscious Memory: A Comparison Between the Theory of Dr Ewald Hering, and the Philosophy of the Unconscious of Dr Edward van Hartmann, with Translations from the Authors: by Samuel Butler* (Bogue, London, 1880).

3 C. R. Darwin, 'A biographical sketch of an infant', *Mind*, 2 (1877), 285–94, p. 294.
4 L. Apostel, 'The unknown Piaget: from the theory of exchange and co-operation toward the theory of knowledge', *New Ideas in Psychology*, 4 (1986), 3–22.
5 M. Donaldson, *Children's Minds* (Fontana/Open Books, Glasgow, 1978), ch. 2.
6 J. Piaget and B. Inhelder, *The Child's Conception of Space* (Routledge & Kegan Paul, London, 1956).
7 Donaldson, *Children's Minds*, ch. 2.
8 ibid., p. 24.
9 J. Dunn, *Sisters and Brothers* (Fontana, London, 1984).
10 ibid., p. 30.
11 J. Ryan, 'Early language development: towards a communicational analysis', in *The Integration of a Child into a Social World*, ed. M. P. M. Richards (Cambridge University Press, Cambridge, 1974).
12 J. S. Bruner, 'From communication to language: a psychological perspective', *Cognition*, 3 (1975), 255–87.
13 A. Lock, 'Introduction: on being picked up', in *Action, Gesture and Symbol*, ed. A. Lock (Academic, London, 1978).
14 L. S. Vygotsky, *Mind in Society: The Development of the Higher Psychological Processes* (Harvard University Press, Cambridge, Mass., 1978), p. 56.
15 H. R. Schaffer, *The Growth of Sociability* (Penguin, Harmondsworth, 1971), p. 13.
16 J. S. Bruner, 'The ontogenesis of speech acts', *Journal of Child Language*, 2 (1975), 1–19.
17 P. Ekman and W. V. Friesen, *Manual for the Facial Action Coding System* (Consulting Psychologists, Palo Alto, Cal., 1978).
18 H. Oster, 'Facial expression and affect development', in *The Development of Affect*, ed. M. Lewis and L. A. Rosenblum (Plenum, New York, 1978).
19 R. L. Birdwhistell, *Kinesics and Context: Essays on Body Motion Communication* (University of Philadelphia Press, Philadelphia, 1970).
20 W. S. Condon and L. W. Sander, 'Neonate movement is synchronised with adult speech: interactional participation and language acquisition', *Science*, 183 (1974), 99–101.
21 K. S. Robson, 'The role of eye-to-eye contact in maternal–infant attachment', *Journal of Child Psychology and Psychiatry*, 8 (1967), 13–25.
22 J. Kagan, 'Attention and psychological change', *Science*, 177 (1970), 826–32.

23 A. N. Meltzoff and M. K. Moore, 'Imitation of facial and manual gestures by human neonates', *Science*, 198 (1977), 75–8.
24 A. N. Meltzoff and M. K. Moore, 'Newborn infants imitate adult facial gestures', *Child Development*, 54 (1983), 702–9.
25 T. B. Brazelton, E. Tronick, L. Adamson, H. Als and S. Wise, 'Early mother–infant reciprocity', in *Parent–Infant Interaction*, ed. R. Porter and M. O'Connor CIBA Foundation Symposia, 33 (new series) (Elsevier, Amsterdam, 1975); E. Tronick, H. Als and L. Adamson, 'Structure of early face-to-face communicative interactions', in *Before Speech: The Beginning of Interpersonal Communication*, ed. M. Bullowa (Cambridge University Press, Cambridge, 1979); L. Murray and C. B. Trevarthen, 'Emotional regulation of interactions between two-month-olds and their mothers', in *Social Perception in Infants*, ed. T. M. Field and N. A. Fox (Albex, Norwood NJ, 1985).
26 C. B. Trevarthen, 'Basic patterns of psychogenetic change in infancy', in *Regressions in Mental Development: Basic Phenomena and Theories*, ed. T. G. Bever (Erlbaum, Hillsdale, NJ, 1982), p. 26.
27 ibid.
28 C. B. Trevarthen and P. A. Hubley, 'Secondary intersubjectivity: confidence, confiding and acts of meaning in the first year', in *Action, Gesture and Symbol*, ed. A. Lock (Academic, London, 1978).
29 R. W. Washburn, 'A study of the smiling and laughter of infants in the first year of life', *Genetic Psychology Monographs*, 6 (1929), 398–537; L. A. Sroufe and J. P. Wunsch, 'The development of laughter in the first year of life', *Child Development*, 43 (1972), 1326–1344.
30 C. B. Trevarthen, P. A. Hubley and L. Murray, 'Psychology of infants', in *Scientific Foundations of Paediatrics*, ed. J. Davis and J. Dobbing (Heinemann, London, 1981).
31 Trevarthen, 'Basic patterns of psychogenetic change', p. 26.
32 T. H. Leahey, *A History of Psychology* (Prentice-Hall, New York, 1980); see ch. 12 concerning 'peripheralism vs. centralism' in psychology.
33 Trevarthen, 'Basic patterns of psychogenetic change', p. 31.
34 D. N. Stern, 'The early development of schemas of self, other and self with other', in *Reflections on Self Psychology*, ed. J. D. Lichtenberg and S. Kaplan (Erlbaum, Hillsdale, NJ, 1983); K. Kaye, *The Mental and Social LIfe of Babies: How Parents Create Persons* (Harvester, Brighton, 1982).
35 D. Frye, P. Rawlings, C. Moore and I. Myers, 'Object–person discrimination and communication at 3 and 10 months', *Developmental Psychology*, 19 (1983), 303–9.
36 B. Sylvester-Bradley, 'Failure to distinguish between people and things in early infancy', *British Journal of Developmental Psychology*, 3 (1985), 281–92.
37 S. W. Jacobson, 'Matching behaviour in the young infant', *Child Development*, 50 (1979), 425–30; R. Over, 'Can human neonates imitate facial gestures?', in *Perceptual Development in Early Infancy: Problems and Issues* ed. B. E. McKenzie and R. M. Day (Erlbaum, Hillsdale, NJ, 1987).
38 T. G. R. Bower and J. G. Wishart, 'Towards a unitary theory of development', in *Origins of the Infant's Social Responsiveness*, ed. E. B. Thoman (Erlbaum, Hillsdale, NJ, 1979), p. 84.

39 A. N. Meltzoff, 'The roots of social and cognitive development, models of man's original nature', in *Social Perception in Infants*, ed. T. M. Field and N. A. Fox (Ablex, Norwood, 1985).

40 L. Lipsitt, 'Learning capacities of the human infant', in *Brain and Early Behaviour*, ed. R. J. Robinson (Academic, London, 1969); H. Papousek, 'Individual variability in learned responses in human infants', in *Brain and Early Behaviour*, ed. R. J. Robinson (Academic, London, 1969).

41 A. MacFarlane, 'Olfaction in the development of social preferences in the human neonate', in *Parent–Infant Interaction*, ed. R. Porter and M. O'Connor, (Elsevier CIBA Foundation Symposia, 33 (new series), Amsterdam, 1975).

42 C. B. Trevarthen, 'Instincts for human understanding and for cultural cooperation: their development in infancy', in *Human Ethology*, ed. M. von Cranach, K. Foppa, W. Lepenies and D. Ploog (Cambridge University Press, Cambridge, 1979), pp. 530–71.

43 C. B. Trevarthen, 'The primary motives for cooperative understanding', in *Social Cognition: Studies of the Development of Understanding*, ed. G. Butterworth and P. Light (Harvester, Brighton, 1982), pp. 77–109.

44 B. Sylvester-Bradley, 'A study of young infants as social beings' (Ph.D. thesis, Edinburgh University, 1980).

45 J. M. Selby, 'Pre-linguistic development and its inherent problems of description', (MA thesis, St Andrews University, 1977); J. M. Selby, 'Feminine identity and contradiction: women research students at Cambridge University' (D.Phil thesis, Cambridge University, 1984).

46 R. A. Hinde quoted in Sylvester-Bradley, 'Failure to distinguish'.

47 J. Dunn, *Distress and Comfort* (Fontana/Open Books, Glasgow, 1977).

48 B. Sylvester-Bradley, 'Negativity in early infant–adult exchanges and its developmental significance', in *Communication in Development*, ed. W. P. Robinson (Academic, London, 1981); J. Kirkland and F. Deane, 'A rejecting baby in a twin set', *Infant Mental Health Journal*, 5 (1984), 47–53.

49 Dunn, *Sisters and Brothers*. See also C. Urwin, 'Observations of aggression between same-aged infants' (unpublished paper, Child Care and Development Group, Cambridge).

50 T. H. Ogden, 'The mother, the infant, and the matrix: interpretations of the work of Donald Winnicott', *Contemporary Psychoanalysis*, 21 (1985), 346–71. See also B. S. Bradley, 'The asymmetric involvement of infants in social life: consequences for theory', *Revue internationale de psychologie sociale* (in press).

51 Trevarthen, et al., 'Psychology of infants', p. 246.

Chapter 9 Infancy and Paradise

1 C. Geertz, *The Interpretation of Cultures* (Hutchinson, London, 1973/1975), p. 9 and p. 5.

2 Other critiques of the equation between infancy and paradise are touched on or developed in: T. M. Horner, 'The psychic life of the young infant: review

and critique of the psycho-analytic concepts of symbiosis and omnipotence', *American Journal of Orthopsychiatry*, 55 (1985), 324–44; C. Urwin, 'Developmental psychology and psycho-analysis: splitting the difference', in *Children of Social Worlds*, ed. M. P. M. Richards and P. Light (Polity, Cambridge, 1986); M. Eliade, *Myths, Rites, Symbols: A Mircea Eliade Reader* (Harper & Row, New York, 1965); R. A. Shweder, 'Rethinking culture and personality theory. III: From genesis and typology to hermeneutics and dynamics', *Ethos*, 8 (1980), 60–94; and B. S. Bradley, 'Infancy as paradise: a theme in the scientific construction of childhood', *Human Development* (submitted for publication). For an explicit, albeit symptomatic, equation between infancy and paradise, see K. Kaye, *The Mental and Social Life of Babies: How Parents Create Persons* (Harvester, Brighton, 1982), pp. 238–9.

3 Genesis 1: 27.

4 I. D. John, ' "The Scientist" as role model for "The Psychologist" ', *Australian Psychologist*, 21 (1986), 219–40; A. Ehrenzweig, *The Hidden Order of Art: A Study in the Psychology of Artistic Imagination* (Weidenfeld & Nicolson, London, 1967), p. 4.

5 C. Steedman, *The Tidy House: Little Girls Writing* (Virago, London, 1982); Cf. M. Donaldson, *Children's Minds* (Fontana/Open Books, Glasgow, 1978), p. 10.

6 J. Bowlby, *Attachment and Loss*, vol. I: *Attachment* (Penguin, Harmondsworth, 1969), p. 368. The case against monotropism was first made in H. R. Schaffer and P. E. Emerson, 'The development of social attachments in infancy', Monographs of the Society for Research on Child Development, 29 (Chicago: University of Chicago Press, 1964), pp. 1–77.

7 S. Freud, *An Outline of Psycho-Analysis* (1940), Standard Edition 23 (Hogarth, London, 1964), p. 188. Quoted in Bowlby, *Attachment*, p. 427; regarding attachment as synonymous with love, see M. D. S. Ainsworth, 'The development of mother–infant attachment', in *Review of Child Development*, vol. III, ed. B. M. Caldwell and N. H. Ricciuti (University of Chicago Press, Chicago, 1973).

8 M. D. S. Ainsworth, S. M. Bell & D. J. Stayton, 'Infant–mother attachment and social development: 'socialization as a product of reciprocal responsiveness to signals', in *The Integration of a Child into a Social World*, ed. M. P. M. Richards (Cambridge University Press, Cambridge, 1974).

9 M. H. Klaus and J. H. Kennell, *Maternal–Infant Bonding* (Mosby, St Louis, 1976); D. W. Winnicott, 'Primary maternal preoccupation', in *Collected Papers: Through Padediatrics to Psycho-Analysis* (Tavistock, London, 1958).

10 T. G. R. Bower, *A Primer of Infant Development* (Freeman, San Francisco, 1979).

11 L. Lipsitt, 'Learning capacities of the human infant', In *Brain and Early Behaviour*, ed. R. J. Robinson (Academic, London, 1969).

12 M. Lewis and J. Brooks-Gunn, *Social Cognition and the Acquisition of Self* (Plenum, New York, 1979).

13 E. S. Spelke, 'Perceptual knowledge of objects in infancy', in *Perspectives in Mental Representation*, eds. J. Mehler, E. Walker and M. Garrett (Erlbaum, Hillsdale, NJ, 1982).

14 M. M. Haith, *Rules that Babies Look By: The Organization of Newborn Visual*

Activity (Erlbaum, Hillsdale, NJ, 1980); J. G. Wishart and T. G. R. Bower, 'A longitudinal study of the development of the object concept', *British Journal of Developmental Psychology*, 3 (1985), 243–58; J. S. Bruner, 'The ontogenesis of speech acts', *Journal of Child Language*, 2 (1975), 1–19.

15 Spelke, 'Perceptual knowledge'; Bruner 'Ontogenesis of speech'.

16 T. G. R. Bower, J. M. Broughton and M. K. Moore, 'Demonstration of intention in the reaching behaviour of neonate humans', *Nature*, 228 (1970), 5172. See also A. Gauld and J. Shotter, *Human Action and its Psychological Investigation* (Routledge & Kegan Paul, London, 1977), as quoted in ch. 1 of this book.

17 C. B. Trevarthen, 'Basic patterns of psychogenetic change', in *Regressions in Mental Development: Basic Phenomena and Theories*, ed. T. G. Bever (Erlbaum, Hillsdale, NJ, 1982).

18 D. N. Stern, 'The early development of schemes of self, other, and "self with other"', in *Reflections on Self Psychology*, ed. J. D. Lichtenberg and S. Kaplan (Erlbaum, Hillsdale, NJ, 1983).

19 C. Trevarthen, 'Descriptive analyses of infant communicative behaviour', in *Studies in Mother–Infant Interaction*, ed. H. R. Schaffer (Academic Press, New York, 1977).

20 J. Piaget, *The Origins of Intelligence in the Child* (Routledge & Kegan Paul, London, 1937/1953).

21 Bruner, 'The organization of early skilled action'; Kaye, *Life of Babies*; Bower et al., 'Intention in reaching behaviour'.

22 S. Hampshire, *Thought and Action* (Chatto & Windus, London, 1965).

23 G. E. M. Anscombe, *Intention* (Blackwell, Oxford, 1963, 2nd edn).

24 'Over-extension' is the term given by child psychologists to the way in which children sometimes wrongly extend the meaning of an adult name (e.g. 'sheep') too far (e.g. to dogs, cats, cows etc.).

25 D. A. Norman, 'Twelve issues for cognitive science', *Cognitive Science*, 4 (1980), 1–32.

26 J. Piaget, *Intelligence and Affectivity: Their Relationship During Child Development* (Annual Reviews, Palo Alto, Ca., 1954/1981); cf. D. Ingleby, 'Psychoanalysis and ideology', in *Critical Theories of Psychological Development* (Plenum, New York, 1987).

27 J. de Haviland, 'Looking smart: the relationship between affect and intelligence', in *Origins of Intelligence: Infancy and Early Childhood* (Plenum, New York, 1975).

28 J. Bowlby, 'The nature of the child's tie to his mother', *International Journal of Psycho-Analysis*, 39 (1958), 350–73.

29 Schaffer and Emerson, 'The development of social attachments'; Bowlby, *Attachment*, pp. 221–2; M. D. S. Ainsworth, 'Object-relations, dependency and attachment: a theoretical review of the infant–mother relationship', *Child Development*, 40 (1969), 969–1025.

30 Trevarthen, 'Descriptive analyses'.

31 A. N. Meltzoff and M. K. Moore, 'Newborn infants imitate adult facial gestures', *Child Development*, 54 (1983), 702–9.

32 e.g. D. J. Lekowicz, 'Sensory dominance in infancy: II. Ten-month-old

infants' response to auditory-visual compounds', *Developmental Psychology*, 24 (1988), 155–71.
33 Kaye, *Life of Babies*; G. A. Richardson, 'Subject loss in infancy research: how biasing is it?', *Infant Behaviour and Development*, 6 (1983), 235–9.
34 e.g. Demos, 'Empathy and affect'; B. Beebe and L. Gerstman, 'A method of defining "packages" of maternal stimulation and their functional significance for the infant with mother and stranger', *International Journal of Behavioural Development*, 7 (1984), 423–40.
35 Genesis 2: 9.
36 UNICEF, *State of the World's Children* (Unicef, New York, 1988).
37 J. Piaget, *Biology and Knowledge* (Routledge & Kegan Paul, London, 1971).
38 E. J. Gibson and E. S. Spelke, 'The development of perception', in *Handbook of Child Psychology*, vol. III, ed. P. H. Mussen (Wiley, New York, 1983).
39 M. Klaus and J. Kennell, *Maternal–Infant Bonding* (Mosby, St. Louis, 1976).
40 S. J. Gould and R. C. Lewontin, 'The spandrels of San Marco and the Panglossian paradigm: a critique of the adaptationist programme', *Proceedings of the Royal Society of London Series B*, 205 (1979), 581–98; S. J. Gould, *The Panda's Thumb: More Reflections in Natural History* (Norton, New York, 1981).
41 R. A. Hinde, *The Biological Bases of Human Social Behaviour* (Prentice-Hall, London, 1974).
42 D. Riley, 'Developmental psychology, biology and Marxism', *Ideology and Consciousness*, 4 (1978), 73–92.
43 Kaye, *Life of Babies*, p. 190.
44 G. Russell, *The Changing Role of Fathers* (Open University Press, Milton Keynes, 1983).
45 C. Lewis, J. Newson and E. Newson, 'Father participation through childhood and its relation to career aspirations and delinquency', in *Fathers: Psychological Perspectives*, ed. N. Beaill and J. McGuire (Junction Books, London, 1982); S. M. Smith, *The Battered Child Syndrome* (Butterworth, London, 1975).
46 UNICEF, *State of the World's Children*.
47 ibid.
48 C. A. Miller, 'Infant mortality in the US, *Scientific American*, 253 (1985), 21–7.
49 B. Cass, 'The feminisation of poverty: what does it mean?', Paper delivered at the Women's Studies Conference, University of Sydney, 20–2 September 1985.
50 N. Frude (ed.), *Psychological Approaches to Child Abuse* (Batsford, London, 1980); J. R. Galler (ed.), *Nutrition and Behaviour* (Plenum, New York, 1984); K. Oates, *Child Abuse and Neglect: What Happens Eventually* (Brunner-Mazel, New York, 1986); I. F. Brockington and R. Knaar (eds), *Motherhood and Mental Illness* (Academic, London, 1982).
51 M. J. Svejda, J. J. Campos and R. N. Emde, 'Mother–infant "bonding": failure to generalise', *Child Development*, 51 (1980), 775–9. Quoted in M. P. M. Richards, 'The myth of bonding', Paper presented at the conference on 'Pregnancy Care for the 1980s', Royal Society of Medicine, April 1981; W. Sluckin, M. Herbert and A. Sluckin, *Maternal Bonding* (Blackwell, Oxford, 1983).

52 M. Polatnick, 'Why men don't rear children: a power analysis', *Berkeley Journal of Sociology*, 18 (1973–4), 45–86.

53 R. Sylvester-Bradley, *The phenomenon of nitrogen fixation*, (CIAT Publications, Cali, Colombia, 1987).

54 R. Spitz, *The First Year of Life* (International Universities Press, New York, 1965).

55 J. Shotter, *Social Accountability and Selfhood* (Blackwell, Oxford, 1984), p. 58.

56 V. Walkerdine, 'From context to text: a psychosemiotic approach', in *Children Thinking Through Language*, ed. M. Beveridge (Arnold, London, 1982).

57 *Shorter Oxford English Dictionary* (Oxford University Press, Oxford, 1972).

58 D. W. Winnicott, 'Mirror-role of mother and family in emotional development', in *Playing and Reality* (Penguin, Harmondsworth, 1971).

59 D. W. Winnicott, 'Primary maternal preoccupation', in *Collected Papers: Through Paediatrics to Psychoanalysis* (Tavistock, London, 1956/1958).

60 D. W. Winnicott, quoted in M. Davis and D. Wallbridge, *Boundary and Space: An Introduction to the Work of D. W. Winnicott* (Brunner-Mazel, New York, 1981).

61 Winnicott, 'Mirror-role', p. 73.

62 B. Sylvester-Bradley and C. B. Trevarthen, 'Babytalk as an adaptation to the infant's communication', in *The Development of Communication*, ed. N. Waterson and C. Snow (Wiley, London, 1978).

63 E. Ochs, 'Cultural dimensions of language acquisition', in *Acquiring Conversational Competence*, ed. E. Ochs and B. Schieffelin (Routledge & Kegan Paul, London, 1983), pp. 187–8.

64 J. Ryan, 'Early language development: towards a communicational analysis', in *The Integration of a Child into a Social World*, ed. M. P. M. Richards (Cambridge University Press, Cambridge, 1974).

65 Shotter, *Social Accountability*, p. 89.

66 ibid., p. 104.

67 ibid., p. 20.

68 D. W. Winnicott, *The Child, the Family and the Outside World* (Penguin, Harmondsworth, 1964).

69 P. J. Caplan and I. Hall-McCorquodale, 'Mother-blaming in major clinical journals', *American Journal of Orthopsychiatry*, 55 (1985), 345–53.

70 Kaye, *Life of Babies*; J. Kagan, D. Lapidus and M. Moore, 'Infant antecedents of cognitive functioning: a longitudinal study', *Child Development*, 49 (1978), 1005–23.

71 T. Gaussen and P. Hubley, 'Babies in special care: some developmental implications of adult–infant interactions', *Association for Child Psychology and Psychiatry Newsletter*, 9 (1987), 15–20; W. Wundt, *Outlines of Psychology* (Leipzig, 1907).

72 A. Oakley, *Women Confined; Towards a Sociology of Childbirth* (Robertson, Oxford, 1980).

73 G. W. Brown and T. Harris, *Social Origins of Depression* (Tavistock, London, 1978).

74 J. Busfield and M. Paddon, *Thinking about Children: Sociology and Fertility in Post-War England* (Cambridge University Press, Cambridge, 1977).

75 J. M. Selby, 'Feminine identity and contradiction: women research students at Cambridge University' (D.Phil thesis, Cambridge University, 1984).

76 S. Prendergast and A. Prout, 'What will I do . . .? Teenage girls and the construction of motherhood', *Sociological Review*, 28 (1980), 517–35.

77 Steedman, *The Tidy House*.

78 S. Ruddick, 'Maternal thinking', *Feminist Studies*, 6 (1980), 342–67.

79 Piaget did most of his work on babies before the 1939–1945 war, but this work only found its way into the thinking of English-speaking scientists after the war. The first English translations of his works on infancy were published in the 1950s.

80 Riley, *War in the Nursery*, ch. 6; L. S. Marcus, *Childhood and Cultural Despair: A Theme and Variations in Seventeenth-Century Literature* (Pittsburgh University Press, Pittsburgh, 1978).

81 W. Blake, *For the Sexes: The Gates of Paradise*, in *Blake: Complete Writings*, ed. G. Keynes (Oxford University Press, Oxford, 1818/1966), pp. 760–771.

82 W. Blake, *Songs of Innocence* and *Songs of Experience*, in *Blake: Complete Writings*, ed. G. M. Keynes (Oxford University Press, Oxford, 1789 and 1794/1966), pp. 111–26 and 210–20.

83 Blake, *Songs of Innocence*, pp. 115–16.

84 Blake, *Gates of Paradise*, p. 770.

85 D. Ault, *Visionary Physics: Blake's Response to Newton* (University of Chicago Press, Chicago, 1974).

86 Gauld and Shotter, *Human Action*; R. E. Palmer, *Hermeneutics: Interpretation Theory in Schleiermacher, Dilthey, Heidegger and Gadamer* (Northwestern University Press, Evanston, Ill., 1969); M. J. Packer, 'Hermeneutic inquiry in the study of human conduct', *American Psychologist*, 40 (1985), 1081–93; Shweder (n. 1 above).

87 K. J. Gergen, *Toward Transformation in Social Knowledge* (Springer-Verlag, New York, 1982); K. J. Gergan, 'The social constructionist movement in modern psychology', *American Psychologist*, 40 (1985), 266–75; K. J. Gergen and M. M. Gergen, 'Narrative form and the construction of psychological science', in *Narrative Psychology: The Storied Nature of Human Conduct*, ed. T. R. Sarbin (Wiley, New York, 1986).

Chapter 10 Psychology as Advocacy

1 F. A. Yates, *The Art of Memory*, (Routledge & Kegan Paul, London, 1966). The work of Frances Yates provides a fascinating connection between the Rosicrucian ideas inspiring Erasmus Darwin's great scientific poem of psychological development (*The Temple of Nature*, especially Canto III; see ch. 3 above) and the idea of the science of babies as a 'natural' museum or memory theatre for those who wish to expatiate on the fundaments of human understanding.

2 J. Hooker, *Of the laws of eclesiastical politie*, Book 1 (1596), quoted in J. Locke, *An essay concerning human understanding*, vol. I, ed. A. C. Fraser (Clarendon, Oxford, 1690/1894), p. 48 (editor's note).

3 J. Swift, 'A critical essay upon the faculties of the mind', in *The Prose Works of*

Jonathan Swift D.D., Vol. I, ed. T. Scott (Bell & Sons, London, 1707/1907), p. 295.

4 e.g. A. Clarke-Stewart, S. Friedman and J. Koch, *Child Development: A Topical Approach* (Wiley, New York, 1985).

5 ibid., p. 5.

6 W. James, *Principles of Psychology* (Dover, New York, 1890/1950), p. 185, vol. I, p. 185.

7 See the discussion of Heidegger in J. M. Robinson, 'Hermeneutic since Barth', in *The New Hermeneutic*, ed. J. M. Robinson (Harper & Row, New York, 1964).

8 M. J. Packer, 'Communication in early infancy: three common assumptions examined and found inadequate', *Human Development*, 26 (1983), 233–48.

9 E.g. S. White, 'Psychology as a moral science', in *The Child and Other Cultural Inventions*, ed. F. S. Kessel and A. W. Siegel (Praeger, New York, 1983).

10 See J. B. Thompson, *Studies in the Theory of Ideology* (University of California Press, Berkeley, 1984), pp. 140–7 and 275–8.

11 This is part of the famous epigraph to Wordsworth's Ode: 'Intimations of Immortality from Recollections of Early Childhood', in *The Poetical Works of William Wordsworth*, ed. T. Hutchinson (Oxford University Press, London, 1920), p. 587. It is often echoed in the literary 'asides' of modern developmental psychology, as in the Editors' introduction to the Wiley Origins of Behaviour series, E.G. M. Lewis and L. A. Rosenblum (eds), *The Effect of the Infant on its Caregiver*, (Wiley, New York, 1974), Preface.

12 B. Bettelheim, *Freud and Man's Soul* (Chatto & Windus, London, 1983). Thanks also to Rob Gordon for this point.

13 On 'language games' see L. Wittgenstein, *Philosophical Investigations* (Blackwell, Oxford, 1958) and P. Winch, *The Idea of a Social Science* (Routledge & Kegan Paul, London, 1958). The full reference to Kierkegaard is S. Kierkegaard, *Repetition: An Essay in Experiment Psychology* (Princeton University Press, Princeton, 1843/1946).

14 Concerning the vision of infancy as anxious in existentialism see S. Kierkegaard, *The Concept of Anxiety* (Princeton University Press, Princeton, 1843/1980). Concerning a similar vision in post-structuralism, see J. Derrida's reading of Rousseau's essay on the origin of language in *Of Grammatology* (Johns Hopkins University Press, Baltimore, 1967/1974), last chapter. Thus, when discussing the origin of language in an anthropological way, Rousseau wrote:

> Upon meeting others, a savage man will initially be frightened. Because of his fear he sees the others as bigger and stronger than himself. He calls them *giants*. After many experiences, he recognises that these so-called giants are neither bigger nor stronger than he. Their stature does not approach the idea he had initially attached to the word giant. So he invents another name common to them and to him, such as the name *man*, for example, and leaves *giant* to the false object that had impressed him during his illusion. That is how the figurative word is born before the literal word, when our gaze is held in passionate fascination.

To this, Derrida supplements:

the other is *first* encountered at a distance, separation and fear must be overcome so that he may be approached as a fellow-being. From a distance, he is immense, like a master and a threatening force. It is the experience of the small and silent [*infans*] man. He begins to speak only out of these deforming and naturally magnifying perceptions. And as the force of dispersion is never reduced, the source of fear always compounds with its contrary.

Concerning the vision of the infant as anxious in feminism see C. Urwin, 'Power relations and the emergence of language', in *Changing the Subject*, ed. J. Henriques, W. Hollway, C. Urwin, C. Venn, V. Walderdine (Methuen, London, 1984) and J. M. Selby, 'Feminine identity and contradiction: women research students at Cambridge University', (D.Phil. thesis, Cambridge University, 1984).

15 G. A. Miller, 'Psychology as a means of promoting human welfare', *American Psychologist*, 24 (1969), 1063–75.

16 The link between psychology and advocacy is explored further in ch. 3 of my doctoral thesis, 'A study of young infants as social beings', University of Edinburgh, 1980.

17 This point is implicit in the excellent rationale for 'participatory research' in 'new paradigm' psychology by R. C. Rosenwald: 'Toward a formative psychology', *Journal for the Theory of Social Behaviour*, 18 (1988), 1–32. The classic exposition of the new paradigm Rosenwald is developing (as am I) is by K. J. Gergen, *Toward Transformation in Social Knowledge* (Springer-Verlag, New York, 1982).

18 The contrast between truth as an accurate representation of reality and truth as what it is better to believe is developed in R. Rorty, *Philosophy and the Mirror of Nature* (Princeton University Press, Princeton, 1979). See Rorty's ch. 1 for the quote from James. The link between faith and 'the choice of the nobler hypothesis' is made in G. Heard, *Prayers and Meditations: A Monthly Cycle Arranged for Daily Use* (Harper, New York, 1949).

Select Bibliography

Ainsworth, M. D. S., 'The development of mother–infant attachment', in *Review of Child Development Research*, vol. III (University of Chicago Press, Chicago, 1973).

Ault, D., *Visionary Physics: Blake's Response to Newton* (University of Chicago Press, Chicago, 1974).

Bloom, L., *Language Development: Form and Function in Emerging Grammars* (MIT Press, Cambridge, Mass., 1970).

Bower, T. G. R., *Development in Infancy* (Freeman, San Francisco, 1974).

Bowlby, J., *Attachment and Loss*, vol. I: *Attachment* (Hogarth, London, 1969).

Bowlby, J., 'The nature of the child's tie to his mother', *International Journal of Psycho-Analysis*, 39 (1958), 350–73.

Brazelton, T. B., E. Tronick, L. Adamson, H. Als and S. Wise, 'Early mother–infant reciprocity', in *Parent–Infant Interaction*, ed. R. Porter and M. O'Connor, CIBA Foundation Symposia, 33 (new series) (Elsevier, Amsterdam, 1975).

Bruner, J. S., 'The ontogenesis of speech acts', *Journal of Child Language*, 2 (1975), 1–19.

Caplan, P. J. and I. Hall-McCorquodale, 'Mother-blaming in major clinical journals', *American Journal of Orthopsychiatry*, 55 (1985), 345–53.

Chomsky, N., Review of Skinner's *Verbal Behavior*, *Language*, 35 (1959), 26–58.

Chomsky, N., *Language and Mind* (Harcourt Brace Jovanovich, New York, 1972).

Darwin, *The Expression of the Emotions in Man and Animals* (Murray, London, 1872).

Darwin, C. R., 'A biographical sketch of an infant', *Mind*, 2 (1877), 285–94.

Darwin, C. R., Notebook on Child Development, Cambridge University Library, (unpublished).

Darwin, E., *The Temple of Nature or the Origin of Society: A Poem with Philosophical Notes* (Johnson, London, 1803).

Derrida, J., *Of Grammatology* (Johns Hopkins University Press, Baltimore, 1967/ 1974).

Donaldson, M., *Children's Minds* (Fontana/Open Books, Glasgow, 1978).

Ferenczi, S., 'The birth of the intellect', in *Final Contributions to the Problems and Methods of Psycho-Analysis*, ed. M. Balint (Hogarth, London, 1931/1955).

Freud, S., 'Screen memories' (1899), in *Collected Papers,* vol. V, ed. J. Strachey (Hogarth, London, 1957).

Freud, S., *The Interpretation of Dreams* (1900) (Penguin, Harmondsworth, 1976).

Freud, S., 'Infantile sexuality' (1905), Penguin Freud Library, 7, (Penguin, Harmondsworth, 1977) pp. 88–126.

Freud, S., 'On narcissism: an introduction' (1914), Penguin Freud Library, 11 (Penguin, Harmondsworth, 1984), pp. 59–98.

Gauld, A., and J. Shotter, *Human Action and its Psychological Investigation* (Routledge & Kegan Paul, London, 1977).

Gergen, K. J., *Toward Transformation in Social Knowledge* (Springer-Verlag, New York, 1982).

Gould, S. J., and R. C. Lewontin, 'The spandrels of San Marco and the Panglossian paradigm: a critique of the adaptationist programme', *Proceedings of the Royal Society of London (Series B)*, 205 (1979), 581–98.

Gruber, H. E., and P. H. Barrett, *Darwin on Man: A Psychological Study of Scientific Creativity* (Wildwood, London, 1974).

Kaye, K., *The Mental and Social Life of Babies: How Parents Create Persons* (Harvester, Brighton, 1982).

Klein, M., 'Some theoretical conclusions regarding the emotional life of the infant' (1952), in *Envy and Gratitude and Other Works 1946–1963* (Hogarth, London, 1975).

Lacan, J., 'Aggressivity in psycho-analysis' in *Écrits: A Selection*, tr. A. Sheridan (Tavistock, London, 1948/1977).

Lacan, J., 'The mirror stage as formative of the function of the I' (1949), in *Écrits: A Selection*, tr. A. Sheridan (Tavistock, London, 1977).

Macanamara, J., 'Cognitive basis for language learning in infants', *Psychological Review*, 79 (1972), 1–13.

Oakley, A., *Women Confined: Towards a Sociology of Childbirth* (Robertson, Oxford, 1980).

Palmer, R. E., *Hermeneutics: Interpretation Theory in Schleiermacher, Dilthey, Heidegger and Gadamer* (Northwestern University Press, Evanston, Ill., 1969).

Papousek, 'Individual variability in learned responses in human infants', in *Brain and Earth Behaviour*, ed. R. J. Robinson (Academic, London, 1969).

Piaget, J., *The Child's Construction of Reality* (Routledge & Kegan Paul, London, 1937/1953).

Piaget, J., *The Origins of Intelligence in the Child* (Routledge & Kegan Paul, London, 1937/1953).

Piaget, J., *Play, Dreams and Imitation* (Routledge & Kegan Paul, London, 1945/ 1951).

Piaget, J., *Language and Thought of the Child* (Routledge & Kegan Paul, London, 1959).

Riley, D., *War in the Nursery: Theories of the Child and Mother* (Virago, London 1983).

Schaffer, H. R., and P. E. Emerson, 'The development of social attachments in infancy', Monographs of the Society for Research on Child Development, 29 (Chicago: University of Chicago Press, 1964), pp. 1–77.

Shweder, R. A., 'Rethinking culture and personality theory III. From genesis and typology to hermeneutics and dynamics', *Ethos*, 8 (1980), 60–94.

Skinner, B. F., 'Baby in a box', in *Cumulative Record* (Appleton-Century-Crofts, New York, 1959).

Skinner, B. F., *Verbal Behavior* (Appleton-Century-Crofts, New York, 1957).

Spitz, R. A., *The First Year of Life* (International Universities Press, New York, 1965).

Stern, D. N., The early development of schemas of self, other and self with other', in *Reflections on Self Psychology*, ed. J. D. Lichtenberg and S. Kaplan (Erlbaum, Hillsdale, NJ, 1983).

Swift, J., 'The difficulty of knowing one's self', in *Prose Works of Jonathan Swift*, vol. IX: *Irish Tracts and Sermons*, ed. T. Scott, (Blackwell, Oxford, 1745/1948).

Thompson, J. B., *Studies in the Theory of Ideology* (Polity, Cambridge, 1984).

Trevarthen, C. B., P. A. Hubley and L. Murray, 'Psychology of infants', in *Scientific Foundations of Paediatrics*, ed. J. Davis and J. Dobbing (Heinemann, London, 1981).

UNICEF, *State of the World's Children* (Unicef, New York, 1988).

Vygotsky, L. S., *Mind in Society: The Development of Higher Psychological Processes* (Harvard University Press, Cambridge, Mass., 1978).

Watson, J. B., and R. Morgan, 'Emotional reactions and psychological experimentation', *American Journal of Psychology*, 28 (1917), 163–84.

Watson, J. B., and R. Rayner, 'Conditioned emotional responses', *Journal of Experimental Psychology*, 3 (1920), 1–14.

Weir, R., *Language in the Crib* (Mouton, The Hague, 1962).

Winnicott, D. W., *Playing and Reality* (Penguin, Harmondsworth, 1971).

Yates, F. A., *The Art of Memory* (Routledge & Kegan Paul, London, 1966).

Illustration Acknowledgements

8.3.1–3   Author.
8.4.1–3   Author.
8.5.1–3   Author.
8.6.1–3   Author.
8.7.1–3   Author.
8.8.1–3   Author.
8.9.1–3   Author.
9.1   Photograph: UNICEF photo/Balcomb.
9.2   Photograph: UNICEF/Bernard P. Wolff.

Index

Keating, 94–6
Kennel, 151, 158–9
Kierkegaard, 179, 203
Klaus, 151, 158–9
Klein, 57–9, 61, 105, 111

Lacan, 7, 57, 60, 62, 116, 178
Lamarckism, 24
language, 6, 10, 29, 38, 45–6, 62–3,
    67–81, 86–7, 124–6, 128, 178;
    acquisition of, 20, 30, 67–81, 92,
    116; 'Language Acquisition Device',
    71, 74–5, 79–81, 130, 152–3; *see also*
    mothers, speech of; vocabulary for
    psychology
laughter, 19, 116–20, 130
learning, 7, 14, 28–44, 106–7, 113,
    118, 132, 157
Leopold, 68
logocentrism, 103, 151–2
Lorenz, 106–7, 110
love, 47–8, 61, 63, 105–21, 122; *see also*
    attachment

Macnamara, 84–5
masturbation, 51, 101
Mead, 4
meaning, 27, 44, 73, 126; *see also*
    interpretation
medical interview, 48
memory, 173–5; of childhood, 13, 49, 59
mental states, 21–3, 33, 42–3, 50, 131,
    138, 144; *see also* experience
mirroring, 160–2
mirrors, 14, 60–4
misery, 115–18; *see also* anxiety;
    crying; illness; pain; poverty
monotropism, 112, 150
Morss, 27
mothers, 5, 29, 35–6, 40, 47, 51, 54,
    57–8, 64, 98–9, 107–12, 131, 150–1,
    159–66, 168; blaming of, 9, 162–6;
    deprivation of, 107–8, 114–15;
    responsiveness of, 113–14; speech
    of, 4, 76, 80, 133–8, 155, 158, 161;
    see also child-care; parental
    behaviour

narcissism, 56–7, 61–3, 144, 146
Narcissus, *see* narcissism
natural history, *see* history, natural
nature–nurture, 173–5
negative aspects of mental life, 3, 115–
    21, 142–4, 152–4, 159–66, 168

object concept, 89–91, 93–5, 98–100,
    102–4, 112
observation, 1, 4, 12–13, 27, 87–90,
    103, 121–2
Oedipus, 47, 51–4, 56–8
oral stage, 51–3, 59; *see also* stages
over-extension, 78, 152

pain, 17, 29, 31; *see also* anxiety;
    illness; misery
Papousek, 41–2, 100
parental behaviour, 22, 36, 40, 117–18
Pavlov, 32–4, 36, 43
Peek-a-boo, 119, 124
people distinguished from things, 101–
    2, 127, 131–2
phallus v. penis, 56
phenotype, 23
Piaget, 8, 27, 85–104, 112, 123, 148,
    152, 158
play, 61–2, 91–2, 119, 124, 130, 133,
    165; play technique, 57
pleasure, 16, 29, 31, 50, 53
political struggle, 41
polymorphous perversity, 51
'positions' (Klein), 58–9
poverty, 9, 156–7
prespeech, 129–30, 133–40
primary process, 50, 58, 88
pro-natalism, 111, 167
psycho-analysis, 7–8, 43, 45–66, 67,
    105; *see also* Freud
psychologist's fallacy, 77, 101
psychology, status of, 2–3, 9–10, 23,
    25, 30, 43, 44, 64–6, 69, 148–50,
    169–71, 173–80

race, 31, 35, 59
rationality, 4, 8, 14, 85–104
recapitulation, 52